ENGAGING
OUR WORLD

Selected Papers from the "Engaging Our World Conference"
Marking the Twentieth Anniversary of the
International Institute for Christian Studies
July 17–19, 2008
Kansas City, Missouri

ENGAGING OUR WORLD

Christian Worldview from the Ivory Tower to Global Impact

William Adrian, Mark E. Roberts & Reggies Wenyika, Editors
Foreword by Daryl McCarthy

W & S ACADEMIC PRESS

Tulsa

Engaging Our World: Christian Worldview from the Ivory Tower to Global Impact

W & S Academic Press, an imprint of Word & Spirit Press
Tulsa, Oklahoma
<wordsp@gmail.com>

Printed in the United States of America if bought there, in the United Kingdom if bought there or in Europe.

Book design and composition by Bob Bubnis / Booksetters, Bowling Green, Kentucky and Mark E. Roberts / W & S Academic Press

ISBN 13: 978-0-9819526-8-0 [case laminate]
ISBN 13: 978-0-9819526-9-7 [paperback]

The paper used in this publication meets the minimum requirements of the American National Standard for Information Sciences—Permanence of Paper for Printed Library Materials, ANSI Z39.48-1992.

Contents

Contents

FOREWORD

As academicians who are followers of Jesus, we are called to make a difference in our world for His Kingdom. Yet many of us live with a tension—how is our research, teaching, and writing contributing to the expansion of Christ's Kingdom and making a difference in the world beyond our classroom?

Our internal tension is exacerbated by the fact that many non-academic believers view those of us in the academy as too abstract and too distant from reality. I suspect that often they are correct in this assumption. "Ivory tower" is a favorite code word for the aloofness of scholars from the rest of the world—from the "real world." In truth, many of us have to admit that we are far more comfortable contemplating the contours of a Christian worldview from an abstract perspective in the quiet of our study than we are engaging with our heart, soul, mind, and body with real-time issues involving broken people in our fallen world.

The academician committed to Christ knows and affirms the critical importance of reflection, thought, research, and scholarship—all part of the Ivory Tower. But as a follower of Jesus, the Christian academician is also committed to leading others to Christ, discipling and mentoring others as together we apply a Christian worldview to the academic, social, and cultural problems that plague humankind.

For some time many Christian scholars have felt the need for a conversation about how a Christian worldview applies in the real world and how we as Christian academicians can make an impact on our planet. We wanted an opportunity to listen to one another, worship together, pray together, discuss and no doubt disagree, and hopefully laugh and cry together along the way as well. Since learning and growth occurs best in community, we needed to come together to do this. We needed a time of expanding our horizons and deepening our moorings as we learned from Him and from one another.

So the *Engaging Our World Conference* was birthed, sponsored by the International Institute for Christian Studies (IICS). IICS was uniquely qualified to host this conference because of its parallel commitments to excellence in scholarship, depth of devotion to Christ, and vision for the world. IICS places Christian academicians and professionals in teaching positions at universities around the world. Over the last several years IICS has hosted a series of academic conferences that have become known as *The Christian Worldview Conference with a Global*

Vision. These conferences attract academicians from a wide range of disciplines and many parts of the globe, and some say that it is unlike any other academic gathering they have attended in its seamless approach to scholarship and a passion for the Christ who is Creator of all things and Lord over all truth.

The *Engaging Our World Conference* combined in equal measure the great Christian traditions of worship and passionate devotion to Jesus Christ as Lord, high standards of intellectual excellence, depth in spiritual formation, and breadth of fellowship across denominational lines, all within the context of a global vision—an understanding that much of the world remains beyond the reach of the Good News and that we as academicians will play a key role in reaching them. A Christian worldview is necessarily Christ-centered and global.

The publisher gathered several key papers from this conference for a broader audience. Now you can join this conversation about a Christian worldview and how it applies to the real world.

The goal of this book is to help Christian academicians and professionals understand how a Christian worldview applies to the rest of the world—beyond the Ivory Tower. How do we make a difference? How can we serve as Jesus's mind, heart, hands, feet and eyes on this planet? How can we spread *shalom*, especially in the area of our expertise? What difference should the Lordship of Christ make in the key issues facing humankind today? How do we connect the Ivory Tower to the *real* world?

I know you will be challenged and blessed and hopefully stretched as you read these words from scholars in various disciplines and from a wide spectrum of theological positions. Above all, I hope you will ask yourself one simple question over and over as you read this book. "What difference does my Christian worldview make?"

This book will help deepen your commitment to understanding and living a Christian worldview. Reading it thoughtfully will force you to reexamine your stereotypes of conversion, evangelism and apologetics and encourage you to think Christianly about your discipline and your life. It will give you new insights on how to apply a Christian worldview in your field and inspire you to impact your world for Christ and His Kingdom

Let's be scholars who truly make a difference in our world for Christ!

— Dr. Daryl McCarthy
President,
International Institute for Christian Studies

PREFACE

The 2008 International Institute for Christian Studies Conference marked the twentieth anniversary of IICS and attracted over sixty presentations responding to the theme "Engaging Our World: From the Ivory Tower to Global Impact" July 17–19, in Kansas City, Missouri. From these we have selected sixteen papers for this volume. They impressed us as communicating effectively one or more dimensions of Christian worldview that we believed would benefit a wide range of readers—from those well read in the literature of Christian worldview to those wondering what a worldview is and how it matters to any specific field of study or action. Having chosen these papers, we were pleased to discern among them significant connections. First, they all express dimensions of a biblical worldview that views creation as God-indwelled. The Hebrew term *shekinah* refers to "The majestic presence or manifestation of God which has descended to 'dwell' among men" *(Jewish Encyclopedia),* imbuing all of life—spirit and matter—with divine favor and targeting it for divine redemption. Christians know this divine indwelling to have consummated in the Word-become-flesh, Jesus Christ, who now indwells believers in the person of the Holy Spirit. Sharing this genuinely hope-filled, crucial linchpin of the biblical worldview connects this group as a community of Christian scholars.

Second, together the papers and their authors express an interesting range of academic and professional focus. Most are teachers or professors in universities around the world, but the group also includes a teacher of English in a Christian high school and a corporate research scientist. Professional fields represented include engineering, theology and biblical studies, education, chemistry, English, history, and management; and most contributors have taught in universities around the globe.

Third, the essays evince a progression in topics. The first addresses the status of the concept "worldview" among scholars. "Christian worldview" has become popular, and perhaps overused, in describing the metanarrative of God in the world. Questions about the meaning and uses of the phrase have emerged among scholars, schools of thought, and academic disciplines. Robert Kurka's essay answers critics who claim that the notion of a Christian worldview as propounded by evangelicals has seen its day. He points to its permanency, showing how it has been indelibly written in the record of Scripture and Western intellectual history and continues to serve Christian faith today.

The next four papers follow an arc in worldview thinking from the beginning of everything to the differing receptions of a biblical worldview in the global South and in the West, with a brief case study of one Western biblical scholar. The story of God begins with the Genesis narrative of creation, and Wayne Brouwer's paper describes that unique biblical worldview in the origin, identity, and ongoing story of Israel, "the one who wrestles with God." Daniel Button's paper describes a different challenge to a biblical worldview in the global South, where the conflict is not secularism versus religion, as it is in the West, because the "Global South missed the Enlightenment." The Judeo-Christian worldview finds a natural home in the South, where the Old Testament is venerated and religious faith, community, and morality cohere with a palpable sense of the supernatural, expressed in great concern for prophecy. Mark E. Roberts' paper explores how the West lost its Christian mind by failing to recognize the dogmatism of the Enlightenment for what it was: the Great Narrowing of human knowledge to a thin slice sired by a skepticism that can never lead to the knowledge of God. Edward Meadors explores the fruit of this skepticism in the "deconversion" story of the once-evangelical New Testament scholar Bart Ehrman.

Six papers focus specifically on relationships between Christian worldview and dimensions of higher education. American and European higher education today is dominated by an Enlightenment perspective that accepts a naturalistic metanarrative of history and relegates religion to the primitive and superstitious past. But it has not always been so, as the paper by Reggies Wenyika and William Adrian shows. It documents the historical and systematic removal of the Judeo-Christian heritage and biblical worldview from the curricula of most American universities. A Judeo-Christian worldview rejects the assumption that there is an impassable gulf between science and religion, and this is especially evident among those authors in scientific disciplines. Papers by Steven Eisenbarth and Kenneth Van Treuren, Dominic Halsmer, and David Ross, all engineers and scholars, describe the role of faith in the practice and ethics within the engineering profession; and the paper by David Leonard argues philosophically for the legitimacy of Intelligent Design as science.

Four papers focus on worldview and language. John Han and Mary Bagley describe the Christian worldview expressed in the popular fiction of John Grisham. Susan Robbins chronicles her experience teaching English in non-English speaking environments and contends that how persons use language expresses a worldview: "language is not value-free." The paper by Rick Williams, an English teacher at a Christian high school, shows how a growing number of Christian and parochial schools and home-school programs teach Christian worldview through literature. And William Wilson considers how today's image-saturated culture has elicited a corresponding homiletic that threatens to displace the authority of the divine word in preaching with the authority of personal emotional response to relativistic images.

The final analytical paper demonstrates why worldviewish thinking, feeling, and acting matters. David K. Naugle focuses on Christians' embrace of a multitude of dualisms that yield compartmentalized lives conformed to materialistic culture and that rob the gospel of its culture-renewing power. Naugle emphasizes that academic enterprises are not "worldview neutral":"Neither life nor scholarship is possible without a foundational point of view."

The final paper testifies personally to the life-giving gospel of Jesus Christ. Kumiko Takeuchi's testimony demonstrates the good fruit the gospel produces in all areas of one's life, from the personal to the public and professional. Its place as the concluding essay emphasizes that Christian worldview matters because it serves the mission of the gospel in God's world.

We thank several groups for making this volume possible:

- all the contributors for cooperating graciously with editorial requests, often on short notice;
- the administrative team at IICS, including the President, Dr. Daryl McCarthy, who consistently encouraged us; and Executive Assistants Joy McBride and Katie Eicholtz, who have responded to all our requests graciously and efficiently; and
- the publishing team at W & S Academic Press.

We send this book out with the prayer and hope that its contents will reach an audience many times greater than those privileged to hear the original presentations.

William Adrian
Mark E. Roberts
Reggies Wenyika
Bartlesville & Tulsa, Oklahoma
June 2009

1

REQUIEM FOR WORLDVIEW EDUCATION: A *PRE-MORTEM* SONG?

Robert C. Kurka

INTRODUCTION

For nearly thirty years, literally hundreds of students at evangelical institutions of higher learning have "cut their worldview teeth" on the following definition:

> A worldview is a set of presuppositions (assumptions that may be true, partially true or entirely false) which we hold (consciously or subconsciously, consistently or inconsistently) about the basic makeup of our world.1

However, during the past five years, these same students are increasingly reading and hearing comments that more and more reflect the following sentiment:

> My own college and graduate theological studies were all done in the context of a modern worldview of education. I completed my graduate studies in 1968 and was interviewed that year to teach

---

1 James W. Sire, *The Universe Next Door: A Basic Worldview Catalog*, 3rd ed. (Downers Grove, Ill.: Inter Varsity Press, 1997), 16.

Robert C. Kurka <rkurka@lccs.edu> is Professor of Theology and Church in Culture at Lincoln Christian Seminary, Lincoln, Illinois, where he also directs the *Issachar Institute,* a center for worldview studies and Christian scholarship. He has contributed chapters to *Evangelicalism and the Stone-Campbell Movement* (Vol. 1, Inter Varsity, 2002; Vol. 2, ACU Press, 2006) and articles to *The Journal of the Evangelical Theological Society, The Stone-Campbell Journal,* and popular periodicals. He has taught in Africa and Asia and lectures for "Perspectives on the World Christian Movement." He holds a BA from Crossroads College (MN), an MDiv from Lincoln Christian Seminary, and a DMin from Trinity Evangelical Divinity School, where he is completing a PhD in Systematic Theology.

in the theology department of Wheaton College. My entire interview was on the question of a Christian worldview. What is it?
How do we develop it? How do we teach it? Wheaton College
soon instituted a course for faculty members that dealt with these
matters. This course and the writing of a paper on a Christian
view of one's teaching discipline became and still is a requirement
for tenure. But today the younger evangelical questions the priority given to Christianity as a worldview. Younger evangelical
Charles Moore writes, "The idea of Christianity as a worldview is
essentially Gnostic. It makes Christianity an idea, a philosophical
viewpoint, a construct. . . .This is the problem that so many young
people in evangelical colleges and seminaries experience. Christianity, when presented as a worldview, is turned into a cognitive
subject to be discussed, debated, and proven. What is lacking . . .
is the personal dimension."[2]

The above words, penned by the late Robert Webber in his 2002
publication, *The Younger Evangelicals,* sent a not-so-subtle signal that
a cherished era of evangelical scholarship and education was changing radically, if not coming to a close. An evangelicalism that had essentially rebuilt its intellectual tradition upon "worldview thinking"
(defined by the Dutch scholars, Kuyper and Dooyeweerd; translated
into the American context by Orr, Van Til, and Henry; and popularized by Francis Schaeffer and James Sire) was now being taken to task
for allegedly adopting a "modernist instrument" as it sought to make
itself presentable at the table of respectable academia. According to the
former Wheaton College theology professor and his cadre of younger
pastors, teachers, and scholars, the present day reality of a *postmodern*
world (suspicious of individualistic, human reason and embracing experiential communitarianism) was now rendering a widely-embraced
approach to Christian learning irrelevant, obscurantist, and most likely, a foreign import in the first place.[3] This shot across the worldview
bow was a prelude to what has now become a cacophony of voices—
not a few from the ranks of *weltanschauung*'s most devoted following,
the Reformed camp—calling their evangelical brethren to significantly alter, if not depart from altogether, a program that is "hopelessly
modern."[4]

---

2 Robert E. Webber, *The Younger Evangelicals: Facing the Challenges of the New World* (Grand
Rapids: Baker Books, 2002), 164–65.

3 Webber writes that he and his younger colleagues do not so much reject "the metanarrative that sweeps from creation to the fall to the redemption and hope of the new heavens and
the new earth" but rather "a Christianity too thoroughly enmeshed with the modern outlook
based on reason and science . . . ideological competitors who have bought into the 'worldview'
method of education to counter secularism and support the Christian worldview." (Ibid., 165).

4 These Reformed voices include John Franke (and his late writing partner, Stanley Grenz),

Typical of these postmodern prophets is Redeemer University College's Theodore Plantinga, who argues that the worldview concept carries with it unfortunate epistemological baggage that cannot be easily removed from its *secular* use (and in his view, Enlightenment origins).[5] Among Plantinga's criticisms are the charges that worldview "falls prey to *visualism,* i.e., the systematic overestimation of the importance of vision in the process of human experience and thought," and that "the worldview notion encourages us to engage in top-down theorizing in which the philosopher (unless someone else turns out to be the expert on worldviews) gets to dictate to people in other disciplines what sorts of theories they should embrace."[6] Other critics have accused worldview adherents of taking the biblical concept of conversion—a personal meeting with the crucified and resurrected Christ—and reducing it into a set of philosophical propositions that simply make Jesus' lordship the most adequate belief system in a world of cognitive competitors.[7] More recently, in a most creative and thoughtful volume, *God's Judgments,* historian Steven Keillor has weighed in with a decidedly non-postmodernist critique of worldview thinking, proposing that "Christianity is an interpretation of history (not an alternative reading of it but an old-fashioned metanarrative interpretation) far more than it is a worldview or philosophy."[8] Suffice

James K. A. Smith, as well as Yale (and former Calvin) philosopher, Nicholas Wolsterstorff, who faults the term *worldview* for its alleged dependence upon "thought, intellection, (and) cognition. It stresses intellect." (Nicholas Wolsterstorff, "Educating for Life," in *Reflections on Christian Teaching and Learning,* eds. Gloria Stronks and Clarence W. Joldersma [Grand Rapids: Baker, 2002], 107). Grenz found fault with worldview (and doctrinal systems) because it (they) tended to replace Christian *experience* (mitigated by the Holy Spirit) as the primary source of authentic faith (cf. *Revisioning Evangelical Theology: A Fresh Agenda for the 21st Century* [Downers Grove, Ill.: InterVarsity, 1993]). Other worldview critics have emerged from the ranks of the Wesleyan tradition, such as Henry Knight III and Roger Olson. Not surprisingly, this worldview negativity is now being prominently voiced in the more popular voices of evangelicalism, notably in Emergent Church leaders, such as Brian McLaren.

5   Theodore Plantinga, "David Naugle and the Quest for a Theory of Everything," *Myodicy* 17 (December 2002),< http://www.alpha.redeemer.ca/tplant/m/MCD.HTM> (accessed October 29, 2007). (Note: The author is saddened by the recent, untimely death of Prof. Plantinga. Our condolences go out to his family and the Redeemer University College community).

6   Ibid., 13.

7   This is the charge brought by Gregory Clark in his "pre-Webber" essay, "The Nature of Conversion: How the Rhetoric of Worldview Philosophy Can Betray Evangelicals," in *The Nature of Confession: Evangelicals and Postliberals in Conversation,* ed. Timothy R. Phillips and Dennis Okholm (Downers Grove, Ill.: Inter Varsity, 1996): 201–18. Clark's article may well be viewed as one of the opening salvos against Christian worldview thinking, coining what has become almost a common mantra among worldview critics; i.e., that the concept did not come into existence prior to the Kantian Revolution (205).

8   Stephen J. Keillor, God's *Judgments: Interpreting History and the Christian Faith* (Downers Grove, Ill.: Inter Varsity, 2007), 15. Keillor argues that "inherent defects in worldview think-

15

to say, the twentieth century, evangelical revival of worldview studies is facing growing criticism from conservative Christianity's twenty-first-century thinkers and leaders. While worldview-oriented programs are apparently prospering, if not even proliferating, among the circles of popular evangelicalism,[9] the transition that is now occurring in the evangelical academy (liberal arts colleges, Bible colleges, and seminaries) from traditional and baby-boomer scholars and educators to what Webber calls "the younger evangelicals" would only seem to suggest that this formidable piece of Christian pedagogy may be on its way out. Clearly, the early strains of a worldview requiem can already be heard among the memberships of conservative scholarly societies (e.g., the Evangelical Theological Society), and within the next quarter century, the funeral song may indeed reach its grand finale. The question, then, that looms in front of us, seems apparent: "Is it time to put to rest an aged 'way of seeing' from a bygone, modern era and allow worldview thinking to die an honorable death?" In other words, is it now incumbent on evangelicals to get on with an approach to Christianity that is more appropriate to our experientially-driven age?

Yet this inquiry may be a bit premature. Maybe "worldview" is not really as modernistic as its contemporary critics claim. Could it actually be the legitimate offspring of a time even more bygone than modernity, a time pre-dating the origins of Protestantism? Could it also be that one can hardly account for the profound influence of Christianity on Western civilization—particularly in the development of science—apart from some notion of Christian worldview? And furthermore, could one possibly even argue that worldview is an inherently biblical motif—much like the concept of trinity—that is less constrictive and rigidly doctrinaire, more holistic and communally-lived—than the models served up by both its practitioners and critics? Since music is considered less reductive than philosophy, given its ability to connect with the imagination and emotions, we will use it as an analogy for describing a concept that is too rich to be caught in the sterile language of the philosopher. Consequently, in the ensuing pages, I will attempt to argue that *weltanschauung* is less a pop tune for a past generation and more a classic for all time; less

---

ing prevent it from adequately addressing divine judgment in history" (14), and like many critics, contends that it cannot extricate itself from a grounding in philosophy. According to this thoughtful author, the tragic occurrences of "9/11" demonstrate the inadequacy of worldview to account for "unique, unpredictable events" (14) since it (allegedly) has no room for the judgments of God (16–17). I will contend, later in this paper, that the concept of "worldview" is not inherently inimical to the notion of divine wrath; moreover, a biblically-driven understanding demands the inclusion of such a lens.

9   Charles Colson's "Breakpoint" columns, Focus on the Family's "The Truth Project," and James Emery White's "Serious Times" are good examples of this phenomena.

an organ-driven Fanny Crosby hymn (no matter how delightful a saint she was) and more an orchestral Bach concerto that never loses its savor and power and is regarded as great music no matter the time or space. While I will candidly admit that some (perhaps, too many) evangelical renderings of worldview carry with it the strains of modernism, I will also attempt to show that this is not due to any imperfection with the composition itself, but rather with a somewhat normal accommodation to the tastes of the given generation—even to the tastes of the current, postmodern audience. In short, I intend to demonstrate that the current crop of choruses announcing the death of worldview thinking are themselves pre-mortem songs or, to borrow Mark Twain's expression, news that has been "greatly exaggerated."

WORLDVIEW: A BIBLICAL AND PRE-MODERN CLASSIC

In what can only be called a case of postmodern irony, David Naugle's great *weltanschauung* defense, *Worldview: The History of the Concept,* appeared in bookstores the very same year as Robert Webber's *The Younger Evangelicals* gave notice of the concept's demise.[10] In this monumental and still largely unparalleled work, Naugle, a philosophy professor at Dallas Baptist University, offers what the title suggests: a historical survey of the term, discussing its development in the hands of nineteenth- and twentieth-century Protestant evangelicals (i.e., James Orr and Abraham Kuyper), as well as in forms less well known (at least to Protestant evangelicals) manifested in the writings of Roman Catholic pontiff John Paul II and Eastern Orthodox theologian Alexander Schmemann.[11] While the customary language of worldview is absent from these representatives of wider Christendom, "imbedded in both traditions is an inner impulse to express their comprehension of Christianity as a *Weltanschauung*."[12] Naugle further comments:

> Nestled in the pope's program of Christian humanism is nothing less than a comprehensive Catholic interpretation of the universe centered on the incarnation of Jesus Christ and the dignity of persons. Since the spirit of Eastern Orthodoxy militates against theological ratiocination, formulating a propositional Orthodox worldview is a rarity. This does not mean that such an entity is missing. . . . Its source is found in the church's liturgy, and from this wellspring Schmemann is capable of outlining an Orthodox perception of life at its sacramental and priestly best.[13]

---

10   David K. Naugle, *Worldview: The History of a Concept* (Grand Rapids: Eerdmans, 2002).

11   Ibid.; see especially pages 4–54.

12   Ibid., 52.

13   Ibid., 53.

Following his discussion of worldview's fairly recent theological pilgrimage, Naugle then turns to the philological and philosophical origins of *weltanschauung*, almost admitting the allegedly non-Christian roots of the concept.[14] Virtually no one disputes that the term was coined by the eighteenth-century Prussian philosopher Immanuel Kant in his 1790 tome, *Critique of Judgment*.[15] Most Kant scholars and commentators (including Martin Heidegger) believe that *weltanschauung* carried with it little more than the notion of our "sense perception of the world" in its original usage, and only achieved the more commonly understood, Enlightenment meaning of intellectual cosmic comprehension in the ensuing generations of German thinkers.[16] Subsequent German philosophers, particularly G. W. F. Hegel and, most significantly, Wilhelm Dilthey, provided this term with much of its present-day content, including the rather paradoxical concepts of the autonomous human mind's ability to process reality—and to shape it through one's own subjective experiences.[17]

This latent relativism would later surface in the writings of Friedrich Nietzsche, as this well-known nihilist would view every *weltanschauung* as merely a human construction (deconstruction?) of the world shaped by the knower's time, place, and culture.[18] Whereas Dilthey appeared to keep his relativism in check, Nietzsche, on the other hand was bent on allowing worldview *perspectivalism* full nihilistic reign. In his conviction that language was largely responsible for shaping one's world, however, he was anticipating the twentieth-century responses of the later Ludwig Wittgenstein and the Frenchman,

---

14 Ibid., 55–186. Naugle will later liken the concept of worldview to Augustine's well-known analogy of "Egyptian gold;" i.e., appropriating pagan notions and employing them in means suitable to Christian truth. He comments: "If we follow Augustine's reasoning, we can propose that believers need to . . . cleanse it of its pagan associations, reform it biblically, and make it a concept submissive to Christ" (259). In this paper, I will argue that while the Enlightenment may have coined the term *weltanschauung*, a distinctive, Christian approach to reality had long been in operation—without the reductive rationalism of its later European expositors.

15 Ibid., 58, 59.

16 Ibid., 59; 68–73; 82–98.

17 Ibid., 68–73; 82–98. A biblically driven and "historical," Christian understanding of epistemology (in large part due to its doctrine of creation) escapes this Nietzschian (and more recently, postmodernist) critique.

18 Ibid., 98–107. Naugle rightly comments that in spite of Nietzsche's "extremist perspectivism," the latter's writing does "contain an essential insight . . . [that] all human beings see things aslant, Christians included. . . . If held in balance, this position can avoid the excesses of both modernist dogmatism and postmodernist skepticism and terminate in a kind of critical realism which recognizes the role of both objectivist and subjectivist factors in the knowing process" (106). The historic Christian Faith's ability to *separate ontology from epistemology* (largely though its doctrine of creation) allows it to escape this Nietzschian (and more recently, postmodernist) critique.

Michel Foucault, who both gave up any idea of knowing anything about objective reality, conceding instead that all we have access to are linguistic constructions. Even more despairingly, in the case of the latter, worldviews are generally used by a powerful elite in order to oppress society's weak.[19]

In actuality, the philological and historical history of *weltanschauung* is nothing short of a narration of how the Western world transitioned from a modernistic ethos to a postmodern one, beginning with a brimming confidence in the ability of human reason to comprehend the cosmos and ending with frustration and cynicism that such a project was hopelessly unattainable and, in practice, patently destructive. Indeed, if David Naugle had concluded his volume at this point, we would have been left with the conclusion that so many of our contemporaries are voicing: i.e., worldview is a failed, modern philosophic program that has finally been exposed for what it is by postmodern thinkers. Rather than taking the approach of earlier evangelicals, who rushed to imitate Augustine's policy of plundering the Egyptians, today's worldview critics would have us run in the other direction from epistemology that itself cannot escape its original Kantian clutches.

But the Naugle story does not end with postmodern deconstructive philosophy. While *weltanschauung* has arguably fallen out of favor with these philosophers (although not a few, prominent, evangelical Christian philosophers, such as J. P. Moreland and William Lane Craig are strong worldview proponents), it has gained another life in the circles of the natural and social sciences.[20] This unexpected vitality is particularly seen in the writings of Michael Polanyi and Thomas Kuhn, two philosophers of science who still tower over the landscape. In brief, Polanyi argued that "faith and belief are the inescapable starting points of the knowing process," whereas Kuhn left an indelible imprint in twentieth-century intellectual history with his well-known and often-cited analysis of scientific paradigm revolution.[21] While Kuhn severely overstates his case for "paradigm incommensurability,"

---

19 Ibid. See especially pages 148–162, and 180–185.

20 Ibid., 187. It should be noted that in spite of postmodernism's toll on continental philosophy, there has been a significant resurgence in Anglo-American philosophy that has been heavily influenced by theists. According to atheist philosopher Quentin Smith, "God is not 'dead' in academia; he returned to life in the late 1960's and is now alive and well in his last academic stronghold, philosophy departments" (cited in *Philosophic Foundations for a Christian Worldview*, edited by J.P. Moreland and William Lane Craig [Downers Grove, Ill.: InterVarsity, 2003], 3). In short, it seems that theistic belief fuels the philosophic discipline whereas the lack of such contributes to its demise. This observation should at least give us caution as we evaluate the younger evangelicals' disdain for worldview and its unholy alliance with philosophy.

21 Ibid., 206–208.

he nonetheless draws attention to the reality that the scientific and scholarly enterprise always proceeds along the lines of an "established pre-understanding of reality," or worldview. This preferred paradigm, then, is subsequently reinforced or ultimately rejected on the basis of its ability to explain the data of reality; hence, we have witnessed the abandonment of Ptolemaic cosmology for one of Newtonian mechanics, and in the last century, the latter's repudiation in favor of a universe described in terms of Einsteinian relativity.[22] Not surprisingly, Kuhn's work has been implemented by a variety of disciplines as they attempt to chronicle their own histories.[23]

The social sciences of psychology, anthropology, and sociology have also been shaped—and are currently being impacted—by the concept of worldview. After briefly surveying the work of Freud and Jung, Naugle offers the following observation:

> [A]ny program of psychotherapy—Freudian, Jungian, or otherwise—is established upon fundamental worldview assumptions, and philosophical underpinnings as such are extremely influential factors in the overall psychotherapeutic process.[24]

More recent publications by the American Psychological Association bear out this positive assessment of worldview's ability to understand the nature of human persons.[25] In addition, applied psychology disciplines like criminal justice utilize worldview thinking in defining

---

22 Ibid., 198–199. Without something like a governing paradigm, contends Kuhn, it is hard to account for new, scientific discoveries, since the very uniqueness of these findings presupposes that in some way, they are deviations from an accepted view (Thomas S. Kuhn, *The Structure of Scientific Revolutions* [Chicago: University of Chicago Press, 1970], 10–22).

23 Kuhn's paradigm doctrine has been appropriated in many and diverse ways, including by those committed to an antirealist constructivism and/or a coherentist view of knowledge. Kuhn himself denied the charge of relativism, although he admitted that there was "no theory-independent way to reconstruct phrases like 'really-there'" since "the notion of a match between the ontology of a theory and its 'real' counterpart in nature now seems to me illusive in principle" (*The Structure of Scientific Revolution*, 206). As intimated earlier, the biblical doctrine of creation *ex nihilo* appears to be the only solution to distinguishing reality from its interpretation(s).

24 Naugle, *Worldviews: The History*, 222.

25 Noted clinical psychologist William R. Miller writes: "I find it quite useful the German noun *Menschenbild*—one's fundamental understanding (picture) of the nature of the human person. It is the person-level parallel to a more familiar term within psychology, *Weltanschauung*—one's world view or broader understanding of reality" (William R. Miller and Harold D. Delaney, *Judeo-Christian Perspectives on Reality: Human Nature, Motivation, and Change* (Washington, DC: American Psychological Association, 2005), 16. Miller then goes on to articulate eight tenets that he believes are necessary to a theistic understanding of human nature: reality of spirit, human beings are not God, sin, agency, spiritual health, relational responsibility, hope, and transformation (16–19).

the disparate models of reality that distinguish a criminal from a so-cially-healthy mind.[26] If *weltanschauung* carries with it an incurable tendency towards relativism as its critics (not to mention its history) suggest, it is interesting to note that in fields like criminal justice there are views of reality that are clearly wrong.

The "twin disciplines" of anthropology and sociology likewise bear the imprint of worldview, especially as they explain how individual persons and society process the reality in which they find themselves.[27] In particular, these fields have brought a more diachronic approach to *weltanschauung*-thinking, focusing attention on such philosophically-ignored features as a worldview's narrative function. Rather than simply providing the synchronic topics (e.g., God, cosmos, human nature, death, etc.) that occupy the attention of philosophers and systematic theologians, anthropologists and sociologists have noted that shared stories or meta-narratives of a culture's origins, purpose, and destiny are very helpful in explaining indigenous behavior.[28] Although these "cosmic myths" can run the gamut from Marx's materialistically-driven history of class struggle to Peter Berger's more general concept of a society-protecting "sacred canopy," this approach has, in essence, elevated these two disciplines to a level where they are regularly viewing individuals and cultures through *system* lenses,

---

26 Clinical psychologists often utilize "worldview-like" language to both analyze and bring correction to an offender's perception of reality. Clinical concepts like *irrational beliefs* and *schemas* assume that the client is in some way thinking incorrectly and irrationally and therefore needs to be taught to either think more logically (in the case of the former) and/or to unpack a flawed life narrative (e.g.; "people I depend upon always leave me in the end," in the case of the latter). See Thomas Bien, "Story and Narrative," in *Judeo-Christian Perspectives on Reality*, 95–112. It is interesting to note that these clinical concepts suggest a worldview understanding that is both synchronic and diachronic in its essential nature, a dual character that has only recently been showing up in theological discussions of the concept.

27 Naugle, *Worldview: The History*, 222–252.

28 The anthropological-sociological understanding of worldview as a diachronic ("story") device has been appropriated in the circles of evangelical *missiology*, particularly in the work of the late Paul Hiebert. A helpful discussion of worldview as both narrative and core beliefs is found in *Understanding Folk Religion: A Christian Response to Popular Beliefs and Practices*, edited by Paul Hiebert, R. Daniel Shaw, and Tite Tienou (Grand Rapids: Baker, 1999); see especially pages 95–132. The influence of Clifford Geertz is clearly seen (and admitted) in Hiebert's work. Interestingly, Hiebert, the *anthropologist* by trade, believes there is such a thing as a *biblical worldview* that God was preparing his Old Testament people to embrace, "in which the incarnation, death and resurrection of Christ could adequately be understood.... Some will argue that there is no such thing as a biblical worldview. If not, then the gospel deals only with limited cultural and social matters at the surface matter" (Paul Hiebert, "The Social Sciences and Missions: Applying the Message," in *Missiology and the Social Sciences: Contributions, Cautions, and Conclusions*, edited by Edward Rommen and Gary Corwin [Pasadena, Cal.: William Carey Library, 1996]: 206 [184–213]). In a recent, posthumously-published volume, Hiebert argues that *genuine conversion* to Christ—usually measured by changes in belief and/or behavior—is precipitated by a change in *worldview*. (Paul Hiebert, *Transforming Worldviews: An Anthropological Understanding on How People Change* [Baker, 2008]).

noting themes and ideas that are common throughout the human race, although expressed at times in dramatically different ways.[29] Such insights have particularly been helpful to evangelical missiologists as they have attempted to articulate evangelistic strategies that result in genuine conversion, not merely "baptized pagans."[30]

As we travel with Naugle through the disciplines and appreciate the prominence that worldview thinking plays in both their formation and their present constitution, a gnawing question still remains: Can the concept of *weltanschauung* — with all its merits — be extricated from its apparently Enlightenment philosophic origins? While we have extolled its successful application in psychology, anthropology, and sociology, we have also seen that these fields can do little more than describe the beliefs and behaviors that undergird individuals and societies—hardly adequate for a faith that is regularly expressed in the rich, experiential language of "in Christ," not to mention in the sacramental events of baptism and eucharist? Did not the great Karl Barth warn us against imprisoning the God of the Bible within a philosophic framework?[31] A "history of the concept" may be intellectually satisfying, but is it ultimately serviceable to such a non-reductionistic religion as Christianity, with its less-than-comprehensible notion of a three-in-one deity? In candid terms we, the evangelical heirs of Kuyper, must ask: Is "Abraham" after Kant or before him? Or more directly: Is the notion of a biblical worldview itself biblical? Once again, we have David Naugle to thank for pointing us in a helpful direction.

THE BIBLICAL BASIS FOR A BIBLICAL WORLDVIEW

For many Christian critics of worldview, the term's strongly cognitive association—quite repugnant to postmoderns—is matched by its failure to yield anything like a norming model of reality, given that all cosmic descriptions are limited by the time, place, and culture of the observer. While many moderns believed that they were engaged in genuinely objective research, in reality they were unable to transcend

---

29 Naugle, *Worldview: The History*, 227–233.

30 Hiebert, "The Social Sciences and Missions," 205–207.

31 Karl Barth, *Church Dogmatics* III/3, ed. G.W. Bromiley and T.F. Torrance, trans. G.W. Bromiley and R.J. Ehrlich (Edinburgh: T. & T. Clark, 1960. 140. Cited in Naugle, *Worldview: The History*, 335). In response to Barth (and his contemporary, evangelical) worldview critics, the words of Carl Henry still ring true: ". . . scholars who deplore the notion of a Christian world view are not immune to sponsoring covertly or promoting an alternative world view while professing to purge Christianity of supposed non-Christian commitments. While Barth dismisses every world view as intellectual barbarism, he has a world view of his own, inconsistent though it may be" (Carl F.H. Henry, "Fortunes of the Christian World View," *Trinity Journal* , n.s. 19 [1998]:168 [163–176]).

their situational finiteness, thereby making any claim of universal knowledge dubious at best and arrogant at worst. With postmodernity's "outing" of the myth of certainty, it now appears that continued discussion of a biblical worldview is impossible and unprofitable. Theodore Plantinga is among those who contend that this inherent relativism renders worldview virtually unusable for Christian consumption, unless it is radically cleansed.[32] But Naugle is not quite ready to cede the concept to merely human convention; rather, he contends, its true—and non-relativistic—roots sink deep into the pages of Scripture itself.

> Worldview in Christian perspective implies the objective existence of the Trinitarian God whose essential character establishes the moral order of the universe and whose word, wisdom, and law define and govern all aspects of created existence.[33]

The opening words of the Bible remind us that reality is not the construction of finite human wisdom but is the creation of the eternal, Triune God, who is independent and transcendent over everything. The biblical creation narrative provides the only real escape from relativism in that it opens with a pre-existent creator who calls into being a bounded (and therefore real) creation that, in turn, is embedded with His plurality-in-oneness and moral authority in its creational diversity and purposeful structure and order.[34]

The first three chapters of Genesis lay out the rudimentary plotlines of a story that will, in turn, organize and interpret the rest of the Bible, as well as potentially our everyday existence. In its seminal narrative, Genesis 1—3 sets forth the determinative events that shape the believing community's responses to life's key questions: 1) Why are we—or is anything, for that matter—here?; 2) What has gone wrong?; and 3) How will it be repaired?[35] Genesis offers a story that answers

---

32 Plantinga, "David Naugle and the Quest for a Theory," 16.

33 Naugle, *Worldview: The History*, 260.

34 Ibid., 261.

35 In a recent *JETS* article, I argued a similar point: "The Bible begins with *ontology*—the (pre)existence of God followed by the creation of his grand, but finite universe. Ontology *precedes* epistemology in the creation narrative; that is, something/one is really there, independent of one's perception about the reality of the cosmos" (Robert C. Kurka, "Before 'Foundationalism: A More Biblical Alternative to the Grenz/Franke Proposal for Doing Theology" *JETS* 50:1 [March 2007]: 152, n. 28.) It is my suspicion that behind some of the current dismissal of "absolute truth" and/or "objectivity" on the part of evangelical worldview critics is a tendency to view Genesis 1—3 (4—11) as largely mythical and ahistorical. While I am not disputing the primarily *literary structure* of the creation account, the Genesis writer is clearly presenting a cosmos that took form *prior* to human observation, a "literal sequence"

these concerns with a three-part drama of God's creation, humanity's (and subsequently, all creation's) fall, and God's promise of cosmic redemption that will be accomplished through the work of the "woman's seed" (Gen 3:15). This meta-narrative, then (one that intentionally incorporates and corrects all cultural meta-narratives) provides the basic information that will ground the rest of God's dealings with his people: His commands, laws, creedal recitations, prophetic utterances, their mission, the nature and work of Christ, the ministry of the Holy Spirit in the church and the world, and finally the *eschaton*, or in Milton's words, "paradise regained." As Nancy Pearcey, student of Francis Schaeffer, has noted so well, "the Bible does not begin with the command to invite Jesus into your heart, but rather with the words, 'In the beginning, God created the heavens and the earth.'"[36]

At the end of the Genesis 1 creation narrative, we encounter the first commission given by God to humanity: "Be fruitful and multiply and rule over creation" (1:28). Lynn White notwithstanding, can such words entail anything but a mandate to view all creation as God's gift to his human creation and to use those capacities that set us apart from the animals in a manner that honors the creator and carefully stewards creation? Present-day worldview enthusiasts have dubbed this the "cultural commission," and, I believe, with good reason, since these words clearly articulate our human purpose and destiny: to consciously recognize and respect God's ownership of the entire cosmos in our work, in our communities (small and large), and in a manner that literally incarnates the Creator in its character and conduct.[37] This is worldview in the thickest sense of the concept, thus making the subsequent Fall, recorded in Genesis 3, a worldview rebellion: i.e., Adam's choosing to adopt the socially-constructed and non-real perspective of Satan instead of faithfully obeying God and creational ontology.

In the Fall narrative we first encounter a plurality of world views—and even the initial charge that worldviews are relative—but clearly only one *weltanschauung* leads to life, whereas the other, unambiguously, spells death (Gen 3:1–5; cf. Rom 5:12ff). While most evangelical theologians would see God's special revelation as more than remedial (he speaks his intentions to humanity prior to the Fall), the intervention

---

that places epistemology in subordination to ontology.

36 Nancy Pearcey, *Total Truth: Liberating Christianity from Its Cultural Captivity* (Wheaton, Ill.: Crossway Books, 2005), 45. The creation-fall-redemption scheme is also a staple in the 1980s' fine works of Albert Wolters, *Creation Regained: Biblical Basics for a Reformational Worldview* (Grand Rapids: Eerdmans, 1985), and Brian Walsh and J. Richard Middleton, *The Transforming Vision: Shaping a Christian Worldview* (Downers Grove, Ill.: Inter Varsity, 1984.)

37 See, for example, Charles Colson and Nancy Pearcey, *How Now Shall We Live?* (Wheaton, Ill.: Tyndale House, 1999), 17.

of sin and its resultant death, destruction, and often godless vision, surely demand divine speech if we have any hope of fulfilling our cultural mandate. And thus, through the use of various and sundry means, the Triune God embarks on a grand worldview-correcting mission that will culminate with the Word become flesh (Jhn 1:14) and a global community that will slowly gain his vision until all is bright, once again, at the *eschaton* (Rev 22:1–5).

In one of his most helpful contributions to a theology of *weltanschauung*, Naugle calls our attention to the prominent use of the term "heart" in Scripture, a term that biblical scholars have long recognized for its holistic connotations.[38] While "heart" has clearly been adulterated with heavy notions of emotion and subjectivity in our time, the biblical writers saw the *kardia* (Heb. *leb*), as a fitting euphemism to describe all that made up the inner person: his or her beliefs, thoughts, values, desires, and commitments.[39] It is both cognitive and affective and the seat of unbelief ("the fool says in his heart there is no God") and trust in Yahweh (the *shema*). Out of the heart proceed human actions, both good and evil.[40] One's visible and not so visible treasures are the products and evidence of the heart, or one's view of what is ultimately real.[41] It is Naugle's contention that this simple, but complex biblical word is Scripture's own term to describe the concept of worldview, a word that defies the reductionism—and relativism—that history's more recent expression, *weltanschauung*, appears to have a difficult time avoiding. While it is possible—and highly probable—that the heart believes and cherishes things that are clearly in opposition to God, it is also possible to have a right (or pure) heart that magnifies itself in justice, righteousness, mercy, and truth.[42] Undoubtedly, much more detailed, exegetical work still needs to be done on the worldview nuances that this term seems to entail.

As I further peruse the Bible's contents, another key worldview-related concept appears to reside in the Wisdom literature and its focus upon living outside of the cult.[43] Sapiential thought is difficult for west-

---

38 Naugle, *Worldview: The History*, 267–274.

39 Ibid., 267. See especially, Alex Nuc, "*Leb*", in *New International Dictionary of Old Testament Theology and Exegesis*, edited by Willem A. VanGemeren (Grand Rapids: Zondervan, 1997) 2:749–754. Nuc summarizes the meaning of *leb* and *lebab* : "In the OT, the words have a dominant metaphorical use in reference to the center of human psychical and spiritual life, to the entire inner life of a person" (749).

40 Cf. Ps 14:1; Deut 6:4–5; Matt 15:18–20.

41 Cf. Matt 6:19–21; Lk 12:32–34.

42 Cf. Jer 17:9 ("deceitful heart") with the "godly heart" in Ps 119:1–3, 7, 10, 30, etc., Matt 5:8.

43 For a recent, excellent discussion on the "communal" nature of OT Wisdom Literature, see William P. Brown, *Character in Crisis* (Grand Rapids: Eerdmans, 1996).

erners to get their hands around, with their preference for neat, succinct, and precise rules and steps of application. Wisdom literature forces us to look at everyday life the way it is—messy, unpredictable, seemingly chaotic and unjust—and assess these realities in a manner that tends to apply the narrative of Scripture (creation-fall-redemption-new creation) to making sense out of a life situation more than importing the direct, terse words of *torah*.[44] It is not surprising to see why the author of Proverbs reminds us that this somewhat tenuous approach to faithful living needs to be carefully submitted to the fear of the Lord.[45] This not-so-clean attempt to honor God's creational intentions and standards may well suggest that our worldview formulation is never going to be an exact science.

The Incarnation provides us with the most ringing and tangible model of what life lived with a true heart (worldview) looks like, as Jesus embodies how humanity thinks and acts when its picture of reality is correct. Scholars such as Ben Witherington have noted the strong presence of wisdom in the sayings of Jesus—often times in conflict with the Old Testament tradition of the Jewish teachers, who displayed a strong preference for neat commandments over against the more fluid expressions of *hokma* (cf. Jn 9:1–3, healing of the blind man".[46] This strong, sapiential element that characterizes the life and ministry of Jesus certainly exposes many of our contemporary programs to imitate Christ (generally, in simple, easy-to-follow steps) as the frauds they really are.

The same thing holds true for those who attempt to read the story of the early church in a search for replicable patterns instead of as a record of what Christian people do when they think, feel, and act when their hearts are regenerated by the Spirit of God.[47] They often do things that are hard to understand by those who look at life very pragmatically (cf. Acts 4:31–37), for their narrative of the world reads very differently from those around them. The early church clearly read the same scriptures as their Jewish counterparts, and yet they lived out these divine words (notably in their inclusion of the Gentiles) in new and fresh ways,

---

44 Brown comments: "What the wisdom literature uniquely contributes to the contemporary discussion is neither hard-and-fast principles nor gripping narratives. This often neglected corpus essentially provides characterizations of character, that is to say, profiles of character embodied in certain 'lives of virtue'" (Ibid., 19).

45 Cf. Prov 1:7, et.al.

46 Ben Witherington, III, *Jesus the Sage: The Pilgrimage of Wisdom*. Minneapolis: Fortress, 1994.

47 Aside from the obvious display of divine healing seen in this miracle, Jesus is exposing the folly of his disciples (and their culture) because they could regularly pass by hurting people and not see significant opportunities to "display God's work" in deeds of kindness. Wisdom foregoes needless and unprofitable theological discussion in favor of embodying the healing grace of God.

evidencing that Jeremiah and Ezekiel's prophecies of changed, human hearts had come to pass. One cannot simply ape the *kardia* that drives the Acts narrative.

Worldview thinking of the more narrative, sapiential variey is also seen in the writings of Paul, in his ethical admonitions for sure, but even more dramatically in his eschatology. Many scholars consider Paul's "now-and-not yet" perspective to be his most significant contribution to biblical theology.[48] But is not this stroke of Spirit-led Pauline genius itself a by-product of a concept of reality that has understood redemption in delayed terms; e.g., exodus, exile, and the promised messiah? Certainly, Christ's death and resurrection is the decisive event that guarantees cosmic restoration, but even this most final of divine redemptive acts denies its adherents immediate satisfaction. While God has given his people a substantial deposit on their future inheritance (the Holy Spirit, Eph 1:13-14), they must live out their hope in much the same manner as their first exodus forebears (cf. Heb 11). This pilgrimage demands the wisdom of the sages as every generation of Christian encounters life situations that their predecessors could have never anticipated. One thing is sure: Perfect solutions to human (and cosmic) problems will never be struck in this life; even partial ones (such as the eradication of slavery as an institution) come only after years, even centuries, of struggle. But struggle we must![49]

It may be argued that these worldview dynamics find their consummate expression in that deliciously enticing (and frequently

---

48 See for example C. Marvin Pate, *The End of the World Has Come* (Grand Rapids: Zondervan, 1995). Paul's eschatological perspective is seen in such admonitions as those he gives regarding the Christian and the state (Ro 13:1–7; cf. 1 Ti 2:2), lawsuits (1 Co 6:1–15), and slavery (Eph 6:5–9; Col 3:22–4:1; Phlm). In each of these (and other) contexts, the apostle is calling upon believers to set aside their need for immediate justice or vindication in favor of a patient, prudent lifestyle that confidently looks forward to its reward at the *parousia*. Our present refusal to demand our rights, in turn, effects a positive response toward the Christian community from the outside world, and, in time, even societal change (as the history of Christianity has demonstrated countless times).

49 McMaster University scholar Stephen Westerholm has recently proposed that Paul's writings (especially the Romans Epistle) need to be read as a "worldview treatise." Westerholm comments: " Even casual readers of his letters sense that Paul was a man completely captivated by a particular way of looking at life. . . . Indeed, for many, Paul's captivation proved contagious: the vision of life that Paul communicated gave new direction and significance to their lives as well. It provided them with a sense of what they should and should not do, and motivation for doing what (in the light of the vision) they were convinced was right and worthwhile. In the two millennia since then, Paul's letters have played essentially the same role for millions of readers: they have proved to be a compelling, illuminating, and treasured guide to life." (Stephen Westerholm, *Understanding Paul: The Early Christian Worldview of the Letter to the Romans*, 2nd ed. [Grand Rapids: Baker Academic, 2004], 10). Since this publication, the author has added another "worldview reading" of a NT book (and genre): *Understanding Matthew: The Early Christian Worldview of the First Gospel* (Baker, 2006).

frustrating!) final volume of the New Testament, John's *Revelation*. In a book that is as much concerned with how God's people live their lives in the present as it is with the future coming of Christ (if not more so!), the Revelator reminds his readers that reality is not merely what it appears to be. While the earth's inhabitants (and especially the Church) experiences a world of satanic oppression, persecution, famine, disease, natural disasters, and death (cf. Rev 6), the true center of the universe is the "throne room of heaven," occupied by the Father, Son, and Spirit, who are, in turn, receiving the worship of unseen, but very real, celestial beings (chaps. 4—5). In fact, the Lamb (the ascended Jesus) is actually in charge of the avalanche of judgments that are poured out upon this cosmos (e.g., "come"—6:1, 3, 5, et al), and ultimately these do not bring about the destruction of Christ's followers but rather of the kingdoms of this world, death, and the devil himself (cf. chap. 20).[50] In reality, God's kingdom is advancing to its final, glorious end, a kingdom ruled not by political and military despots but rather populated by his saints, many of whom may spill their blood as martyrs (cf. 6:9–11; 14:13; 20:4). This portrait of reality may indeed be counterintuitive, but the one who is "the faithful witness" (1:5) assures us that this unveiling (admittedly, in a highly symbolic, apocalyptic format) represents the true state of affairs. Consequently, he exhorts his people to "hear what the Spirit says" (2:7, 11, 17, et al) and "be victorious" over the evil forces that deceptively present themselves as god over this universe. Could there be a finer (or more imaginative!) portrait of a worldview centered in the triune God, his redemption in Christ—in both present and future dimensions—and the necessity for Christians to exercise a trans-sensual wisdom that recognizes that what meets the eye may not really be the case!

The corrected sight offered in the Book of Revelation further reminds us of one of the major sub-themes of the New Testament; i.e., that it is precisely through the regenerative work of the Holy Spirit that we are able to recognize that Jesus is "the Messiah" (cf. Matt 16:16, 17—"this [Christological confession] was not revealed to you [Peter]

---

50 See G. K. Beale, *The Book of Revelation*, NIGNTC (Grand Rapids: Eerdmans, 1999). The notion that the Book of Revelation is, among other things, a quintessential presentation of the biblical worldview, has recently taken the form of a workshop in Lincoln Christian College and Seminary's "Bible and Worldview Seminar." In this unique workshop (at least, among the many popular worldview-oriented seminars), LCS dean and NT scholar Robert Lowery argues that the "The Worldview of the Book of Revelation" is primarily a *theo-/christo-centric* view of reality that, in turn, ensures the completion of God's kingdom on earth, rather than a book of futuristic emphases that often dominate discussions of the Apocalypse in local churches.

by flesh and blood"). As we then consider this Spirit-fueled, cosmic vision, common ecclesiastical practices literally explode with new meaning. The well-known baptismal confession, "Jesus is Lord," (Rom 10:9; 1 Cor 12:3) is a commitment to centering all of life around his rule. The sacraments themselves are visual and existential experiences of what is really real (forgiveness, life, and community). On another note, Paul's use of military imagery to describe the Christian journey or Jesus' call to enter the "narrow gate" remind us that reality is more than what humans conventionally see. Such conventional sight is, in fact, the product of demonic deception.[51] Evangelism becomes a worldview encounter, such as the kind described in Acts 17:16 ff, where Paul preaches the gospel to pagan intellectuals by summarizing the biblical narrative (creation-final judgment) in a manner that clearly exposes the inadequacies of Stoic and Epicurean explanatory systems.[52] The *Areopagus Address* is also a fitting demonstration that Christians can point out the faults with other belief systems and do it with respect, since we are cognizant that false ideas, not human beings, are the enemy (cf. Eph 6:12). Not surprisingly, Paul's use of a worldview apologetic is being more frequently drawn upon in our postmodern culture that is pluralistic, biblically ignorant, and certainly intolerant of those who tell them they are wrong. In my own experience, such an approach has even facilitated a more constructive atmosphere for dialogue and more healthy forms of Christian witness.[53]

---

51 Cf. Eph 6:10–18; 2 Cor 10:3–5; Matt 7:13–14.

52 The apologetic nature of this passage has long been recognized. See especially the classic work by Bertil Gartner, *The Aeropagus Speech and Natural Revelation* (Uppsala: C. W. K. Gleerup, 1955), and the brief, but poignant discussion of D.A. Carson in his *The Gagging of God: Christianity Confronts Pluralism* (Grand Rapids: Zondervan, 1996), 496–505. Carson most helpfully draws attention to Paul's use of a biblical storyline in this speech to make intelligible his proclamation of the gospel to an audience confused about Jesus and the resurrection (v. 18).

53 In the fall of 2007, I was invited to speak at a public assembly called by churches in a small, rural community that had recently become home to a "witch school." Rather than allowing this venue to become a forum to fuel fear and hostility towards the wiccans , I chose to take the "Areopagus Approach" and engage the participants in a worldview discussion; first describing, then comparing and contrasting the understandings about reality that govern both *pagans* (in the technical, not pejorative sense) and Christians. This presentation had a calming effect upon all in the audience (including a few wiccans) and encouraged believers to befriend, pray for, and constructively evangelize their neighbors (as well as reminded the "witch school crowd" that their worldview is being abandoned in large numbers by adherents in the world that Phillip Jenkins describes, a southern hemisphere that is becoming rapidly Christian, in large part due to the Gospel's ability to address the key issues of life). *The Chicago Tribune*, in fact, took note of the peace power of worldview: "Instead of leading a pep rally against the witches, the professor at Lincoln Christian College and Seminary delivered an academic lecture comparing Wicca and Christianity…When the meeting was over, many of the opponents appeared calm. They vowed to turn down their anger and increase their prayers. Lewis (CEO of the witch school) was pleasantly surprised." (Megan Twohey, "Witch

Allow me to transition to a less obvious, yet no less important example of the New Testament's giving evidence that believers are presumably operating with a distinctive *weltanschauung*. In his 2003 essay, "A Christian World-View and the Futures of Evangelicalism," Craig Bartholomew further demonstrates the value that a biblically-driven, Christian worldview brings to contemporary Christians. In this thoughtful piece of theological reflection, the author agues that worldview is practically necessary for believers to properly understand the "central church activities such as evangelism and discipleship"; moreover, "it even influences the way we read the Scriptures."[54] Using the Lord's Prayer to illustrate his point, Bartholomew notes that the words "hallowed be your name, and your kingdom come, your will be done on earth as it is in heaven" are practically meaningless if we lack some prior knowledge about who this God is, his character and nature as one who is totally distinct from *his* creation and its creatures; a holy God who, alone, warrants worship and praise. In order to hallow his character or name, we have to have some idea of what it is. The basic introduction to this God, of course, is provided in the opening chapters of Genesis.[55] Furthermore, any concrete idea of what God's heavenly kingdom looks like in this-world form is also derived from the biblical story of creation in which we are given a vision of a perfect, harmonious, universe—" a world in which God is acknowledged in every area of life as he made it."[56] Thus, when Christians pray the Lord's Prayer, they are committing themselves to intentionally work and live in this creation-sized, divine restoration project. Obviously, the Church's all-too-frequent lapse into dualism (in which some areas are deemed sacred and others are not, and some vocations are "ministry," whereas others are "secular jobs") is out of sync with the creation-generated petitions of the model prayer. The absence of believers in politics, economics, the arts, etc., is evidence that we really have not grasped the scope intended in Jesus' prayer.[57] Bartholomew further notes that the this lack of creational perspective not only restrains Christians from seeing every sphere as a potential ministry field, but also puts *creation itself* at risk. He aptly comments:

School Fails to Charm Town," *Chicago Tribune* 10/28/2007).

54 Craig G. Bartholomew, "A Christian World-view and the Futures of Evangelicalism," in *The Futures of Evangelicalism: Issues and Prospects*, edited by Craig Bartholomew, Robin Parry, and Andrew West (Grand Rapids: Kregel, 2003): 201 (194–220).

55 Ibid., 201.

56 Ibid., 201.

57 Ibid., 202.

Creation flourishes as it fulfills its God-given intentions. In God's good but fallen world the well-being of creation thus depends to a significant extent on the structures of creation being directed in obedience to God rather than in rebellion against God. In our modern, Western democracies with their welfare nets and high standards of living it is too easy to forget the human cost of bad politics and disastrous economics.[58]

Craig Bartholomew's essay provides us with a fitting conclusion to the biblical conclusion to our discussion of worldview's biblical basis. Without something like a *weltanschauung* in place, the earliest disciples of Jesus would be clueless about fundamental things like prayer and the scope as well as manner of their "Great Commission" mandate. Jesus' Model Prayer *presumes* a grand meta-narrative that the genuine believer will cherish in his/her heart. Furthermore, as recipients of the indwelling Holy Spirit, such a vision will be divinely enabled and empowered—often in highly anticipated ways—as the ensuing history of Christianity so eloquently testifies.

MEDIEVAL CHURCH HISTORY—"BEFORE ABRAHAM (KUYPER), I (WORLDVIEW) AM"

Evangelical Protestantism has long regarded the development of later patristic-medieval Catholicism as largely a negative turn in the history of the Church, resulting in a distorted aberration of the more pristine Christianity described in the New Testament. While we rarely express it in such brazen terms, many of us have inherited a Protestant myth that assumes that little went right between the years of Augustine to Luther and that the sixteenth-century cultural developments in disciplines like science were solely the product of the Reformation. Today, many of us have come to realize that Christianity enjoyed golden days long before Calvin. Thanks to scholars such as Rodney Stark, evangelicals now are acknowledging their deep debt to their Roman Catholic theological forebears, who years prior to the Reformation (much less Orr and Kuyper) demonstrated the reality of a notion like biblical worldview in their thought and actions.[59]

Stark ably calls attention to the development of a discipline deemed theology in the hands of early Christians due to their faith's unique

---

58 Ibid., 202.

59 See Rodney Stark, *For the Glory of God* (Princeton, N.J.: Princeton University Press, 2003), especially Chapter 2: "God's Handiwork: The Religious Origins of Science," 121–199; and his more recent, less-technical work, The *Victory of Reason: How Christianity Led to Freedom, Capitalism, and Western Success* (New York: Random House, 2005).

ability to be expressed in communicable propositions drawn from the plotlines of an understandable story (cf. New Testament "creeds" and the *Areopagus Address*, discussed previously).[60] This distinctive theologizing capability, then, is seen at work in the ancient Church's construction of its great ecumenical statements of faith (*regula fidei*, Athanasian, Nicene, and Apostles' Creeds), that in turn defined the beliefs and corresponding behaviors that enable the faith to withstand its internal, aberrational voices (e.g., Gnosticism), as well as re-shape the character and values of its largely-pagan environment. Such convictions about the true nature of reality (grounded in the doctrine of creation) gave rise to social practices and developments heretofore not seen in the Roman Empire: women's rights, children's rights, fair treatment of slaves, the creation of hospitals for the sick and needy, etc. In his *Cities of God*, Stark argues that because of its this-worldly concern, Christianity prospered in the *urban* areas (more so than in rural environs, as often presumed) precisely because these societal problems were (and are) so magnified in populated places.[61] While ancient pagan religion could offer only temporal, ecstatic, and highly individualistic spiritual experiences, Christianity, on the other hand, brought a steady, even-handed, and community-building agenda that slowly but gradually won out (although often persecuted, at first). Although church historians are still suspicious about the true intentions of Constantine's Edict of Toleration (was it more a pragmatic matter than heartfelt?), there can be little argument that his Christianity-empowering reign is evidence that he saw a distinctive, humanity-unifying ethos among those who practiced a faith in Jesus.[62]

It would not be difficult to document the development of many positive cultural developments (e.g., education, law, even early forms

---

60 Stark comments: "Sometimes described as 'the science of faith,' theology consists of formal reasoning about God. . . . Theology necessitates an image of God as a conscious, rational, supernatural being of unlimited power and scope who care about humans and imposes moral codes and responsibilities upon them, thereby generating serious intellectual questions such as: Why does God allow us to sin? Does the
Sixth Commandment prohibit war? When does an infant acquire a soul? . . . To fully appreciate the nature of theology, it is useful to explore why there are no theologians in the East. . . . The East lacks theologians because those who might otherwise take up such an intellectual pursuit reject its first premise: the existence of a conscious, all-powerful God" (*Victory of Reason*, 5–6).

61 Rodney Stark, *Cities of God: The Real Story of How Christianity Became an Urban Movement and Conquered Rome* (San Francisco: Harper, 2006). See especially pages 113–116, "When Doctrine Matters."

62 Ibid., 189–94. Stark writes: "Constantine was not responsible for the triumph of Christianity. By the time he gained the throne, Christian growth had already become a tidal wave of exponential increase. . . . If anything, Christianity played a leading role in the triumph of Constantine, providing him with substantial and well-organized urban support" (189).

of agricultural technology) that came about in the medieval period as a direct result of the Church's doctrine and its application. This has been ably done in several recent volumes.[63] For the purposes of this paper, let me simply call attention to the rise of science in the west.[64]

Centuries prior to the Protestant Reformation, Catholic theologians were well on the way towards developing a cosmology that would enable the scientific revolution of Copernicus, Galileo, and Newton. Because of their belief in the biblical doctrine of creation and its attendant truth that this cosmos bears the glory of God, these "worshipping schoolmen" were able to transcend the limits of Greek atomism and systematically envision a heliocentric universe and a round earth, long before the notable church rebels gave these premises articulation.[65] The well-known Aristotelianism that characterizes Reformation–era Catholicism, was repudiated by these earlier thinkers, in favor of a trans-sensual understanding of reality that is drawn from the pages of Scripture. Sadly, facing the twin challenges of Islam (which was Aristotelian in its scientific outlook) and Protestantism (which was not), the Roman church took the unfortunate step backward in its scientific research, probably due to a fear that somehow, new scientific insights would better play into the hands of Christianity's dissidents (Protestants) who seemed bent on ridding themselves of all things traditional.[66] While science clearly thrived in the more open world of Protestantism, such success was largely the result of earlier Catholic scholarship. The words of the great Roman Catholic historian of science Stanley Jaki well remind us that the development of a "live-birth" science came about from a move to place

> the ultimate in intelligibility (God) . . . on a level transcending both man and nature during the Middle Ages. . . . Its most articulate spokesmen were medicant friars committed to an evangelical vision of man and world, a vision in which the order, beauty, and peace of nature were a shining reflection of the Creator and Father of all.[67]

---

63 Stark, *Victory of Reason*, 19–23.

64 Ibid., 22–33. In stark contrast [pun intended] to the hubris of later Enlightenment scientists, these medieval schoolmen did their work recognizing that "in order to love and honor God, it is necessary to fully appreciate the wonders of his handiwork. Because God is perfect, his handiwork functions in accord with immutable principles. By the full use of our God-given powers of reason and observation, it ought to be possible to discover these principles." (22–23).

65 Stark, *For the Glory of God*, 22–33.

66 Ibid., 22–33.

67 Stanley L. Jaki, *The Road of Science and the Ways to God* (Chicago: University of Chicago Press, 1978), 33.

Call it my bias, but such a vision seems to be the product of something like a biblical worldview. It seems that the subsequent Protestant acquisition of science inherently brought with it a *weltanschauung* heritage from the religion of Rome.

These pre-Kuyperian manifestations of worldview thinking (if indeed, I am correct in this assessment) also remind us that all attempts to think and live Christianly are not necessarily good and healthy. The same faith-based climate that gave rise to transformational developments in science and medicine (medieval church), also attempted to apply this "whole sphere" ideology through the highly regimented, forced, and artificial means often dubbed Christendom. (Legislated and church- or state-enforced worldview is never a particularly good thing, as Calvin was to find in his Geneva project, years later). And who can forget the infamous, medieval version of literally returning "every square inch" (even, geographically!) to Christ's lordship in the Crusades?

These, and other episodes, are graphic reminders that the worldview war we wage cannot be fought successfully with conventional weaponry but only with those endued and sanctioned with divine power (2 Cor 10: 4).

Suffice to say, worldview thinking—and living—apparently enjoyed a rich long heritage *before* the nineteenth- and twentieth-century Protestants appropriated the *weltanschauung* language of modernity to describe the robust practice of "taking every thought captive to Christ." While the development of Christian theology, a this-worldly spirituality, and the rise of science, give ample tribute to the implicit existence of a concept like what these later evangelicals deemed "biblical worldview," it was left to those in the twilight years of Christianity's second millennium to coin or, more accurately, to appropriate a term to identify what believers had been doing from the Church's earliest years. It certainly cannot be denied that the adoption of Kantian language has not always produced a worldview formulation that matches the cognitive—and affective—richness of the Bible's "heart" (too often, Christian worldview discussion has been highly, if not exclusively cognitive), but this shortcoming should not cause us to jettison the concept. Rather, we should be challenged to regularly, re-examine what the Scriptures present as *weltanschauung* so that we will not settle for modernity's, corrupted, reductionistic version, as well as pursue an on-going, serious study of the Church's history in order to gain an understanding of what a biblical worldview looks like in practice—and what it does not.

With this said, and not without a bit of trepidation, I will now attempt to offer my own proposal of what a Christian worldview ought to contain. In keeping with this paper's musical parlance, I hope that the following suggestions will serve to reinforce that this classic is a timeless piece that should not be put to rest by either modern or postmodern audiences.

KEEPING A CLASSIC ALIVE AND UNADULTERATED: A PROPOSAL FOR A THICK CHRISTIAN WORLDVIEW

It seems to me that a biblically-driven, historically-informed, comprehensive, and classical rendition of biblical worldview should attempt to incorporate the following elements:[68]

1. It should be narrative-driven, cognizant that Scripture is primarily a story—a cosmic story—that invites its "readers" into the divine drama of the Triune God's redemption and ultimately consummation of a universe that He has created and sovereignly maintains in spite of a multi-dimensional Fall. This divinely-inspired meta-narrative, then, brings a necessary corrective to all other myths that attempt to make sense out of humanity's place in this cosmos (usually, local stories); in a real sense, one could say that the biblical story is God's gift of worldview. Given, then, that the bulk of the biblical narrative is concerned with God's calling of a global people—redeemed by the work of Christ—who, in turn, will manifest this true worldview, one can echo the conclusion of Christopher Wright that the Bible's grand narrative is inherently missiological.[69] Consequently, the biblical faith cannot help but be evangelistic in its essential orientation, no matter how distasteful such a notion is to a postmodern culture.

2. It should be *didactic* or creedal in terms of reflecting clear biblical, historical, and ecumenical conclusions drawn from the scriptural narrative; e.g., God as Trinity, creation, the deity and humanity of Jesus Christ, Jesus' sin-atoning death and resurrection, all humans as the

---

68 In order to facilitate a biblical naturalization of *weltanschauung*, Naugle has suggested a worldview concept composed of the following four elements: 1) robust objectivist notions about the existence of God and his order for the moral and the structures of creation; 2)"heart" and its essentially spiritual orientation and view of reality that determines one's way in the world; 3) presence of sin and a Satanic strategy to blind the human heart concerning the truth of God and his creation; and 4) necessity of Christ's redemptive work and grace in order to facilitate a proper understanding of God and his world (*Worldview: The History*), 290. In a very recent contribution to worldview thinking (generally positive and constructive), J. Mark Bertrand offers his own list of four pillars that provide the foundation for a distinctive, biblical notion of worldview: 1) creation; 2) order; 3) rationality; and 4) fear. (*[Re]Thinking Worldview* [Wheaton, Ill.: Crossway, 2007], see especially pages 41–74.

69 See Christopher Wright, *The Mission of God: Unlocking the Key to the Bible's Grand Narrative* (Downers Grove, Ill.: Inter Varsity, 2007); see especially pages 33–74. .

imago dei, sinfulness of humanity, salvation by God's grace appropriated by human faith, the Church as the Body of Christ, the future, personal and physical return of Christ as savior and judge, recreation of the cosmos. While Christian traditions may differ on some of the "specific scheming" of some of these beliefs (e.g., meaning and mode of baptism, Calvinistic and Arminian understandings of election and predestination, et al.), a Christian worldview will primarily be negotiated by these cardinal doctrines (that are fundamentally *christo-centric*) rather than denominational distinctives. The ecumenical creeds can well be our guide in discerning these core beliefs.

3.   In fact, it should be *Christ-centered*—in both its understanding of the nature of redemption (cross and resurrection) as well as in its attempt to think and practice an authentic, God-shaped view of reality (i.e., mind of Christ, Phil 2:5; Col 3:2), a model definitively incarnated in the earthly life and ministry of Jesus himself.

4.   It should be *exegetically accountable*. While the key beliefs of the biblical narrative are fairly without dispute, these, as well as our distinctive evangelical traditions should always be submitted to on-going, careful, and honest scriptural exegesis (a genuine exercise in *semper reformanda*). Particularly in the case of the latter (tradition), we must be vigilant in holding our understanding of Scripture to the biblical text itself.

5.   It should be a *communal conversation*, involving the study of Scripture, doctrine, and application as a corporate enterprise—within and outside of our traditions, both locally and in dialog with the global Christian community.[70]

6.   Given its understanding of creation, it should embrace a distinctive *epistemology*, i.e., a *critical realism* that recognizes that there are ontological realities regardless of what we see or do not see. This approach to knowing, in turn, demands that we persistently pursue the truth of the way things really are—in the Word and the world—taking care to present our findings accurately and fairly, without the spin that so characterizes much public discourse in our time. This approach also implies that we will correct deficient ideas and practice as reality demands.

7.   Given the reality that it is so very difficult to see things ontologically, or as they really are, a robust biblical worldview should include *a strong notion of spiritual warfare*—an awareness that from Eden, the Enemy has done all that he is able to convince human beings to observe

---

70   The case for global Christian conversation has been eloquently made by Phillip Jenkins in his fine work, *The Next Christendom; The Coming of Global Christianity* (New York: Oxford University Press, 2002). According to Jenkins, our Southern Christian brothers and sisters will serve to keep our biblical perspective "more conservative in terms of beliefs and moral teaching" due to their "very strong supernatural orientation" (2–3).

and understand reality in ways that undermine the way it really is. This "deconstructive" approach can run the gamut from seeing the universe as the tormented abode of capricious and often malevolent spirits (animism) to a modernistic hubris that assumes that we have everything completely figured out with our science and technology (or, for that matter, the postmodernist assessment that very little can really be known). The recognition that we are engaged in an on-going battle for the mind (cf. 2 Cor 10:5; Eph 6:10ff) should, if nothing else, continually cause us to undergird all of our pursuits with prayer (Eph 6:18).

8. While a well-rounded biblical worldview should possess a serious view of *human frailty* and *fallenness*—and be extremely cautious about assuming the truth of our perceptions and observations—it should, nonetheless, include a fairly good dose of what Calvin referred to as "common grace." [71] In other words, we should not be so consumed with a hermeneutics of suspicion, that we, in turn, fail to see the hand of God in the thoughts and pursuits of unregenerate people. If indeed there is an ontology to reality given in creation, we should not be surprised when non-Christians in virtually every field get things *right* (after all, the whole cosmos belongs to, and breathes the Lord). While we may rightly question their interpretations of the data, the givenness of God's general revelation determines that certain beliefs, theories, and practices are valid because they correspond to the nature of the cosmos, whether such assessments are made by Buddhists, Hindus, Muslims, Jews, or Christians. Medical research and practice demonstrates this creational independence every day. Furthermore, given the thick, spiritual fabric to the universe, we should not be shocked if non-Christian religions occasionally outperform churches in their spirituality—our prayer lives often pale in comparison to our Muslim neighbors—because in this universe in which the Lord brings rain to the just and the unjust, certain things are simply the way they are. Clearly, common grace is not salvific, and I am certainly not implying that other religions are just as true as Christianity (cf. Heb 1:1-2), but its existence clearly should keep us in an informed dialogue with our unbelieving world, rather than in a protective, evangelical cocoon.

9. Given our nature as finite space-, time-, and experience-limited creatures (as well as fallen) and given that our knowledge of reality is an on-going, ever-corrective process, our understanding and practice of

---

71 Kevin Vanhoozer has recently edited a commendable effort in addressing the omission of common grace from many construals of a Christian worldview, especially, but not limited to, those coming from a Reformed perspective. See *Everyday Theology: How to Read Cultural Texts and Interpret Trends*, edited by Kevin J. Vanhoozer, Charles A. Anderson, and Michael J. Sleasman (Grand Rapids: Baker Academic, 2007).

a Christian worldview should reflect a *genuine humility*. We should always be aware that this side of the eschaton, there will always be a myopic character to our Christian sight.

10. It should manifest a *historical awareness,* giving evidence in its pronouncement and plans an understanding of what good and faithful applications of *weltanschauung* have brought, as well as the harm done when it is ignored or applied in deficient ways. This awareness will provide us a needed meter by which we may assess present-day articulations of Christian faithfulness; i.e., have these been tried before? How have they fared? How did the reality of the fall limit the application of good, reminding us that perfection is indeed, eschatological? This often-omitted point of historical awareness in worldview formulation suggests two additional characteristics of a Christian *weltanschauung:*

11. It should carry a strong note of *eschatological confidence and contentment.* We have already observed the worldview implications of Pauline eschatology—"now and not yet"—but much of contemporary evangelical social and political practice has evidenced that we don't really understand the "not yet." Too often, Bible-believers have presented their agenda as an all-or-nothing enterprise, giving their opponents very little opportunity to re-evaluate and modify their understandings and practices. The abortion debate has frequently been marked by such polarities. A far better, eschatologically-driven approach would suggest that we take small, baby steps, as we attempt to reverse the ravages of Roe v. Wade, finding some sense of satisfaction in decisions like the Supreme Court's recent decision to uphold partial-birth abortion restrictions, knowing that full justice on this issue will only be realized at the *parousia.* This contentment, is not to be understand as passivity or as surrender—we are to work diligently as agents of the kingdom of God—but rather as a guard against both zealous dominion theology on the one hand and severe disappointment and discouragement on the other.

12. Acknowledging Steven Keillor's insightful call for the recognition of *God's judgment* in comprehending the flow of history, a robust understanding of biblical worldview should also include a regular time of reflection that carefully asks the painful question so often verbalized by the Old Testament prophets: "Are we witnessing the judgment of God upon our culture?" Obviously, this part of the *weltanschauung* process needs to be applied with much prudence and caution, for we have seen some notable and embarrassing examples of intemperate and even destructive applications of "prophecy" in our culture: e.g., the Kansas church that disrupts military burials with its pronouncements that such deaths are God's judgments upon a nation that

tolerates homosexuality. Yet we are often missing an Augustine-like philosophy of history that understands that civilizations collapse if they are built upon the shoulders of man—even if such cultures look ostensibly "Christian." If I might put it in a Keillor-like way, "Is Jeffersonian democracy a mark of the divine city or the human one? Is the United States in what may be its twilight years, merely producing the harvest that its earlier seed was bound to sow? Was 9/11 a judgment of God upon a 'city' that has actually been constructed with secular mortar and covered with a godly façade?" These are surely not pleasant questions nor ones that are answered with the simplistic responses of an anti-American political left. But a full-orbed biblical worldview cannot do without the unsettling questions of a prophet.

13. This call for a prudent, prophetic element to *weltanschauung*, reminds us that worldview formulation is highly *sapiential* in its essential character; i.e., it carefully attempts to understand what God is doing in this world in contexts where the Bible often does not directly speak, given Scripture's own, real-world setting. As we have discussed earlier, the Wisdom tradition (so magnificently embodied in Jesus) addressed the practical issues of human existence not by slavishly reciting isolated bits of the Torah (more a pharisaical practice) but by applying a godly wisdom to them. Such wisdom is messier than merely amassing together a few, choice texts, and it is humbly driven by a conscious and intentional "fear of the Lord" that defies easy reductionism. This sapiential component causes us to be reticent about designating our understanding of a contemporary situation, *"the* biblical position," preferring instead to claim more modestly that a biblical view should carry with it "certain key elements" (such as what we are charting out, here). While most of us in the evangelical academy would agree that "God is not a Democrat or Republican," one would probably not know that from more than a few of the worldview programs that have been developed in the biblically conservative community. Whereas, the kind of worldview approach that we believe is genuinely biblical generally attempts to thicken a discussion of real-life situations (e.g., we see the victims of the problem of AIDS as more than those directly carrying the HIV virus, due to our complex understanding of the Fall; likewise, we see treatment and cure in ways larger than either condoms or abstinence due to our complex understanding of redemption), these popular approaches tend to minimize discussion. In reality, they actually undermine James' wise counsel to the Christian community: "If any of you lacks wisdom, you should ask God" (Jas 1:5). Such wisdom is inextricably linked with the work of the indwelling, Holy Spirit.

14. Lest our characteristics of worldview be thought of as simply better processes of *cognition*, let us be clear that our *practice of life*—our

relationships, our work, our play, our dreams and values, our habits, et al—is the true arena where *weltanschauung* is played out. Life is where the issues of heart are truly seen, a reality that is as humbling as it is dynamic. As Jesus so well reminded us, there is an inseparable link between our treasures and our worldview (Matt 6:21), and it is in the experiences of daily living that our theory reveals itself to be but a cognitive model. Genuinely biblical worldview thinking is seen in corresponding worldview living, and only the God-Man himself demonstrated a pure heart in every word, deed, and relationship. Indeed, let us not forget this communal element in our pursuit of thought-life integrity. Jesus ably demonstrates that our holiness is not a matter of becoming separated from human community but rather of living in it and more specifically creating community where too often only fragmented individuals reside.

15. Finally (only in the terms of this paper!), a biblical worldview should be conceived in terms of *covenant*. This means that we are always mindful that our pursuit to think and live according to the ways of God and in the mind of Christ is a serious responsibility that inherently comes with His grace. We consciously engage this deep, thick, messy, and difficult enterprise of biblical worldview because of what He has done for us and hence out of our gratitude and love for him. The New Testament's portrayals of the Church as "God's household" and "Christ's Bride" reinforce this covenantal theme; i.e., *to be holy as the Lord, our God is holy* (cf. Lev 19:2; Eph 1:5), further reminding us that we are a covenant people whose *wisdom* attracts the *admiration of the nations* (Deut 4:6–8) and moreover, the *attention of "the rulers and authorities in the heavenly realms"* (Eph 3:10).[72]

CONCLUSION

We began this paper by citing two contemporary evangelical statements about worldview, the first a definition authored by one of

---

72 I can well anticipate the criticism that this worldview proposal will elicit from some (many) who will contend that I have made the concept far too complex. These critics will probably contend that a truly practical Christian worldview should lend itself to simple, succinct formulation. While this criticism undoubtedly has some merit—fifteen elements is fairly bulky—it also betrays a subtle, modernistic premise: i.e., that deep truths must be reducible to simple, mechanistic properties or they are not relevant (pragmatism). This approach (often popularly summarized in the acronym KISS—"Keep It Simple, Stupid") actually can tend to subvert authentic Christian discipleship by reducing such to a series of how-to steps and skills instead of the holistic and hard approach to life that accompanies "taking up one's cross" (Matt 10:38). Furthermore, in a culture that has become defined by quick-fix flashpoints and demonization, a more reflective, careful, cautious, and considerate approach to speech and deed would seem to be in order, an approach that is more likely to come from my complex model. Perhaps, it might be helpful to think of these fifteen elements as a matrix more than a linear construct; i.e., a network of intersecting and inseparable elements (lived in Christian community) rather than a series of independent, progressive steps that must be mastered individually.

this generation's most venerable proponents of the concept and the second penned by a former practitioner turned critic who, in effect, unleashed a postmodern critique against weltanschauung that, in particular, questioned its value as any more than a cognitive model. In our subsequent discussion detailing both the Enlightenment origins of the term but more importantly the biblical underpinnings of a concept, expressed in the holistic and musical term heart, we have attempted to argue a case made so eloquently by David Naugle, namely, that worldview is a "Christian (new) birthright" that should not be exchanged for a tempting and more fashionable bowl of postmodern porridge. While admittedly some classical evangelical schematics of worldview have leaned too heavily on narrow, modernistic versions, the notion deserves to live on in this new millennium in its more scriptural and ecclesiastical-historical forms. James Sire has clearly heard the classical tune. In the fourth edition of The Universe Next Door (2004) as well as in its companion volume, Naming the Worldview, Sire offers a revised, Naugle-inspired rendition of his previous, cognitive-heavy definition:

A worldview is a commitment, a fundamental orientation of the heart that can be expressed as a story or in a set of presuppositions (assumptions which may be true, partially true or entirely false) which we hold (consciously or subconsciously, consistently or inconsistently) about the basic constitution of reality, and that provides the foundation on which we live and move and have our being.[73]

Fittingly, at the conclusion of this latest printing of the worldview classic, he adds these words about a distinctly, theistic worldview:

To accept Christian theism only as an intellectual construct is not to accept it fully. There is a deeply personal dimension involved with grasping and living within this worldview, for it involves acknowledging our own individual dependence upon God as his creatures, our own individual rebellion against God and our own reliance on God for restoration to fellowship with him. And it means to accept Christ as both our Liberator from bondage and Lord of our future. . . . And it leads to an examined life that is well worth living.[74]

---

[73] James W. Sire, *The Universe Next Door: A Basic Worldview Catalog, Fourth Edition* (Downers Grove, Ill.: Inter Varsity, 2004), 17; cf. also, *Naming the Elephant: Worldview as a Concept* (Downers Grove, Ill.: Inter Varsity, 2004), 122. In *Naming the Elephant*, Sire openly credits Naugle with provoking his "refined definition," as well as his own growing dissatisfaction with his earlier rendering (18–19; cf. also, chapter 7).

[74] Sire, *The Universe Next Door*, 4th ed., 250.

Commitment, fundamental orientation of the heart, story, constitution of reality, personal dimension, grasping and living, present and future, examined life—these are terms more befitting a *weltanschauung concept* that is truly a biblical and sacred classic rather than an out-dated and pedestrian modern composition, not to mention the trendy but temporary alternatives offered on the postmodern chart. If Sire's recent writings are indicative of the full sound that will mark twenty-first century worldview studies, the mournful sound of taps will have to be delayed—perhaps until the final blast of the archangel's trumpet.[75]

---

75 See also *Living at the Crossroads: An Introduction to Christian Worldview*, by Michael Goheen and Craig Bartholomew (Grand Rapids: Baker Academic, 2008), as perhaps another promising indicator that the more well-orbed and thick worldview formulation espoused in this essay may well be on the way.

2

GENESIS AS MISSIOLOGICAL WORLDVIEW: INFORMING THE FOUR MAJOR QUESTIONS OF BOTH PRE-MODERN AND POST-MODERN TIMES

Wayne Brouwer

If the Bible begins at Mt. Sinai as the initial documents of the covenant between Yahweh and Israel, what is the purpose of Genesis? To gain an answer we must pay careful attention to the literary development of the text of Genesis.

It is fairly obvious when reading Genesis in a single sitting that there is a marked shift in the text between chapters 11 and 12. The first eleven chapters of Genesis are further removed from our day to day experiences, having more of a mythological character to them like the cosmological origins stories found in many ancient societies. At the same time, although chapters 12—50 seem to enter our historical arena more fully, they feel something like the ancestor hero stories that are told in nearly every culture to define its identity.

COMPETING WORLDVIEWS

The "mythical" qualities of Genesis 1—11 ought not to be interpreted as synonymous with either "untrue" or "non-historical." Myths are stories that summarize worldviews in elided prose, giving snap-

Wayne Brouwer <brouwer@chartermi.net> is professor of Religion and Studies in Ministry at Hope College, and adjunct professor of Theology and Ministry at Western Theological Seminary, both in Holland, Michigan. He has published numerous articles and more than a dozen books, including *Covenant Documents: Reading the Bible again for the First Time* (2009), *Political Religion* (2007), *The Literary Structure of John 13—17: A Chiastic Reading* (2000), and *Being a Believer in an Unbelieving World* (1999). He holds degrees from Dordt College (AB), Calvin Theological Seminary (MDiv, ThM) and McMaster University (MA, PhD).

shots of the value systems that drive a culture, or providing hooks on which to hang the unspoken but ubiquitous understanding of a society's identity. So it is that the stories told by way of myths may be cartoon-like fairy tales, or they may be selected emblematic events from the actual unfolding of a community's early history, or a combination of both. Myths, by their very nature, do not intend to be read as scientific description or journalistic documentary. They serve instead to carry the fundamental values and worldview understandings of the culture in a manageable, memorable collection of tales.

In this respect, Genesis functions as an extended historical prologue to the Sinai covenant, answering a number of important questions that arise simply because Israel has been shaken loose from four hundred years of enslaved slumber and is now being reshaped as the marriage partner of God in a divine mission that is not yet fully clarified. Genesis gives the context to the Suzerain-Vassal treaty formed in Exodus 20—24. It takes important moments from both the distant and recent past, and uses these as the shepherding banks which direct the flow of the people's river of identity. Because there is no authorial self-disclosure within the pages of Genesis we are left to speculate about its specific origins. Still, there is an important clue that emerges when the Hebrew nomenclature for God is analyzed. Most often, especially beginning with the stories of Abram in Genesis 12, Yahweh is used to name the divinity. According to the book of Exodus, this name emerged in Israel through the deity's self-disclosure to Moses in the encounter at Mt. Horeb (Exo 3). Thus, if one is to listen to the internal testimony of the literature of the Bible, Genesis is understood to function as a companion volume to the covenant documents of Israel's national identity formation at Mt. Sinai. Therefore, Genesis must be read not as a volume pre-existing in a disconnected primeval world, but rather as the interpretation of events leading up to the engagement of Yahweh and Israel at Sinai in the Suzerain-Vassal covenant established there. Genesis is the extended historical prologue of the Sinai covenant.

Viewed this way, the message of Genesis is readily accessible. To begin with, the cosmological origins myths of chapters 1—11 are apologetic devices that announce a very different worldview than that available in the cultures that surrounded Israel. The two dominant cosmogonies in the ancient near east were established by the civilizations of Mesopotamia (filtered largely through Babylonian recitations) and Egypt. Cosmogonic myths describe the origins of the world as we know it, providing a paradigm by which to analyze and interpret contemporary events. Scattered across these cosmogonic myths are four methods of creation:

- **Fabricating**: divine acts on undifferentiated primordial matter that result in elements of the world as we know it.
- **Conflict Resolution**: deities battling with one another or with the original powers of chaos, with the result that the winners get to shape natural elements out of the losers.
- **Sexual Generation**: either the intragender replication of a god to form other gods or natural substances, or the sexual interaction between gods and goddesses bringing into existence offspring which give name or shape or power to visible entities.
- **Declaration**: creation through the spoken word.

The Genesis account of creation contains a small nod toward the first of these, but expends the bulk of its energy using the last. The world as we know it was produced by the divine creative word.

Not so with the Egyptian origins myths. Distilled from the various records that are available to us, the generalized creation story goes roughly like this. *Nun* was the chaos power pervading the primeval waters. *Atum* was the creative force which lived on *Benben*, a pyramidical hill rising out of the primeval waters. *Atum* split to form the elemental gods *Shu* (air) and *Tefnut* (moisture). *Tefnut* bore two children: *Geb* (god of earth) and *Nut* (goddess of the skies). These, in turn gave birth to lesser gods who differentiated among themselves and came to rule various dimensions of the world as we now know it. Humanity was a final and unplanned outcome, with these weaklings useful only to do the work that the gods no longer wished to do, and to feed the gods by way of burning animal flesh in order to make it accessible.

Similar, and yet uniquely nuanced, are the cosmogonies of ancient Mesopotamia. The name *Mesopotamia* literally means "between the waters." It denotes that region of the near east encompassed by the combined watersheds of the Tigris and Euphrates rivers. Early civilizations here, enveloped by a somewhat different climatic environment than that found in Egypt, reflected this uniqueness in their origin myths. *Apsu* was the chaos power resident in the primeval waters. *Tiamat* was the bitter sea within the primeval waters upon which earth floated. *Lhamu* and *Lahamu* were gods of silt (at the edges of earth) created from the interaction of the primeval waters and the bitter seas. The horizons, *Anshar* and *Kishar*, were separated from one another by the birth of their child *Anu* (sky). *Anu* engendered *Ea-Nudimmud*, the god of earth and wisdom.

All of these gods were filled with pent-up energy and this caused them to fight constantly. Since they existed within the belly of *Tiamat*, *Apsu* got indigestion and made plans to destroy all his restless and noisy children, i.e., the rest of the gods. In order to survive, *Ea* cast a spell which put *Apsu* asleep. Then *Ea* killed *Apsu*, but his remains formed new gods, all of which were now in bitter struggle with each other and with their older relatives. Among the gods, *Marduk* rose as champion, quelling the fights and resurrecting order. To celebrate his success, *Marduk* created Babylon, which thus became the center of the universe and the source of all human civilization. These late-on-the-scene beings were created from the spilled blood of the gods, and they were deliberately fashioned as slaves who would do the work that the gods no longer wished to do.

The Genesis creation story is very spare when placed alongside these other cosmogonic myths. In summary, it declares that God existed before the world that is apprehended by our senses was brought into being. It also asserts that creation happened by way of divine speech rather than through the sexual interaction of deities or as the animation of guts and gore left over and emerging out of their conflicts. Moreover, creation was an intentional act that took place by way of orderly progression:

Day 1: Arenas for Light and Darkness
Day 2: Arenas for Sky and Sea
Day 3: Arenas for Earth's dominant surfaces
Day 4: Inhabitants of Light and Darkness
Day 5: Inhabitants of Sky and Sea
Day 6: Inhabitants of Earth

In the balanced rhythm of poetic prose the Genesis creation story shows how divine planning and purpose brought the world into being specifically as a home for humanity. These creatures are not the by-product of restless fighting among the gods. Nor are they a slave race produced in order to give the gods more leisure. In fact, according to the Genesis account, human beings are the only creatures made in the image of God, thus sharing the best of divine qualities.

A comparison of the values that underlie these various creation myths shows the differences that are fundamental for shaping distinct worldviews:

EGYPT AND MESOPOTAMIA	GENESIS
Divinity exudes throughout the natural order	Divinity is separate from the natural order
There is an eternal dualism of good and evil	All is created good, and evil enters only later as a usurper
All things originate by devolution, with successive generations of creatures always crasser, baser, or less important than earlier ones	All things originate by intentional divine plan and are developed into species that occupy unique homes in the natural order
Humanity is an afterthought, a bother, and a slave race	Humanity is the reason for all the previous creative activity and alone shares divine character and purpose
The reason for humanity's existence is toil	The reason for humanity's existence is creativity, relationship, and rest

If, as the literature itself requires, the creation stories of Genesis 1—2 are part of a lengthy historical prologue to the meeting of Yahweh and Israel at Mt. Sinai, these cosmogonic myths are not to be read as the end product of scientific or historical analysis. They are designed to place Israel in an entirely different worldview context than that which shaped their neighbors. Humanity's place in this natural realm is one of intimacy with God, rather than fear and slavery. The human race exists in harmony with nature, not as its bitter opponent or only helpless minor element. Women and men together share creative responsibility with God over animals and plants.

Moreover, there is no hint of evil or sin in the creation stories themselves. In fact, the recurring refrain is that God saw the coming-into-being of each successive wave of creation and declared it to be good. There is no eternal dualism of opposing forces that in their conflict engendered the world as we know it. Nor is the creative energy of human life itself derived from inherent powers of good and evil which, in their chasing of one another, produce the changes necessary to drive the system. Instead, evil appears only after a fully developed created realm is complete, and then enters as a usurping power that seeks to draw away the reflected creativity of the human race into alliance with forces which deny the Creator's values and goals. Evil and sin are essentially linked to human perspectives that are in competition with the one declared true and genuine by the creation stories themselves.

In Genesis 3—11 there appear to be two divine attempts to recover the pristine qualities of the original creation. First, after the initial humans step out of the worldview of the Creator and enter the perspectives of the tempter, the Creator displays graciousness in delaying the sentence of death upon them and also by providing promises that this conflict need not end their existence. Instead, the human creatures are driven out of the Garden of Eden in what seems to be a desire to pull them to their senses through the restlessness of homelessness. They become exiles, and their descendents, in order to compensate, build cities in an apparent attempt to regain civility. All these efforts fail, however, and the cancer of disobedience explodes in acts of killing and violence.

Then comes the second recovery effort. Just as his name seems to imply, Noah is heralded as one who will bring "comfort" from the afflictions of both sin and the curses of God that accompany it (Gen 5:29). What takes place, however, is the famous flood story (Gen 6—9) in which God designs a massive "do-over." The natural realm is destroyed except for a floating biological bank called the ark. Noah and his family are spared the ravages of a massive flood intended to wipe out the terrestrial dimensions of the universe created in Genesis 1. All that survive are the few humans and the species restorers that have been kept safe in the big boat.

In God's instructions to Noah following the flood (Gen 9:1–7) there are clear echoes of the divine mandate given to Adam and Eve in the Garden of Eden (Gen 1:28–30). In other words, the tale of the flood is as much a story of re-creation as it is of judgment and destruction. A new element is added however, one which would be vital for Israel to understand as it stood before God at Mt. Sinai. After the words of blessing by which Noah and his family are given earth again as their home, there are words of self-reflection by the Creator (Gen 9:8–17). For the first time, chronologically speaking, the idea of a "covenant" enters the biblical record. Interestingly here, though, it is shaped in the manner of a Babylonian Royal Grant rather than a Hittite Suzerain Vassal treaty.

The Babylonian Royal Grant was a formula by which kings could record their acts of beneficence. Unlike the Suzerain Vassal covenant it did not bind the receiver of the gift into some form of specific responsive obedience. Instead, it assured the one who had received the gift that this was intended by the king, and could not be revoked by others. Sometimes, in fact, a maledictory oath accompanied the donation, assuring the recipient that the burden of following through on the gift remained the responsibility of the giver. The maledictory oath was a promise, made at the expense of personal well-being, that the king would guarantee the gift.

THREE KINDS OF COVENANTS

In ancient Israel's world there were three dominant covenantal structures that shaped relationships locally and internationally:

- **Parity Agreements** were made between equal parties for mutual benefit (cf. Jacob & Laban in Gen 31:36–54)

- **Royal Grants** were the gifts of kings to those on whom they wished to show favor, and did not by themselves require a long-term reciprocal behavior (cf. God's gifts and promises in Gen 9:8–17)

- **Suzerain-Vassal Covenants** were social constructs shaping a reciprocal relationship between a ruler and people (cf. Exo 20 – 24)

This is clearly expressed in the divine promise of protection and continuation of earth's natural order in Genesis 9:8–17. There will never again be a catastrophic destruction on the scale of the great flood just finished, nor will any other initiative be launched either by the Creator or by any other threatening power to attempt the annihilation of life on planet earth.

A sign accompanied this assertion, but not as a reminder to humanity. Instead, God declared that the bow in the heavens will frequently appear as a recurring memory jogger for the deity. There is no word for "rainbow" in the Hebrew language; the term used in this divine speech is simply "bow," like the weapon a hunter brought into the forest after his prey or an archer stretched with arrows on the field of battle. Understood as it was initially intended, the "bow" thus takes on sinister significance. Whenever God viewed the bow, it was curved with tension, ready to release its projectiletoward heaven. The implication would be clear to the ancient Israelites. God was taking a self-maledictory oath as part of this Royal Grant to spare creation; in it the deity professed self-annihilation if no other solution was found to bring safety and everlasting continuity to the natural order, including the human race. This, in anticipation, heightened the significance of the role of the divine mediator both in its Israelite context and beyond.

In the end, neither remedy intended to countermand the intrusion of evil into the world order which had been created "good" had any lasting merit. On the one hand, Eden's exiles fabricated cities where, rather than finding a return to the garden, they compounded the menace and suffering of sin. Similarly with the other initiative: the re-creation attempted through Noah failed, as the stories immediately following show. Noah's son Ham ridiculed his drunken father, resulting in a sharp curse placed upon his descendents (Gen 9:20–25). Then the entire human community gathered itself into a monolithic empire that threatens to become self-sufficient (Gen 11:1–9). Suddenly evil resided not only in specific individuals who did bad things, but took on a corporate face. As God challenged this power play, the story turned in a new and decisive direction.

THREE STORY CYCLES

If Genesis 1—11 is analogous to the cosmogonic myths that informed the societies among which young Israel was wrestling for a place, the rest of the book has a character not unlike that of the ancestor hero stories which also shaped other national cultures. Once again, comparing the tales of Abraham, Isaac, Jacob, and Joseph to the mythology of neighboring civilizations does not imply that these biblical tales are false or untrue. Rather, it is helpful to see the manner in which the literature functions in defining the identity of the emerging culture, and ancestor hero stories provide a genre of comparison. In other words, the narratives of the patriarchs are not merely documentary history through which Israel could fashion a set of lively bedtime stories. Instead, the very heart of Israel's identity was shaped as the nation reflected on certain aspects of the lives of its forebears. For this reason there is no complete history of Abraham or entire biography of Isaac or fully-developed life of Jacob. Indeed, one would be hard pressed to formulate these from the limited amount of historical information given about each.

The purpose of these stories, particularly since they appear to emerge from the Sinai-covenant-making events of Exodus, is instead to provide a basis for Israel to understand who she is as a nation. This becomes more apparent when the essential focus of each major story cycle is probed.

Although later references to Israel's ancestral parentage would emerge as the standardized phrase "Abraham, Isaac and Jacob," in reality the second part of Genesis contains three major story cycles in which Isaac is only a footnote to two, and Joseph is added as a key player in the drama. In rough overview, Genesis 12—50 may be outlined in this manner:

- Abraham Story Cycle (chapters 12—25)
- Jacob Story Cycle (chapters 26—36)
- Joseph Story Cycle (chapters 37—50)

Each of these story cycles adds a unique element to Israel's self identity when read backwards from the covenant making ceremony at Mt. Sinai. In this way they form, with Genesis 1—11, a deliberate extended historical prologue to the Suzerain Vassal treaty by staging that event over against the prevailing worldviews of the day and within a certain missional context that illumines the purpose of Israel's existence and the reason why Yahweh takes such interest in this tiny nation.

The Abraham Story Cycle

Abram is an Aramean from the heart of Mesopotamia whose father Terah begins a journey westward that Abram continues upon his father's death. Whatever Terah's reasons might have been for moving from the old family village—restlessness, treasure-seeking, displacement, wanderlust—Genesis 12 informs us that Abram's continuation of the trek was motivated by a divine call to seek a land which would become his by providential appointment. This is the first of four similar divine declarations that occur in quick succession in chapters 12, 13, 15 and 17. Such repetition cues us to the importance of these theophanies, but it ought also cause us to look more closely at the forms in which the promises to Abram are made.

In brief, Abram's first three encounters with God are shaped literarily as Royal Grants. Only in Genesis 17 does the language of the dialogue change and elements are added to give it the flavor of a Suzerain Vassal covenant. This is very significant.

For Israel, standing at Mt. Sinai in the context of a Suzerain Vassal covenant-making ceremony, the implications would be striking. First of all, the nation would see itself as the unique and miraculously-born child fulfilling a divine promise. Israel could not exist were it not for God's unusual efforts at getting Abram and Sarai pregnant in a way that was humanly impossible. Second, they were the descendents of a man on a divine pilgrimage. Not only was Abram *en route* to a land of promise, but he was also the instrument of God for the blessing of all the nations of the earth. In other words, Israel was born with a mandate, and it was globally encompassing. Third, while these people had recently emerged from Egypt as a despised social underclass of disenfranchised slaves, they were actually landowners. Canaan was theirs for the taking because they already owned it. They would not enter the land by stealth but through the front door; they would claim the land, not by surreptitious means or mere battlefield bloodshed, but as rightful owners going home. This would greatly affect their common psyche: they were the long-lost heirs of a kingdom returning to claim their royal privilege and possessions.

Genesis 12 — **Royal Grant: Land**	*Abram's Response:* Leave the Land
Genesis 13 — **Royal Grant: Land**	*Abram's Response:* Fight over the Land
Genesis 15 — **Royal Grant**: Son	*Abram's Response:* Connive to get Ishmael as Son
Genesis 17 — **Suzerain-Vassal**: **Land, Son; Renaming, Circumcision**	*Abraham's Response:* Faith & Trust (cf. ch. 22)

Fourth, there was a selection in the process of creating their identity. They were children of Abraham, but so were a number of area tribes and nations descending from Ishmael. What made them special was the uniqueness of their lineage through Isaac, the miraculously-born child of Abram and Sarai's old age. Israel had international kinship relations, but she also retained a unique identity fostered by the divine distinctions between branches of the family. Fifthly, in the progression of the divine dialogue with Abram there was a call to participation in the mission of God. As the story of Abram unfolded, it was clear that this commitment to God's plans was minimal at best until the change from Royal Grants (Gen 12, 13, 15) to the Suzerain Vassal Covenant of chapter 17. Each time Abram was given a gift, he seemingly threw it away, tried to take it by force, or manipulated his circumstances so that he controlled his destiny; only when God took formal ownership of both Abram and the situation through the Suzerain Vassal Covenant of Genesis 17 was there a marked change in Abram's participation in the divine initiative. The renaming of Abram and Sarai to Abraham and Sarah were only partly significant for the meaning of the names; mostly they were a deliberate and public declaration that God owned them. To name meant to have power over, just as was the case when a divine word created the elements of the universe in Genesis 1 and Adam named the animals in Genesis 2. Furthermore, in the call to circumcise all the males of the family, God transformed a widely used social rite of passage symbol into a visible mark of belonging now no longer tied to personal achievements like battlefield wins or hunting success, but merely to the gracious goodness of God and participation in the divine mission.

ABRAHAM AND THE SACRIFICE OF ISAAC (GENESIS 22)

This incident is identified as a test of Abraham's faith. In light of his response to earlier Royal Grant promises (12: he leaves the land; 13: he tries to take the land by force; 15: he connives to get a son), Abraham is now called to declare his loyalty to the God who has ratified a Suzerain Vassal covenant with him (Gen 17). While the test may seem overly demanding (kill your only son, the one given miraculously and the heir to your identity and promises), other considerations help us understand it better.

First, it was not unusual for people at that time to believe that deities required human sacrifice. The unusual twist in this story is that Yahweh, by stopping the bloodshed of Isaac, is not one of these other deities, and does not delight in human sacrifice.

Second, Yahweh provides an alternative offering, a ram divinely placed on the scene. Third, the place is named "Moriah," which can ambiguously mean either "Yahweh sees" or "Yahweh will be seen," both of which are correct (Yahweh sees the faith of Abraham; Yahweh is more clearly seen by Abraham), and thus illuminate the idea presented in the text that "Yahweh provides" the sacrifice.

Fourth, this idea is further confirmed by future references to the location of the site. In 2 Chronicles 3:1 this mountain is specified as the future location of Solomon's Temple. This would tie the animal sacrifice to the Temple rituals of a later century. It would also put the events of Genesis 22 on the very spot where Jesus would be crucified some twenty centuries hence in another intense Father—Son engagement.

But what was that divine mission? Only when Israel heard the rest of the covenant prologue and then followed Moses to the promised land would it become clear. Still, in recalling the tale of father Abraham in this manner, Genesis places before Israel at Sinai the important element of unique identity: we came into this world miraculously as a result of a divine initiative to bless all the nations of the earth; therefore we are a unique people with the powerful backing of the Creator and participating in a mission that is still in progress.

The Jacob Story Cycle

Only a few details of Isaac's life are told on the pages of Genesis, and they occur in the transitional paragraphs from the Abraham Story Cycle (Gen 12—25) to the Jacob Story Cycle (Gen 26—37). Isaac is to have a wife from within Terah's larger family back in the old country, and this is accomplished through clear divine intervention and leading (ch. 24). To Isaac and Rebecca are born twins who are opposites in character, and always in competition with one another (ch. 25). Rather than emerging with an identity of his own, Isaac seems doomed to repeat his father's mistakes (ch. 26).

After those few notes, Jacob takes center stage. He is a conniver from birth (Gen 25:21–34) who is favored by his mother (Gen 25:28; 27:1—28:9), cheats his family (father Isaac, 27:1–39; brother Esau, 25:29–34, 27:1–39; uncle Laban, 30:25–43; daughter Dinah, 34:1–31), works for his uncle Laban to earn wives Leah and Rachel (Gen 29:15–30) and cattle (Gen 30:25–43), is cheated by his uncle (Gen 2 9:25–27), afraid of his brother (Gen 32:3–21), a cowardly wrestler with God (Gen 32:22–32), and finally receives the covenant blessing and mandate (Gen 35:1–15).

While all of these stories are fascinating in themselves, two significant themes emerge as dominant. First, in the character of Jacob the nation of Israel will always find herself reflected. After all, it is Jacob who bequeaths his special covenant name "Israel" to the community formed by his descendents. Hearing about Jacob and his exploits would be like reading a secret diary mapping Israel's psychological profile. Even before leaving Egypt, the people were wrangling with Moses about burdens and responsibilities, seeking ways to shift workloads and blames elsewhere. Once the wilderness trek began, a variety of conniving subterfuges showed up, including complaints about who really had a right to lead. The spirit of Jacob remained with his namesakes.

Second, the meaning of the name "Israel" and the circumstances surrounding it became a defining moment in Israel's theology. Rarely does the text of Genesis crack open to reveal an origin outside of its narrative timeline, but as the tale of Jacob's night-long wrestling match concludes, there is indeed a note that identifies the organized nation of Israel as the audience reviewing these matters (Gen 32:32). The story itself is more sordid than it appears at first glance. Jacob and his amassed company are heading back home to Canaan. Jacob hopes that his brother Esau has miraculously had a bout of amnesia and is excited to welcome him with no dark thoughts about Jacob's nasty subterfuge a few decades earlier. But Esau has a good memory, and the report quickly arrives that the maligned brother is racing toward Jacob's retinue at the center of an aggressive army seeking revenge.

Always the manipulator, Jacob strategizes ways to save his skin. First he splits the caravan in two, hoping Esau will target the wrong camp. Then large gifts are sent ahead in the expectation that Esau will be slowed by the herds offered and his men distracted by the feasts of fresh roasted meat they take. Perhaps a little drunkenness might accompany the barbecue rituals, and because of these subterfuges, Jacob's groups will be able to slip by in the night.

But Jacob knows the depth of his guilt, and his manic attempts at self-preservation continue. He sends his wives and children and remaining possessions across the Jabok River while he remains behind. This is a sinister and cowardly move, for it exposes Jacob's family to the possible onslaught of Esau's army without the moderate natural moat of the river to make their position more defensible. Meanwhile Jacob himself is sitting in the protection of the hills, and will have the advantage of hearing the screams of his children and wives as they are slaughtered as a warning order to escape, even if they do not. Jacob is always the conniver and a master of self-preservation.

Yet it is here, in the quarters where he had taken such pains to make himself safe, that he becomes most vulnerable. "A man wrestled with him till daybreak" (Gen 32:24). We know even less about this figure than the little that Jacob seems to know. Nevertheless, both he and we are to infer that this was a divine engagement and that God would not allow Jacob's hiding to keep him aloof from the court of heaven or from a confrontation with himself and the tests of righteousness. At the same time, a divine graciousness in the story reminds us that the divine messenger does not overpower or overwhelm Jacob but continues to grapple with him and even provides a blessing he does not deserve. This, then, is the meaning of "Israel"—one who wrestles with God.

Looking back at Jacob, Israel at Mt. Sinai would see herself. She carried the conniving DNA of her forebear in her social makeup. But here at Mt. Sinai she also carried his divinely appointed name. In the Suzerain Vassal covenant Yahweh formulated with her, the wrestling continued. Yahweh and Israel were bound in an embrace that would change them both.

The Joseph Story Cycle

Although Abraham hears a disembodied voice and Jacob has a vision of heaven one night at Bethel, it is Joseph whose Genesis record is entirely shaped by dreams. He enters the narrative as a self-absorbed privileged son who foolishly antagonizes his family by reporting nighttime revelations that he is the most important among them, destined to be their lord and master (Gen 37:2–11). His arrogance precipitates a plot among his siblings to get rid of him (Gen 37:12–35), and this brings him to Egypt as a slave (Gen 37:36; 38:1–6). Now the dreaming takes center stage again as Joseph is unjustly thrown in prison (Gen 39:7–23), where he meets two men from the Pharaoh's court who are awaiting adjudication on treason charges (Gen 40:1–4). They each have dreams (Gen 40:5–8), which Joseph is able to interpret (Gen 40:9–19) in a way entirely consistent with the events that follow (Gen 40:20–22).

Joseph's unique skills come to the attention of the Pharaoh two years later, when the ruler's night-time reveries plague him like a nightmare and Joseph is brought in to make sense of it all (Gen 40:23—41:36). This earns Joseph a spot as co-regent of Egypt (Gen 41:37–57), and it is from this position that he becomes savior of his family during the ensuing famine (Gen 42—46). Joseph's tale ends with his sons Manasseh and Ephraim gaining equal status with Jacob's other sons in the inheritance distributions (Gen 48—49), and Joseph's burying his father with honors in Canaan (Gen 50:1–14) while keeping alive the dream of the whole family returning there one day when the current crisis had passed (Gen 50:15–26).

In its focus on dreams, the Joseph story cycle that concludes Genesis deals with two issues. First, it answers the question of how this nation of Israel, springing from such illustrious stock, become an enslaved people in land not their own. Second, it creates a vision for the way in which the future is brighter than the past; along with their forebear Joseph, they need only take hold of the dream of God for them.

THE METANARRATIVE OF GENESIS

When viewed through its obvious literary development, the book of Genesis is reasonably perceived as an extended historical prologue to the Sinai covenant. It provides the information necessary for Israel to understand why Yahweh is establishing this treaty with this particular people and what will be the outcome of it. In its pages are described the divine explanations about the character of reality, including creation's original goodness and the devastating effects of sin. Genesis informs Israel of God's long-standing plan to reassert divine connections with all the races of humanity, and that this is now to be done through a particular community shaped by way of this Suzerain Vassal covenant. Furthermore, Genesis describes Israel's unique, miraculous origins, and spells out something of her edgy character. Finally, it unfolds the more recent history that tells why Israel was in Egypt rather than in Canaan, where she belonged.

In effect, the literary design of Genesis, in its largest arcs, has this shape:

- **Chapters 1—11: Origins Story Cycle**
  What is the nature of reality?
  It is divinely good, but thoroughly contaminated by evil

- **Chapters 12—25: Abraham Story Cycle**
  Who are we as a unique people?
  We are miraculously born to be God's witness to the nations

- **Chapters 26—36: Jacob Story Cycle**
  What is our character as a people?
  We are deceitful connivers who wrestle with God

- **Chapters 37—50: Joseph Story Cycle**
  How did we get to Egypt?
  By dreaming our own dreams
  How did we get out of Egypt?
  By dreaming the dreams of God

Genesis, then, cannot be separated from Exodus, because, first, it is addressed to the nation of Israel standing at Mt. Sinai, gaining its new identity through the Suzerain Vassal covenant being made there. Furthermore, Genesis is not an independent text of either mere ancestor stories or chronologies of creation and national origins. Because it is literature that illumines the Sinai covenant, it gives information pertinent only to that event. Chapters 1—2 are not so much about the documentation of timelines and details in the divine creative activity as they are a clearly articulated worldview over against the current understandings of humanity and the natural realm found in neighboring nations. The Sinai covenant makes sense only if there is a sovereign creator who still has a stake in human society. Furthermore, although sin and evil are part of the pervasive common earthbound experience, these are not co-equal or co-eternal with God or good or the way things are supposed to be. Finally, in Israel's unique patrimony is a story that separates this nation from the rest of humanity not in anthropological superiority but only in its mission and mandate.

The four worldview questions addressed on the pages of Genesis linger throughout history as critical issues of human life and society. As Modernism swept the sacral world out of the heavens, Post-Modernism continues to look for meaning somewhere in the clouds of dust below. The four questions of Genesis serve as a link between the biblical record and current quest for meaning.

1. What is the nature of the universe in which we are living? Is it a random collection of happenstance occurrences that is at best the provenance of chaotic fate and at worst weighted against us by vindictive unseen powers? Or is it the product of a loving and intelligent and personal deity who is still seeking restoration and renewal with the human race after our centuries of bratty willfulness that have nearly annihilated civilization?

2. What is the unique purpose and meaning of the "church" or the "people of God?" Does religion (or at least Christianity) make one deluded and irrelevant? Is there meaning that goes beyond repetitive ritual to be found in becoming part of a religious movement? Why is "mission" so important to the church, and what is the truest nature of that mission? Are we still on the journey of Abraham, and what is the blessing we are holding out to the nations of this world?

3. Who are we in our core beings? Just because we were born and raised in the church, does that mean we are more noble, more pious, more godly, more deserving, than others who did not have the same heritage? What does it mean to be a scrapping human being? Who are we fighting for, even in our "religious wars?" What happens to us when God comes down to wrestle with us? Who is winning? Who is losing? And what does the wrestling itself mean for how we understand our nature and our place in life?

4. How did we get to Egypt? How did we get to Chicago, to New York, to Johannesburg, to Moscow, to Des Moines, to Mexico City, to Kyoto, to La Paz, to Padunkaville? What are the dreams we are chasing in our mad pursuit of self? In what prisons do we find ourselves the morning after we've seen our names in bright lights? Is there another dream to see, a vision to grasp, a world still waiting to be born that gives us a context in which to live and move and breathe and grow again? How are we going to get out of Egypt? When will we begin to dream the dream of God?

THE MORALLY WEIGHTED GENEALOGIES OF GENESIS

This grand perspective of Genesis is confirmed by another literary overlay that subtly weaves together all of the smaller sections of Genesis. A recurring textual device in the book is the phrase "These are the generations of . . ." (2:4, 5:1, 6:9, 10:1, 11:10, 11:27, 25:12, 25:19, 36:1, 37:2). When surveying the book through this grid, several ideas emerge. First, the initial story of the creation (Gen 1:1—2:3) does not begin with this phrase, and therefore stands apart from the rest of sections that follow. Second, these subsequent ten sections—each beginning with the phrase—appear to be morally weighted, so that the dominant evaluation in each is either positive or negative with respect to responsive obedience or disobedience to God. Third, there is a progression to the series, which highlights the unique character and role of the group that will ultimately emerge as the nation of Israel.

The outcome is an unfolding explanation of human history which moves from original perfection (the creation story of Genesis 1:1—2:3) through the corrupting influence of individual expressions of sin and rebellion (the "generations" of "heaven and earth" and "Adam") into a divine response that targets an individual for salvation (the "generation" of "Noah"); this is followed by a communal rebellion (the "generation" of the "Sons of Noah"), precipitating a divine counteraction that produces a community designed for obedient witness (the "generations" of "Shem" and "Terah"). Along the way this family experiences separations tracking the line of the missional community (the "generations" of "Isaac" and "Jacob") in distinction from others (the "generations" of "Ishmael" and "Esau").

CREATION PLUS TEN "GENERATIONS"

One literary device that shapes Genesis is the initial statement of the moral goodness of God's creative activity (1:1—2:3) followed by the explication of ten "generations," each of which is morally weighted as seeking original goodness (+) or not (-):

2:4—4:26 "Heaven and earth" (-)

5:1—6:8 "Adam" (-)

6:9—9:29 "Noah" (+)

10:1—11:9 "Sons of Noah" (-)

11:10–26 "Shem" (+)

11:27—25:11 "Terah" (+)

25:12–18 "Ishmael" (-)

25:19—35:29 "Isaac" (+)

36:1—37:1 "Esau" (-)

37:2—50:26 "Jacob" (+)

By the time Genesis ends, Israel at Mt. Sinai is placed in an interpreted natural order shaped by a particular worldview, has been informed about its unique calling and character, and understands the reason for Yahweh's recent political battle and victory over the Pharaoh of Egypt in order to reclaim Israel as a redemptive community of witness. In response to the failed attempts at winning back humanity by way of the homeless restlessness of Adam and Eve and their early decedents just outside the Garden of Eden and again through the re-creative efforts to restart the human race through Noah following the purging flood, Israel now can see its place as a nation with a peculiar identity that is intended to become a city on the hill providing a divinely inspired lifestyle and religion, in contrast to those which are more or less the products of human invention gone bad.

When distilled into a diagram, Genesis may be portrayed in this manner (see below). All of this begs another question. What does it feel like to have God move into the neighborhood? What is life like when God is the chief resident at the heart of the community?

Answering these questions necessitates further covenant documents. The books we know as Leviticus and Numbers probed those issues for ancient Israel; these and the rest of the books of the Bible have become our "Scripture" precisely for this reason, as the journey with Yahweh and the divine mission continues to unfold.

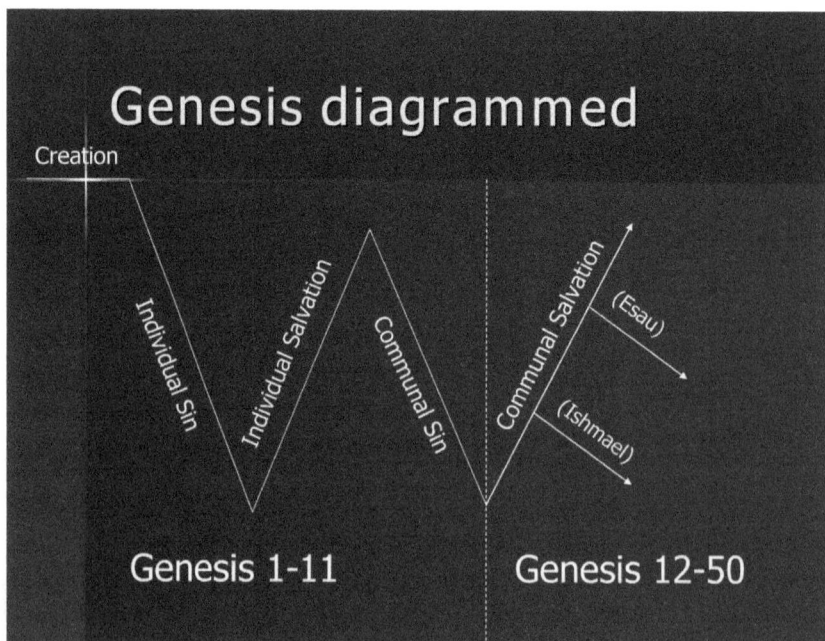

Genesis diagrammed

Creation

Individual Sin

Individual Salvation

Communal Sin

Communal Salvation

(Esau)

(Ishmael)

Genesis 1-11   Genesis 12-50

3

WORLDVIEW WARS IN THE GLOBAL SOUTH: A CASE STUDY OF UGANDA CHRISTIAN UNIVERSITY

Daniel C. Button

Christianity today has become largely a Global South phenomenon. But what is the Global South? Conventionally, the term "Global South" refers to Africa, Asia, and Latin America, and thus far its application has been primarily restricted to a religious context rather than a political one. Even more narrowly it applies to a specifically Christian framework, because the similarities of condition which give it meaning are to be found within the parallel developments and growth of Christianity in these three major regions south of the equator, especially within the post-colonial dynamics of the past 50 years. If this were all it meant, simply a numerical shifting of numbers of affirming Christians from the Northern to the Southern hemispheres, there would be little worth talking about. But underlying the numerical shift

Daniel C. Button <drbutton@ucu.ac.ug> is a lecturer in the Theology Faculty and Head of the Department of Foundation Studies at Uganda Christian University in Mukono, Uganda. He also chairs the African Areopagus Society (promoting dialogue between faith and science). He has been a mission partner with Crosslinks (UK) and Global Teams (USA) since 1997, is ordained in the Church of Uganda (Anglican), and has taught in Africa since 1991, primarily in Zimbabwe and Uganda. He has authored or edited several student textbooks, including Christian Ethics, and Understanding Worldviews, and written various articles on science, theology, and education in the African context. Currently a PhD candidate through St. John's College, University of Nottingham, he holds an MDiv from Columbia International University and BAs from Bethel College (Minn.) and the University of Minnesota.

is a more subtle yet far more significant shift in the nature of Christianity as practiced and believed.

To assert that Christianity today has become largely a Global South phenomenon is actually to make a controversial yet compelling observation that worldwide Christianity is undergoing a seismic upheaval, no longer dominated by a linear progression from European Reformation through Enlightenment Rationalism to Modernity, Liberalism, and now Postmodernism in its varied forms, but growing and taking shape in a quite different and unexpected direction: perhaps worryingly for some, an uncontrolled and uncontrollable one.

The recently concluded GAFCON (Global Anglican Future Conference) is just one example of a Global South movement which has taken shape quite rapidly (in Anglican terms) to suddenly emerge as a perceived threat to the historic structures and modern progressive developments of the Anglican Communion. Why is GAFCON so significant now, when it would not have been even 20 years ago? Prof. Lamin Sanneh a highly respected Global South historian, notes that, "The average Anglican is black, [African], female, under 30, evangelical, has 3 children, lives on two dollars a day, walks three kms for water and is related to someone with HIV/AIDS."[1] This picture is so distant from the Church of England or the Episcopal Church in America as to give one pause. Of the 80 million members of the Anglican Communion worldwide, 17 million are found in Nigeria, 9 million in Uganda, and 7 million in Kenya. These three African nations alone account for more than 40% of the global Anglican population,[2] and this picture represents the general trend in many denominations and certainly in the Christian Church as a whole.

To some the transition of 'normative' Christianity from West to South may seem like a straightforward statement of fact; to others it may sound like a provocative assertion based on rather spurious evidence of sheer numbers over real substance; and to others, especially Western evangelicals despairing of the church in Europe and America, it may be a statement of wishful thinking rather than certain conviction. Whatever one's assessment may be, it should be clear that this is at least a *significant* phenomenon, the implications of which need to be considered by the Western Church as well as the Global South, especially in the context of the global configuration of competing worldviews. An important related observation however, is that Christianity

---

1 In Chris Sugden; "Anglican update: on the verge of a great future?" in *Evangelicals Now*, Dec 2006.

2 These statistics have been widely published and circulated. Taken here from Bishop Joel Obetia's "Chairman's Communication to the COU Board of Mission", 29 March 2007.

and the Christian Worldview—perhaps even more so in the Global South than in the West today—are not necessarily synonymous, and may even, at certain points, appear to be at odds with each other. This unnerving observation will be explored later in this paper.

Before proceeding to the issue of the Christian Worldview in the Global South, a word on the title of this paper may be helpful. In using the term "wars", I am not referring to the possibility or likelihood of a major clash of civilizations, as predicted in Huntington's seminal work of 1996[3], although if such a major clash does occur it will certainly be played out on African soil, as were both world wars, and even more so the cold war quest for post-colonial political dominance. What I am referring to is the much more gradual and subtle war being played out every day in newspapers, media, churches, universities, political parties, and cultural institutions. This is the battle of competing world-views or, to use a phrase resonant even within secular parlance today, the "battle for hearts and minds". If the major lines of battle have truly shifted to the Global South and the developing world, then it becomes imperative that the Western Church, if it wants to remain relevant in this changing environment, begins to understand the nature of Global South Christianity, not to mention the challenges, fears, threats and crises being faced by our "comrades in arms" in the spiritual and philosophical battle of worldviews. It is my assertion that the worldview wars taking place "under the radar" in the Global South will ultimately be of far greater significance than the physical wars being fought in Iraq and Afghanistan over these past eight years.

Uganda Christian University as a Microcosm

The purpose of using a Global South University curriculum as a case study by which to enter into the nature of worldview wars is two-fold. First, as Charles Malik famously pronounced, "This great western institution, the university, dominates the world today more than any other institution: more than the Church, more than the government, more than all other institutions—challenging one to reach the world."[4] Education in the developing world has become the primary means of escaping poverty, achieving social mobility and financial success, and reaching and maintaining a relative level of security for the extended family both present and future. Even one person with a degree in a large extensive family will have an impact on the welfare of everyone. In Uganda today, despite previous generations unable to gain even a basic education, studies have

---

3 Samuel Huntington, *The Clash of Civilizations* (London: Simon & Schuster, 1996).

4 Charles Malik as quoted in Africa Evangelistic Enterprises Newsletter, May 2005. See also Charles Malik, "The Two Tasks", 1980 Address to Wheaton College.

shown that Ugandans place an extremely high value on education, and will spend on average upwards of 25% of their total income on school fees for their children.[5] Despite a $320 per capita income[6], and a $2000 per year tuition, UCU is oversubscribed and demand remains very high.

Furthermore, universities in the Global South have seen extraordinarily dynamic growth. In 1975 Makerere was the sole university in Uganda, basically established for the purpose of civil service training. Not until 1988 was a second university opened, a regional Islamic university. However, over the same period enrolment at Makerere shot up from a previously stable 2,500 to nearly 30,000. Due to market pressures, university education was finally privatized in the early 1990s. By 2000 there were 10 universities in Uganda, by 2005 there were 17. Today there are at least 27 and still not meeting the demand. Only 63,000 of Uganda's 26 million population are presently enrolled at university, and only 2% are enrolled in any form of tertiary education.[7] What is more interesting however, is that of all these new universities, more than half are faith-based institutions. Even in the so-called secular universities, the predominant worldview of both staff and students is faith-based (either Christian or Islamic), religion plays a central role, and the secular bias of the West does not rule out faith-based dialogue or curricular influence.

This leads to the second reason for using UCU as a case study. Joel Carpenter argues that these new faith-based universities "form a great 'knowledge industry' reaching around the world in complex networks of institutional interaction."[8] He observes a surprising characteristic common to many of these universities: an evangelical Christian ethos. He continues: "'Evangelical University' may look like an oxymoron to the average academic [in the West], who knows that the world in which she lives and moves is resolutely secular . . . yet there are new universities arising out of Protestant movements for evangelization and spiritual renewal in many parts of the world."[9] In his assessment, he concludes, "Any attempt to investigate the relationship between the spread of evangelical forms of Christianity in the non-Western world and the forces of globalization would do well to consider these educational movements."[10]

5 A.B.K. Kasozi, *University Education in Uganda*, (Fountain Pub: Kampala, 2003), preface p. xvii

6 "Vision 2035: Working Draft for National Dialogue", National Planning Authority, May 2008.

7 Compiled from Uganda Bureau of Statistics Population & Housing Census Report, 2002, released March 2005. Also A.B.K. Kasozi, op.cit. pp 1-4.

8 Joel A. Carpenter, pre-publication chapter in *Interpreting Contemporary Christianity: Global Process and Local Identities*, ed. Ogbu Kalu, (Grand Rapids: Curzon and Eerdmans, 200_?) from "New Evangelical Universities: Cogs in a World System or Players in a New Game?" p. 1.

9 Ibid., p. 1

10 Ibid., p. 2

The university therefore, is a critically important player in the global marketplace of ideas, philosophies, and worldviews, both in the Western world and in the Global South. The difference is that just as Christianity has taken a new direction in the Global South, so too is university education proceeding in a new direction from that of its secular Western parent. Ironically in both cases, the Global South may justifiably claim that it is more closely adhering to the path of original intent, while the West, through the last two centuries, has in fact embarked in the new direction. Universities in the developing world are coming of age, but the secular institutions which promoted their development did not foresee that their offspring would reject the very philosophical underpinnings which produced them—just as the original medieval Christian institutions could not have predicted the rampant secularization of their 19th and 20th Century offspring in Modern Europe and America.

As a microcosm of the worldview wars in the Global South, Uganda Christian University is an excellent representative. Established as a university in 1997, Chartered in 2004,[11] it nevertheless has a prior 90 year history as the flagship theological college of the Anglican Church in much of East Africa. At its inception, it had roughly 250 students; 5 years later it had 2,500; by its 10th anniversary in 2007 the growth had to be capped off at 7,000 students in 12 different departments to maintain standards of quality over quantity, yet the demand for places remains overwhelming. UCU was established firmly as a Christian institution, not merely in name but in substance, with a clear evangelical statement of faith embedded in its instruments of identity; oversight by the Anglican Church of Uganda as its Trustee body; an educational commitment to the "Integration of Faith and Teaching"; a full time academic employment policy mandating personal testimony of salvation and commitment to Christ; an open admission policy requiring students to "respect the Christian ethos of the university"; and a curriculum requirement across all disciplines incorporating four Christian foundational courses: Old Testament, New Testament, Worldviews, and Ethics. All of this underpins the many institutionally sponsored student activities, fellowship groups, mission and evangelism outreaches, etc., which fall under the domain of the Chaplaincy. The Christian identity of UCU is summarized in its motto, "God, the Beginning and the End", and its mission statement includes the key phrase, "[preparing] students for thoughtful, productive lives of Christian faith and service. . . ."[12]

---

11 Charter granted 20th May, 2004; gazetted 14th Jan 2005 under *The Uganda Christian University Charter Notice*, sec. 102(3) of the Universities and other Tertiary Institutions Act, 2001.

12 The full statement reads, "Uganda Christian University is dedicated through teaching,

Ugandan Archbishop Henry Luke Orombi, one of the foremost Anglican leaders of the Global South movement, and also the Chancellor of Uganda Christian University, has been a staunch supporter of a collaborative Christian mission between Church and University. One goal of such collaboration would be to learn about Islam, and to combat militant Islam, which Orombi sees as "the greatest threat to our social, political and cultural heritage."[13] A second goal is to combat a doctrinal dry rot stemming from the West:

> Today, the undermining of Biblical authority so rampant in the established, mainline Western churches is attacking the church from within with a false gospel. Christians should counter these malign influences by seeking to 'extend the influence of Word and Spirit throughout the culture—in the universities, the military, the houses of government, and the marketplace.[14]

At UCU's recent 2008 graduation ceremony he charged students to follow the principles of Christ-like servant leadership while making an impact in all realms of society. "If only Ugandans would learn this simple lesson—that it is our corporate responsibility to take action when something needs doing." He also reiterated that, "The Church of Uganda founded this institution not for any private or material benefit it might receive but to offer the riches of education to the young people of this country."[15]

Likewise the guest speaker at the same event, Egyptian Presiding Bishop Mouneer Anis of the Province of Jerusalem and the Middle East, said this:[16]

> My brothers and sisters, it is not enough to note and be proud of the shift in the "centre of gravity of Christianity" to Africa, but we should be determined that this shift should not be just numerical but have a great impact in the quality and the effectiveness of the Church and its institutions. It is my dream, which I hope will be yours as well, that the Church in Africa should shape the global Christian mind in the third Millennium as it did in the first one. Not only that, but that we should play a leading role in changing the face of Africa and in overcoming the threats and challenges

scholarship, service, spiritual formation, student development and social involvement to the preparation of students for thoughtful, productive lives of Christian faith and service in their respective professions and places."

13 "Archbishop warns of threat of militant Islam", *Church of England Newspaper*, Feb 9, 2007.

14 Ibid.

15 Chancellor Archbishop Henry Orombi, unpublished graduation address, UCU, 6 June 2008.

16 President Bishop Mouneer Anis, unpublished graduation address, UCU, 6 June 2008.

that we face today. I am confident that Uganda Christian University is a major player already in fulfilling this dream. It is true to say that you, who will graduate today, are strategically positioned at the core of our "African Hope" and that the Gospel and the mission of our Lord and Saviour Jesus Christ are at the heart of this "hope".

While many colleges in the USA have a similar Christian foundation, it is only within the past two decades that some of these colleges likewise have moved toward university status. The difference is that in Uganda, UCU alone attracts nearly 14% of the total university student population in the country, and is only one of many faith-based institutions, thus giving Christian universities an enormous potential impact in society and the nation.[17] One may ask, does this accurately reflect the demographics of the country, or is this an artificially contrived grasping of educational control by religious institutions? Uganda, similar to much of sub-Saharan Africa, claims more than 80% Christian affiliation, with 12% Muslim and some degree of Traditional African religious adherence. The question is not whether Uganda is a Christian country, or whether the locus of Christianity has indeed shifted to the Global South, but what sort of Christianity is it?

WHAT SORT OF CHRISTIANITY IS THIS?

These encouraging statistics of the growth of Christianity only tell one side of the story. Western Christians understandably wonder, how can a country claiming over 80% adherence to Christianity be so rife with major social problems of endemic corruption, tribalism, despotic leadership, religious syncretism, HIV/AIDS, polygamy, witchcraft, war, poverty, domestic violence, defilement, gender disparity, infant and maternal mortality, and other symptoms of social dysfunction which would seem to counter the claims of real Christian transformation? It may be worth noting that many African Church leaders are equally concerned and are addressing these overwhelming problems honestly and openly, despite the painfully slow process of change. Bishop Joel Obetia, a former lecturer at UCU, describes this dichotomy:

> Although the outer man of Africa may be decaying and wasting away with AIDS, wars, hunger and natural disasters, there is an inner man that is daily being renewed and strengthened by God in the spirit. It is this part of Africa that shares freely amidst tragedy, which smiles and celebrates "in spite of", which the world needs to see and interact with.[18]

---

17 Op. cit. "Vision 2035", May 2008.

18 Bishop Joel Obetia of Madi-West Nile Diocese, "Chairman's Communication to the COU

But there is still a serious underlying problem. On the surface, Christianity has grown to an amazing degree in Uganda in just over 100 years. Yet under the surface, the problems of Africa seem as intractable as ever. Is Christianity in Africa merely surface religion without substance? Why is there such paucity of visible evidence of genuine worldview transformation in the larger society? Or worse, does the adopted practice of Christian ritual *preclude* a transformation in world-view thinking? In other words, is it possible that Christian religious *observance* may in some ways act as a barrier to real *transformative* Christian experience, including the adoption of a genuine Christian worldview?

The simple answer is yes, nominal Christianity is a real problem in the Global South. A reasonable comparison may be drawn with Medieval Christianity in Europe, where *practice*, even deep loyalty to one's religion, did not necessarily imply a transformed life or a wholly adopted system of underlying beliefs. As Christianity has become a successful, accepted, and public aspect of the culture to which the majority subscribes, the assumption is made that everyone who participates in that culture is a Christian. Those who attend church, become baptized as infants, take on a Christian name, and involve themselves in various culturally Christian activities are as equally "Christian" as those who undergo a born-again, salvation experience. In Uganda, the distinction is made not between those who are Christian or non-Christian, but between those who are Christian and those who are "saved". It is common practice to introduce oneself as a saved person, while others will readily admit that they are Christians but *not* saved. (*Not* being a Christian implies one is a Muslim—or perhaps of another religion, but the idea that a person simply has no religion is a foreign concept.) Thus, large numbers of Christian students may attend Uganda Christian University without being saved and with little or no concept of a Christian Worldview. This goes a long way toward understanding the charges of syncretism. But while the West may accuse the Global South Christianity of being compromised by paganism, the Global South sees the Western Church as having sold out to materialism, science, and liberalism.

Philip Jenkins' recent book *The New Faces of Christianity* opens with a very telling story of two bishops "participating in a Bible Study, one an African Anglican, the other an American Episcopalian. As the hours went by, tempers flared as the African expressed his confidence in the clear words of Scripture, while the American stressed the need

---

Board of Mission", 29 March 2007.

to interpret the Bible in the light of modern scholarship and contemporary mores. Eventually, the African bishop asked in exasperation, 'If you don't *believe* the scripture, why did you bring it to us in the first place?'" [19] This simple personal encounter tells a much larger story, exemplifying the gulf between Western and Global South Christianity. Archbishop Benjamin Nzimbi of Kenya exclaimed, "Our understanding of the Bible is different from theirs. We are two different churches."[20] Jenkins recognizes this "sharp global division" between the older yet more progressive Christianity of North America and Europe[21], which has been more accommodating to the secular worldview of the society in which it exists, and the new, yet more conservative, traditional Christianity of the Global South churches. And this brings us to the crux of the problem. Why do these two great Christian bodies seem to be so different, and moving in such different directions?

Speaking in such generalities can be misleading. There is no shortage of liberal Christian viewpoints in the Global South nor of conservative traditionalism in the West. But the issue is the general trend or direction of these two bodies, and the major emphasis of each form of Christian belief and practice. My contention is that the root cause of the divergence is the worldview context in which each Christian body has matured and developed. In other words, there is a war of worldviews taking place in both geographical contexts, and the nature of these philosophical and spiritual battles have tremendously shaped the forms of Christianity which have emerged. To put it rather crudely, the Global South missed the Enlightenment.

Western European and North American Christianity has long been embroiled in a battle for domination—some would say for survival—with philosophies and principles emerging from the Enlightenment. Rationalism, empiricism, naturalism, the scientific method and the scientific revolution, liberalism, modernity, and more recently pluralism and multi-culturalism have all emerged out of Enlightenment thought to challenge the Judeo-Christian culture, its values and ethical foundation. Many have referred to this as a great "Culture War", viewing the older Judeo-Christian culture at war with a spectrum of secular post-Enlightenment philosophies arrayed against it. Yet in effect, this is really a battle of worldviews, in which each has been heavily influenced by—and found areas of compromise and accommodation with—the other. Charles Colson agreed with political scientist James Kurth in

---

19 Philip Jenkins, *New Faces of Christianity*, (Oxford Uni Press: 2006), p. 1

20 Ibid., p. 1

21 Ibid., p. 1

contending that the most significant "clash" would not be *between* civilizations as predicted by Huntington, but *within* Western civilization: the clash between the Judeo-Christian worldview and the Secular or Naturalistic worldview.[22] This ongoing battle has been the defining condition in which the Christian Church has developed over the last 400 years in the West. The most obvious illustration of this worldview war can be seen in the Creation—Evolution debate, ever-changing in shape and scope, always on the frontlines with victories claimed and lost on both sides, yet unresolved still after 150 years.

But none of this is true of the Global South. In the Global South, the great worldview battle is *not* between Christianity and Secularism. Unlike in the West, Christianity is the newcomer, not on the defensive but on the offensive, not trying to ward off secular enlightenment philosophies, but trying to bring the Good News of Christ into a context of Traditional Religion and Paganism. Here, both sides of the worldview wars are steeped in faith, religion, and belief in the supernatural. The Enlightenment never came to Africa, and the problems facing Christianity in Africa are not those facing the West. The battle is not framed in terms of a spiritual-supernatural worldview versus a secular-naturalistic one, but rather in terms of *which* spiritual-supernatural belief system is superior? The battlefield is actually more complex than in the West, in that Christianity, Islam, and Traditional Religion—all worldviews with a strong foundational belief in the spiritual realm, all theistic, all believing in supernatural powers without question—are all competing for the hearts and minds of a population struggling with huge challenges of poverty, disease, corruption, and under-development. This happens not so much in terms of which worldview is true or false, but in terms of which one is *better*. In other words, is the blood of Christ *more* powerful than the demons, or the jinn, or the spirits of the ancestors? Is Christian healing *more* reliable than that of the witch-doctors or traditional healers? Christianity has been widely accepted but has not automatically eliminated, nor fully replaced, the worldviews that were present before. The transition is gradual, evangelism has leaped ahead of deep understanding, and therefore the Western Church easily sees African Christianity as syncretistic, describing it as "a mile wide and an inch deep".

Philip Jenkins has highlighted some of these major differences. He writes, "Southern churches are quite at home with Biblical notions of the supernatural, with ideas like dreams and prophecy. Just as relevant in their eyes are that book's core social and political themes, like

---

22 Charles Colson and Nancy Pearcey, *How Now Shall We Live?* (Tyndale House, Wheaton: 1999) p. 19.

martyrdom, oppression and exile."[23] The conservative Christianity in the Global South "includes a much greater respect for the authority of Scripture, especially in matters of morality; a willingness to accept the Bible as an inspired text and a tendency to literalism; a special interest in supernatural elements of Scripture, such as miracles, visions, and healings; a belief in the continuing power of prophecy; and a veneration for the Old Testament, which is treated as equally authoritative as the New."[24] Biblical stories of animal sacrifice, atonement, polygamy, faith healing, miracles, demonic possession, witchcraft, and even child sacrifice, all resonate strongly within the African worldview, even those which are no longer practiced by a believing majority. They are well known, relevant to African life, and of continuing interest to Christians. In other words, Global South Christians read the Bible differently than their Western counterparts. While doctrine is not decided by majority vote, the weight of numbers in the Global South may eventually mean that standard university "theology" will be Global South theology, whereas culture-specific interpretations will be seen as "North American or European theology" rather than "African theology".

TEACHING THE CHRISTIAN WORLDVIEW IN THE GLOBAL SOUTH

As we now turn to look at a brief overview of the particular content of the "Worldviews" course at UCU, we should recognize that all the issues thus far discussed reflect a dimension of teaching quite different from that in the West in terms not only of content and structure but of *purpose*. Dr. Phineas Dube, a Zimbabwean and internationally renowned speaker on Christian leadership, recently addressed UCU on the topic of education and worldview.[25] He underscored that Western style education is devoid of the relational elements of African identity and worldview and is to a large extent responsible for the crisis of African leadership today. Before Western learning came to Africa, the emphasis of education was on being respectful to others; all values had to do with how to treat another human being. That was the worldview— not unlike the Biblical imperative to "do unto others." The primary purpose of education was not learning abstract knowledge but preparing oneself to be a human being within the context of the community. Those who received Western education left the village, learned a world of new

---

23 Op. cit. Jenkins, Preface. In reference to Philip Jenkins, *The Next Christendom,* (New York: Oxford University Press, 2006).

24 Jenkins, Philip, "Reading the Bible in the Global South", *International Bulletin of Missionary Research,* April 2006: vol. 30, No. 2, pp. 67-8.

25 Phineas Dube: Comments from talks and informal interview at UCU Leadership and Mission Week, 15-22 June, 2008.

things, but did not learn who they were; they ended up with an identity crisis. If they went back to the village with their parents, there were two very different worldviews living under the same roof. Two systems of government emerged in Africa, one national and distant from people's understanding, the other rural and based in community. Dube noted that while there was much of value to be found in Western education, it lacked the defining characteristics of the African worldview. "Robert Mugabe," he noted poignantly, "is one of the most educated men in Zimbabwe, holding six degrees from the West. And now my country is dying at the hands of educated men."

Students in African universities today stand at the epicentre of a clash of competing worldviews: the old yet still powerful African Traditional Worldview, the newer but dynamic and maturing Christian Worldview, an aggressive and influential Islamic Worldview, and the formidable challenges of the Secular worldview from the West. Any worldview course worthy of the name must somehow address the diversity and challenges of this Global South context. "Understanding Worldviews" is the third of four Christian Foundation courses taught at UCU and is probably the most transformational in its intent. In teaching this course, there has been a gradual evolution from a Western-based to a more African-based approach driven by what the course is trying to accomplish in the lives of the students. The purpose of the course, as stated in the Introduction, is first to learn to comprehend Christianity as a holistic worldview rather than merely as a religion. Secondly, students learn how to analyze and critique *other* worldviews, subjecting them to the same critical standard enforced upon Christianity. Once this has been mastered, the emphasis shifts to *forming* a Christian worldview as the fundamental foundation of one's life. The book suggests that this may be the most important practical application of anything the student learns at Uganda Christian University.

The course is structured by a large lecture (400 students) of 2 hours followed by a 1–2-hour small group tutorial session over 12 weeks in which students raise issues and ideas in a discussion format, stemming from their independent reading and assignment questions. Required reading comes from two textbooks and our own student workbook, which is a continuously evolving product of each year's teaching experience. The textbooks, including Colson & Pearcey's *How Now Shall We Live*[26], and David Burnett's *Clash of Worlds*[27], have been helpful and insightful in a broader context of understanding other worldviews, but

---

26 Charles Colson and Nancy Pearcey, *How Now Shall We Live?* (Tyndale House, Wheaton: 1999).

27 David Burnett, *Clash of Worlds*, (London: Monarch Books, 1990).

are not specifically relevant to the African context. The Colson book in particular views the Christian Worldview in mortal combat with secular forces attacking it on all sides, which is not the case in Africa.

UCU's own publication, "Understanding Worldviews", contains the following chapters:

1. What is a Worldview?
2. Competing Worldviews (Western Secular and African Traditional)
3. Creation and Cosmos: Naturalism and the Christian Worldview
4. The Value of Human Life
5. The Problem of Sin and Evil: The Christian Worldview Perspective
6. The Problem with the World: Other Worldview Perspectives
7. A Multitude of Solutions: Other Worldview Perspectives
8. The Solution: Salvation in Jesus Christ: the Christian Worldview Perspective
9. The Christian Worldview and Family
10. The Christian Worldview and Work
11. The Christian Worldview and Civil Society
12. Revision of Readings

While Chapter 1 is a fairly standard introduction to Worldviews, Chapter 2 emphasizes the African Traditional and Western Secular Worldviews—along with Islam and others—as examples of competing systems, showing underlying philosophies and beliefs (such as African worldview models of the spiritual and physical realms), together with the manifestations of those beliefs in their respective cultures. African writers have been included expressing in their own words issues of culture, ancestral spirits, social problems, and the diverse interactions between Christianity and Culture. Standard Western authors such as Paul Hiebert are included on issues of worldview transformation and conversion, but the most relevant example of a Christianity which was *not* sufficiently transformed by a Christian worldview—the Rwandan genocide—is addressed by Archbishop Kolini of Rwanda.

Chapter 3 attempts to bring a basic naturalistic understanding of origins from a Western scientific perspective into an African context where such is virtually unknown. To elucidate this difference, I have surveyed classes in which less than half of my UCU students have ever *heard* of dinosaurs let alone have any idea of what they are or where they came from; few if any have any knowledge of the Big Bang Theory; and Evolution is merely a term some are aware of, but few know what it means. Those who do, usually condemn it out-of-hand as a ridiculous innovation of those who don't believe in God. (Yet these students are anything but ignorant. They all speak several languages, most have a thorough understanding of various cultures and religions, they know their Bibles, and they could debate all day on the powers of faith healing, demons, ancestral spirits, miracles, and other competing spiritual facts of life. They simply have little or no science background from secondary school.) We therefore begin with a Christian view of the Cosmos reflected in the words of Dorothy Sayers: "We have rather lost sight of the idea that Christianity is supposed to be an interpretation of the universe."[28] We then move to a basic introduction of scientific discoveries of earth and the universe, emphasizing the difference between science as a *method* of discovery, and naturalism as a non-theistic *interpretation* of science, and finally discuss the various responses of Christianity to science and to a naturalistic worldview.

Chapter 4 looks at human life, assessing issues of value and purpose in an evolutionary model as compared to the biblical view of creation and the "Image of God" in man. The problem of sin and evil in Chapter 5 again highlights issues which are unique to the African context. One such is a pervasive failure to differentiate between sin as a feature of human lostness outside of Christ and sin which may continue after new life in Christ. The result is a common misconception that any time one sins, he/she loses his salvation and is destined for hell unless he repents and is once again forgiven. Chapters 6 & 7 help students to assess the claims of other worldviews—with particular emphasis on Islam—in relation to the major problem of the world and the solutions offered. Chapter 8 moves into a straightforward Christian view of salvation, emphasizing real transformation and a change of lifestyle rather than mere cultural Christianity or the affirmation of certain creeds and propositions.

The last 4 chapters move into the application of the Christian Worldview into various key issues of life: Marriage and Family, Work, and Civil Society. In each case, there are many issues arising unique to either Global South or African Christianity. For example, traditional marriage in Africa is a process rather than an event, including several stages and a brideprice. Marriage is between families, not just individuals; problems of inter-tribal marriages, child brides, and taboos of totems, are all important. "Christian marriage" is basically seen as "Western marriage", but traditional marriage is not readily accepted by the Church. Add to this the terrible dilemmas of singleness and childlessness in African society, and the challenges of polygamy, and one can easily see that Christian worldview on marriage and family must be taught in a wholly different manner than in the West.

---

28 *Dorothy L. Sayers, 1937-1944: From Novelist to Playwright*, vol. 2 of the *Letters of Dorothy Sayers*, ed. Barbara Reynolds, (New York: St. Martin's Press, 1998), p. 158.

In conclusion, UCU is attempting to communicate the transformative nature and power of the Christian Worldview to students standing on the frontlines of a significant worldview war, in terms and in a manner which reflects the changing dynamic of Global South Christianity, and for the purpose of moving students from mere Christian religious adherence to a dynamic, active and life changing faith in the person of Christ and the message of the gospel.

4

How the West Lost Its (Christian) Mind and Can Find It Again

Mark E. Roberts

Introduction

Medieval Europe was united conceptually by a Christian worldview, although not in all points identical with what we would consider a purely biblical worldview today. Nevertheless, its mind was stamped with clearly Christian features: A distinctively Augustinian worldview grew in influence in the early medieval period, while an equally distinctive Aristotelian-Christian worldview, scholasticism, dominated late medieval Europe. A Christian worldview continued to unify Europe in significant ways even when sundered by the Reformation and Counter-Reformation; but it began to lose its nearly uncontested influence with the challenge of the seventeenth- and eighteenth-century Enlightenment. At present, Christian worldview in the West stands as a weakened competitor with the now-dominant naturalistic worldview.

So how did the West in the last millennium lose its Christian mind? Here are two answers, followed by explanation:

(1) The simplest answer: *It shifted from pursuing knowledge based on trust* (in God and in testimony to personal knowledge of him) *to* knowledge based on (trusting in thoroughgoing) doubt.

(2) A slightly less simple answer: It lost it because while it rightly sought to advance beyond the limitations of late medieval scholasticism, its Enlightenment adventure actually shrunk the domain of

Mark E. Roberts <mroberts@oru.edu> directs the Holy Spirit Research Center at Oral Roberts University and, as an adjunct professor, teaches New Testament in its School of Theology & Missions and Humanities at other colleges. He is publisher of Word & Spirit Press and a BreakPoint Commissioned Centurion. He holds the BA (Mississippi College), MA (The Ohio State University), and MA and PhD (Vanderbilt University).

human knowledge instead of expanding it by rejecting knowledge that the new worldview of naturalism did not produce. The old knowledge it rejected came to include knowledge of God and of common morality and, as such, ceased to be a recognizably Christian mind.

Augustine: Knowledge from Trust

In explaining the loss of the Christian mind, I begin by illustrating its existence, exemplified in Augustine. In their fine worldview book *The Collapse of the Brass Heavens*,[1] authors Zeb Bradford Long and Douglas McMurry trace Augustine's journey to faith, expressed especially in his Confessions, which took him through several different worldviews before finding his home in Christ.[2]

(1) He journeyed through sensual indulgence, through New-Age-like Manicheanism, and then through both the Platonic and skeptical philosophies of his day *en route* to Christ. The skepticism was the current expression of more ancient Greek skepticism, which denied that humans can know anything with certainty or insisted that nothing be believed without being proven. Skepticism then and now discounts the transmission of truth through credible testimony.

(2) But Augustine came to see that much genuine knowledge comes only from the testimony of others. He recognized that knowing who his parents were depended wholly on others' testimony (in his pre-DNA days);[3] and over time, he came to see that the Bible is, in the main, trustworthy testimony of others' experience of God and his revelation.

(3) Augustine recognized other crucial qualities of Christian knowledge: that it is personal—it is knowledge of the living God; and that it is powerful. Bradford and McMurry claim that his experience of the power of God's Word decided his epistemology. Augustine lived during the waning years of the Western Roman Empire in which pagan moralists such as Seneca and Cicero decried the savagery of gladiatorial sport and widespread sexual immorality and sought a means to renew the culture. Augustine witnessed such renewing power, which he recounts in several episodes:

---

1 subtitle, *Rebuilding Our Worldview to Embrace the Power of God* (Grand Rapids, Mich.: Chosen Books, 1994): chapter 6, "Before the Brass Heaven: Augustine," 63–72.

2 Prof. Daniel Robinson says Augustine set for himself "the task of recovering the philosophical wisdom of the ancients in order to render it serviceable to the cause of Christianity." "Lecture Eighteen: The Light Within—Augustine on Human Nature," in the course book for Robinson's *The Great Ideas of Philosophy, 2nd edition* (Chantilly, Va.: The Teaching Company, 2004) 71.

3 *Confessions* VI.7

- His best friend from boyhood fell ill and, while unconscious and near death, was baptized by a local priest. He recovered and deepened his devotion to God. Augustine joked about his friend's unconscious baptism, which his friend rebuked sternly, warning Augustine of trifling with God's power. (65)
- A student in Rome was coaxed into watching gladiators and became enslaved to bloodlust. Neither philosophy nor Manicheanism could free him, but Augustine witnessed God's liberating him. (68)
- Augustine wanted freedom from sexual lust and was visited in Rome by an African friend who testified of his conversion to Christ and his deliverance from lust. (70)
- A short time later, Augustine had his famous garden experience with a portion of the book of Romans, in which he "took up and read" from the epistle, "put you on the Lord Jesus Christ and make not provision for the flesh and its concupiscence." (70) His new life as a believer began that day.

"Augustine had discovered that there is a power to free human beings from savagery and lust: the power of Christ as described in the Bible. Augustine was to rebuild his worldview around that power." (71)

Long and McMurry summarize: "Augustine established a number of foundational principles that guided Western culture for more than a thousand years:

1. *Knowledge is power.*

2. *There are three possible sources of knowledge:*

   a. The rational knowledge attained by skepticism (later, [with empiricism] the foundation for modern science);

   b. The occult, Gnostic knowledge, knowledge of neo-pagan religions [such as Manicheanism] (the foundation of today's New Age beliefs);

   c. The Word of God, openly proclaimed in Jesus and the Bible.

3. *The power most likely to tame our self-destructive, savage nature comes from the third source."* (71)

I add:

4. *This knowledge is personal and relational, more than merely calculative.*

5. *And it arises from trust in credible witnesses, not from the doubt of skepticism that demands rationalistic (or, later, empirical) proof.*

ARISTOTELIAN SCHOLASTICISM: KNOWLEDGE AS CONTEMPLATION OF PERFECTIONS

With the reintroduction and study of the texts of Aristotle, by the end of the medieval period, through the Reformation and Counter-Reformation of the sixteenth century, Aristotelian scholasticism, with Thomas Aquinas as its exemplar, dominated the young Christian schools. Its central features included the following:[4]

(1) An epistemology that values traditional authority (with Aristotle second only God) and deductive reasoning from authoritative premises. Disputations (*disputatio*) are the basic form of discourse in universities. What distinguishes these from scholarly debates today is the kind of argumentation that would persuade. Effective arguments stayed on the accepted grounds of established authority and deduced from premises provided by authorities, such as Augustine and Aristotle, for example. Later thinkers would argue that such a form of thought prevented the discovery or creation of new knowledge.

(2) An ordering of everything into a hierarchy of perfections, the Great Chain of Being, atop which is God, the perfect One. In this hierarchy, the immutable (unchanging; stipulated of the heavens and celestial beings and phenomena) is superior to the mutable (e.g., earthly, sub-lunar beings and phenomena). This understanding resists new ideas about astronomy, since heavenly bodies are and should be nearly immutable.

(3) This hierarchy orders also the souls (human, animal, and plants) and the "substantial forms" they govern. At the top of the Chain is God, who is incorporeal and pure actuality. Beneath him are angels, who are incorporeal and pure intellect but imperfect. Humans come next, with a reasoning soul, a corporeal body, and free will to choose between good and evil. At the bottom of the chain, after animals and plants, are stones, which are wholly body and lack soul and its behaviors.

(4) God has built into all the parts and the whole of creation a *telos* toward the fulfillment of his purposes; that is the true nature of each and every thing.

(5) The goal of knowledge in scholasticism is "the contemplative understanding and appreciation of perfections and purposes." Such

---

4 Details about scholasticism come from the handout and lecture by Alan Charles Kors, "The Dawn of the Seventeenth Century: Aristotelian Scholasticism," from his course, "The Birth of the Modern Mind: The Intellectual History of the 17th and 18th Centuries," available through The Teaching Company, http://www.teach12.com.

knowledge directs one upward both in contemplation (thinking on higher, more nearly immutable things is superior to thinking on lower, mutable things) and action (rising above bodily desires toward heavenly ones).

This system is not only contemplative, rather than active, but also doxological. But Enlightenment thinkers such as Francis Bacon, René Descartes, and others found it also sterile and moribund; and they pioneered new thought that formed the modern mind even as it abandoned the Christian mind.

BEYOND SCHOLASTICISM: EXPERIMENTS TOWARD ENLIGHTENMENT

The Enlightenment shifted Western culture dramatically—*from* trust in tradition, religion, and revelation *to* trust in reform and revolution fueled by distrust in traditional sources of authority and, simultaneously, trust in the ability of the individual person to use reason to gain certainty in knowledge and improvement in society.

While I am critical of the views of knowledge, the epistemologies, of the Enlightenment, I want to be fair regarding motives leading toward it.

- The Renaissance and Reformation motto of *ad fontes* ("to the original] sources!") devalued things of immediately preceding centuries (medieval thought and institutions) in favor of ancient, classical sources (which included far more than merely Aristotelian thought). At the same time it valued sharpening of individual critical judgment (expressed in, for example, Erasmus' critical edition of the New Testament and the rise of text criticism), which would often challenge established authority, as it did especially in the Reformation and as especially Descartes would do—he a Roman Catholic who behaved with the individualism of a radical Protestant.
- Religious wars across Europe in the century after Protestant Reformation fueled a secularist impulse.
- Scientific revolution—often led by sincere Christians, such as Francis Bacon—fueled distrust in medieval reliance on authority and fired excitement about social improvement.

Francis Bacon (1561–1626): "Knowledge is Power" for Love of God and Neighbor

Bacon is widely known in histories of science for rejecting scholasticism as futile for increasing human knowledge and also for replacing deductive scholasticism with the inductive method of inquiry, coupled with observational experimentation. A new "instauration" (beginning, or renewal) is his own term for his project. He is also well known for identifying and critiquing the causes of error in thinking as the Idols of the Mind. And he is rightly identified with the maxim "knowledge is power." But he merits mention in this presentation for other reasons, not as widely known or emphasized.

(1) Bacon's Christian motivation: Bacon's enthusiasm for the inductive knowledge of creation arose from his fervent Christian belief that the world was in its eschatological last days and that God had given humanity new thought to enable it to ameliorate, if not reverse, the effects of the Fall through (what we now call) science and technology. Bacon's Christian motivation for both his rejection of scholasticism and advocacy of induction and experimentation is often overlooked or reinterpreted by scholars.[5] But he saw his labors as expressing God's redemptive love for the well being of others.

(2) Bacon's fragmentation of knowledge: Bacon insisted that theology and natural philosophy (i.e., science) should be separated, largely because scholastic theology, with its medieval cultural authority, had so bound the roots of the human enterprise of knowledge that it could not grow. Rather than revising theology and maintaining the unity of all of knowledge (*scientia* meaning, simply, "knowledge"), Bacon's split, along with his advocacy of human power over nature, paves a road that later thinkers will travel in greater and greater numbers without keeping as guardrails Bacon's Christian conviction that charity must guide use of his method. Bacon's separation of theology and, essentially, science influences the conversion of learning and knowledge of God and God's creation from the personal, I-Thou model Augustine exemplifies to the mechanistic, impersonal, and calculative, I-it method of knowledge that the Enlightenment, after Descartes, exalts as the supreme model for all knowledge.[6]

---

5 E.g., the widely used introductory college text *About Philosophy*, now in its 9th edition, offers a nicely designed one-page biographical note about Bacon (140; Robert Paul Wolff and R. Eugene Bales; Upper Saddle River, N.J.: Pearson Education, 2006). It mentions his family, education, and fascinating public and political life, including the financial scandal that drove him from public life; then his major publications and the theory that he may be the true William Shakespeare! But not a word about how his Christian faith motivated the work for which he remains famous. This omission joins claims by several contemporary Bacon scholars that Bacon manipulates religious language in his writings to serve his aim of, in Stephen A. McKnight's words, "transmuting Christian hope for a spiritual salvation into a secular dream of material comfort" ("Francis Bacon's God," 74; *The New Atlantis*, Fall 2005: 73–100). An interview of McKnight on the Mars Hill Audio *Journal* (80.1, May/June 2006) challenges this interpretation of Bacon and helped launch me on this current study. McKnight, professor emeritus in history at the University of Florida, develops his argument in *The Religious Foundations of Francis Bacon's Thought* (University of Missouri Press, 2005).

6 The same edition of the Mars Hill Audio *Journal* (80.2) has an interview with Tim Morris &

René Descartes (1596–1650): Reducing Knowledge to the Rationally Certain via Doubt

Descartes joins Bacon in rejecting scholasticism and in approaching his work as a sincere Christian. In fact, his expressed motive for developing an approach to certain knowledge is evangelistic: that infidels might be persuaded of the truth apart from any prior belief in God or in the truth of Scripture.[7] A further fact that may elicit our sympathy for Descartes' bold break with the past is the sheer number of rival systems competing for allegiance in his day. Jacques Barzun lists them: "the old Aristotelianism and new Stoicism, Epicureanism, atheism, and Pyrrhonism, the complete skepticism that went so far as to deny one's own existence."[8] Descartes the geometer, for whom mathematics modeled the best in thinking, took the bait of seeking epistemological certainty and was willing to jettison all he had ever learned to achieve it. He dared to defeat skepticism with skepticism, wanting to put the bar so high that nothing could challenge the knowledge he defined.

His well-known rationalistic method of four rules[9] was both one of analytical inquiry and one of thoroughgoing doubt. Everything was to be doubted except that which it was impossible to doubt. Following that prescription led to the incorrigible insight that if in fact he were doubting, then "he" had to exist in order to doubt, leading to the famous formulation *cogito ergo sum*. From this certainty of his mind's existence (not, however, of his body's), Descartes believed he could build a house of knowledge that passes the high criterion of certainty, including even the knowledge of God and of the immortality of the soul, thus fulfilling his evangelistic aim.

Because his story is now old to us, we likely do not marvel at what Descartes rejected in his own new beginning. Robert Paul Wolff helps us regain some perspective:[10]

> Descartes' proof of his own existence is one of the high points in the history of philosophy. It is also, in a way, the high point of unbridled individualism in Western civilization. Imagine a

---

Don Petcher, "on science, Christology, and why segregating nature from supernature doesn't do justice to either," which addresses the unintended legacy of some of Bacon's work.

7 in *Collapse of the Brass Heaven* 74–75

8 *From Dawn to Decadence: 500 Years of Western Cultural Life: 1500 to the Present* (New York: HarperCollins, 2000) 200.

9 (1) "accept nothing as true which I did not recognize to be so"; (2) "divide up each of the difficulties which I examined into as many parts as possible": (3) "carry on my reflections in due order . . . . from the most simple to . . . the most complex"; (4) "make enumerations so complete and review so general" to omit nothing" *Discourse on Method*, Part II, quoted in *About Philosophy* 51

10 *About Philosophy* 53 (emphasis author's)

philosopher who proposes to base the entire edifice of scientific, mathematical, and religious knowledge *not* on the collective learning and wisdom of humanity, *not* on the evidence of the laboratory, not on the existence of God, *not even* on the first principles of logic, *but simply on the fact of his own existence!*

Descartes succeeded in demonstrating rationally the existence of his mind, but the bar of certainty is so high that he did not succeed in persuading most unbelievers of the existence of God or of the non-material and everlasting soul. In simple terms, setting the bar so high allowed almost nothing to pass the test of certainty. And therein lies a part of the problem that Descartes' way of thinking passes on to us: Inasmuch as Cartesian rationalism, along with the opposing empiricists and the synthesizing Immanuel Kant, form modern Western thought, this legacy shrinks the field of knowledge people indwelt from pre-Enlightenment times. That is, what counts as knowledge shrinks progressively as the criteria for knowledge are specified more and more rigorously. At this point not only academic philosophy but civilization itself confronts an epistemological Continental Divide: What criteria will cultural authorities use to distinguish knowledge from all else, whether opinion, intuition, hunch, conviction, guess, or sincerely held belief?

Did Descartes truly believe that he and others following his lead could live in the house of knowledge he built according to such rigorous standards? Long and McMurry quote Descartes himself to show that he fudged: While he believed others should live in the house once it was completed, he acknowledged that he must lodge, in the meantime, in his current home. That included obeying "three or four maxims" that did not first meet the criterion of certainty. Descartes elaborates: "The first was to obey the laws and customs of my country, adhering constantly to the religion [Catholicism] in which by God's grace I had been instructed since my childhood" (74). Thus Descartes the builder keeps knowledge from a system he rejects in favor of a new system without first ensuring that the old knowledge will pass the test he is now constructing. Descartes too, like Augustine, proceeded by trust in the testimony of others, but unlike Augustine, he aims for a model of knowledge that excludes such trust.

Long and McMurry identify other flaws in the Cartesian system that gives us the modern mind:

(1) Descartes' emphasis on rationality distorts the nature even of scientific discovery. Long and McMurray comment that "most major scientific discoveries are not birthed in rational thought. They arise

not from conscious logical processes but out of revelations from the subconscious. Rational deductions come later as an attempt to prove the point" (79). Descartes himself had three dreams in 1619 that he believed were from the "Spirit of Truth" and revealed the "foundations of the wonderful science" (79).

(2) Descartes' rationalist epistemology results in the mechanization of the universe, empty of wonder. In this way, the work of Descartes and Bacon tend to the same result, erecting as the supreme model of knowledge the knowing of the other as an It, an object without personal dimensions or relations to the subject. While this picture of the creation of knowledge may be adequate to certain projects, when it is valued as the model of all knowledge, its impersonality tends to transfer to all other objects of inquiry. Moreover, in practice this approach to creating knowledge proceeds as if impersonal matter is all that exists to be known and as if methods proper for the study of impersonal matter are the model for methods for the study of anything, including personal subjects. At the least, this one-size-fits-all epistemology encourages categorical fallacy.

Empiricists Push Back and Toward Atheism: John Locke, Thomas Hobbes, and David Hume

Other thinkers of the time resisted the rationalism of Descartes and others on two main counts:

(1) The high criterion of rational certainty excludes a lot of presumed knowledge that can never meet the lofty criterion, yet such knowledge continues to impress itself upon us so that we cannot ignore it. While anything that meets the Cartesian criterion is truly knowledge, that criterion does not include all that should count as knowledge.

(2) Much, if not all, knowledge comes to us through our senses, even if sensations do not produce incorrigible certainty. Thus empiricists subordinate the reason of the rationalists to the senses.

Empiricists, by definition, emphasize how much knowledge, if not all, derives from our senses. This epistemological choice tends toward atheism quickly, although among the three named for this sub-section, no one accuses John Locke (1632–1704) of atheism. However, philosophers reflecting on Locke's empiricism conclude that it excludes knowledge of the non-material God of the Bible inasmuch as no one claims to experience God through physical senses. Thus the claim of knowledge of God would be nonsense to the empiricist, using both the original denotation of that term and its ongoing and contemporary connotation—foolishness.

With Thomas Hobbes (1588–1679) and David Hume (1711–1776), empiricism leads easily to materialism and, simultaneously, to determinism and atheism (although some insist that Hobbes himself stops shy of unqualified atheism;[11] but truly his effect on culture was atheistic). But not all thinkers, let alone all people who give any thought to what they know and how they know it, accept a compulsion to be only a rationalist or only an empiricist or to be a thoroughgoing, dogmatic materialist. Yet some blending of the two epistemologies has become the prevailing epistemology of the West, as it increasingly tastes and sees what powers the two together manifest in modern science and technology. And in either epistemology, the activity of knowing is experienced and expressed as an essentially impersonal activity, an I-it transaction in a mechanistic world. Such beliefs and practices militate against traditional knowledge and especially against knowledge of God.

Immanuel Kant (1724–1804): Synthesizer and Father of Modern Autonomy

Kant completes the revolution in epistemology that Descartes began, and he offers a way out of the determinism within which materialism in the hands of Hobbes and Hume seemed to imprison humanity. But the costs for Kant's brilliant contributions haunt us to this day.

Regarding epistemology, Kant synthesized rationalism and empiricism thus: He acknowledged the great power of the rational mind by recognizing its many cognitive activities, such as discerning cause and effect, unity, plurality, possibility, necessity, and reality. These acts of the mind Kant named "categories." But he also acknowledged that much knowledge comes to us through our senses, appeasing some empiricists. Sensation is then processed by the mind's categories, and the result is what nearly all will recognize to be knowledge. As good a solution as this seems to be, it has one great drawback: the knowledge we end up with is not knowledge of the external world. It is instead knowledge created by our own minds' stamping their *a priori* categories upon the raw stuff of sensation. So Kant saves knowledge, he offers a way for rationalists and empiricists to come together, but the knowledge we end up with is really not of the external world but only of our own knowing machinery and activity. That is, we end up

---

11 So Daniel N. Robinson, *The Great Ideas of Philosophy*, 2nd ed. (Chantilly, Va.: The Teaching Company, 2004) III: 54–64.

with profound subjectivism. In its own way, Kantian epistemology surrenders pre-Enlightenment knowledge of God perhaps as much as Hume's materialism, and it underwrites much post-Enlightenment theology and study of religion.

Regarding ontology, materialists such as Hobbes and Hume convinced many that human free will is illusory, that any thorough material conception of reality rendered all actions merely mechanical reactions to preceding causes. (Hume denies the existence of causation altogether, but he recognizes that no one can live without the fiction of causation.) Kant takes seriously the materialist denial of free will but finds in the amazing mind an escape from the world of mere appearance. That material world is not finally all that there is. Rationality is itself another dimension of existence that is not subject to laws that determine action in the material world. But when humans act rationally, that is, when they reason, especially about ethical matters, and when they choose to act in accordance with reason, then they have performed freedom, because they have behaved autonomously—as their own law-givers.

Kant, as a sincere Pietist, believed the Bible and its Golden Rule (Matt 7:12). But freedom for him consisted not in merely obeying God on the basis of divine revelation. Such response to an external law is not a rational act. Only when one has rationalized an action and performed autonomously is one free. Since Kant began with deeply biblical convictions, his ideal of autonomy may have produced ethically acceptable results. However, others adopting his views without similar prior convictions could end up justifying their unethical actions by claiming that they are merely performing their freedom. In fact, Kant's philosophy is the way that individual autonomy was lofted into the Enlightenment firmament as perhaps its brightest star. What Kant intended rigorously has been taken rather loosely in the ensuing centuries, and today the typical member of the Western world paraphrases Kant poorly when presuming that he or she is individually a law unto him- or herself and is and ought be acknowledged to be free to do pretty much whatever he or she wishes to do with only the most minimal of boundaries— essentially, not hurting another person in an empirically demonstrable way. (This of course does not include unborn babies, whose personhood one may doubt, or persons with whom one performs immoral sex acts, because harm is not evident empirically immediately.) Kantian autonomy has devolved almost into contemporary social anarchy, a result Kant surely did not intend.

How the West Can Find Its Christian Mind Again

The West lost its Christian mind when, in pursuit of knowledge more rigorous than that of scholasticism, it adopted new methods and rules of knowledge that came to exclude any claims to knowledge that did not meet the new criteria, whether of rationalists such as Descartes or of empiricists such as Hume and Hobbes. Or if one chose the Kantian solution, one contented oneself with radically subjective knowledge.

Theologian Michael J. Buckley, S.J., pushes further. He has investigated the rise of modern atheism perhaps more than anyone else has.[12] His general thesis (developed in two books) is that Christian theologians themselves are largely to blame for the rise of modern atheism, because in their apologetics they adopted the objectivist, mechanistic view of reality suggested by the new [philosophy and] science (Newtonian physics, in particular), which gave "primacy to [knowledge from] inference and 'scientific evidence'" over that from religious experience. Moreover, the same Christian apologists, influenced as they were by Enlightenment philosophy, simultaneously denied that such religious experience produced real knowledge. That is, in order to defend the faith, they conceded crucial foundational issues to their opponents, from which Buckley believes their apologetic, faith-building project could never recover.[13]

He concludes *Denying and Disclosing God* by distinguishing two modes of knowledge:

> This book argues that inference simply cannot substitute for experience. One will not long believe in a personal God with whom there is no personal communication, and the most compelling evidence of a personal God must itself be personal. To attempt something else as foundation or as substitute, as has been done so often in an attempt to shore up the assertion of God, is to move into a process of internal contradictions of which the ultimate resolution must be atheism. (138)

Enlightenment epistemology, its rules for what counts as

---

12 *At the Origins of Modern Atheism* (New Haven, Conn.: Yale, 1987); and *Denying and Disclosing God: The Ambiguous Progress of Modern Atheism* (idem, 2004), the published form of the D'Arcy Lectures given at Oxford in 2000.

13 Philosopher Alvin Plantinga warns against precisely this accommodation by Christians to anti-theistic assumptions in his now-famous 1983 inaugural address at the University of Notre Dame, "Advice to Christian Philosophers," later published "With a special preface for Christian thinkers from different disciplines" in *Faith and Philosophy: Journal of the Society of Christian Philosophers*, vol. 1, permanently copyrighted October 1984. Journal web site: www.faithandphilosophy.com

knowledge, rejects religious experience as merely private and personal, maintaining that genuine knowledge is public and, it would seem, impersonal, that is, objective. Christians simply cannot accept this definition of knowledge and are right to reject this false dichotomy. Theological ethicist Oliver O'Donovan displays the riches of Christian truth, refracted through the Augustinian prism, in his correction of the Aristotelian conception of reason that persisted through the epistemological turn of the Enlightenment and reached us today. [14] Aristotle contrasts theoretical from practical reason, the former concerned with truth, the latter with decisions (6). O'Donovan joins a long list of philosophers seeking to identify the genus of reason that gives rise to these two species, and he finds it in love. Theoretical reason, exemplified in the natural scientist who exalts his detached, objective, dispassionate explorations and experimentations—"Just the facts, ma'am"—expresses love and passion for truth and is therefore practical (12). Practical reason, which O'Donovan considers here within ethics, includes both moral reflection and moral deliberation. Reflection is particularly theoretical because it takes stock of the world and discriminates among loves and hates before deciding on actions that seek to influence this world (13). Uniting both species of reason is love,[15] whose object is "the 'enjoyment' of its object, . . . a relation in which we stand," not another use of the object or even something we do, although love causes action (16; 1 Jhn 3:18).

For our purposes, O'Donovan's analysis shows the close relation between love and knowledge; and this, of course, coheres quite obviously with Christian theism, which affirms that God is love and that the chief duty of humanity is to love God fully and neighbor at least reflexively. In loving we know and grow in knowledge, or, as Augustine says, "we know only as we love" (11). This view of knowledge demands the bursting of the narrow confines of Enlightenment knowledge. Human knowledge is much greater than that crowned by the most rigorous rationalist and empiricist criteria. And even though this Augustinian understanding points in a distinctively Christian way to this broader conception of knowledge and reason, C. S. Lewis points out that numerous ancient and medieval thinkers thought of knowledge in similarly broader terms: In "The Poison of Subjectivism," Lewis anticipates that some readers will be surprised that he includes morality within reason.[16]

---

14 *Common Objects of Love: Moral Reflection and the Shaping of Community* (Grand Rapids, Mich.: Eerdmans, 2002) 11.

15 which O'Donovan describes as "an attitudinal disposition which gives rise to various actions without being wholly accounted for by any of them" (16).

16 in *Christian Reflections* (1967, 1995 by C.S. Lewis Pte. Ltd., published in the United States

If you are surprised that I include this [our judgement of good and evil] under the heading of reason at all, let me remind you that your surprise is itself one result of the subjectivism I am discussing. Until modern times no thinker of the first rank ever doubted that our judgements of value were rational judgements or that what they discovered was objective. It was taken for granted that in temptation passion was opposed, not to some sentiment, but to reason. Thus Plato thought, thus Aristotle, thus Hooker, Butler and Doctor Johnson. The modern view is very different. It does not believe that value judgements are really judgements at all. They are sentiments, or complexes, or attitudes, produced in a community by the pressure of its environment and its traditions, and differing from one community to another. (164)

Christian knowledge informs us that even as love itself originates in God so also does knowledge, knowledge of anything. The Book of Proverbs frames its whole collection with this axiom from 1:7: "The fear of the Lord is the beginning of knowledge." Fear here may be distinct from love in some respects, but both terms point to the contemplation of the ultimate Other with the attitude his unique being deserves. Knowledge begins in and with God and its *telos* is fullness of knowledge of him. As the story of the Enlightenment illustrates, seeking knowledge independent of God leads not to more and better and freer knowledge but to withering, narrowing knowledge that will wound and disease the people or culture operating with such truncated knowledge. The pressing social issues and controversies of our time, especially the poisonous fruits of the so-called sexual liberation, make the point simply by mention.

There is clear Scriptural precedent for such efforts to establish knowledge apart from the fear of and love for the Lord. In the Garden of Eden, Eve succumbed to temptation by doubting God's word, or knowledge, and embracing the offering of another knowledge by the serpent (Gen 3). And the contrast between Zechariah and Mary when each was visited by Gabriel appears in their different responses to God's word, or revelation, his knowledge (Luke 1). Mary exemplifies discipleship with her question of means—"how shall this be since I'm a virgin?"—and full acceptance of God's will: "may it be to me according to your word." But Zechariah behaves as a proto-Enlightenment philosopher. He surely recognizes Gabriel as the Lord's messenger and

by Eerdmans, Grand Rapids, Mich.). Other works developing this insight include Lewis' *The Abolition of Man* (1944, 1947; renewed 1971, 1974, all by C.S. Lewis Pte. Ltd., published in the United States by HarperCollins, New York.); and J. Buziszewski's *What We Can't Not Know* (Dallas: Spence Publishing, 2003).

his words as God's own. But his question is not of means but of doubt: "How shall I know this?" (NKJV). Zechariah says (paraphrased), "I'm not sure about this. What else can you give me to go with what you've said so I can believe?" Finally, Jesus passes his wilderness testing, demonstrating that he is the faithful Son, by grounding his knowledge and conduct of life solely on the word of God and rejecting the tempting alternatives that would betray loyalty to his Father (Matt 4:1–11).

THE CHRISTIAN PROJECT IN THE WORLD THAT HAS LOST ITS MIND

The Christian project in a world that has lost its Christian mind is to truly possess—or be possessed by—a Christian mind and to express it confidently in all of life, without worrying about how to convince others of its truthfulness using the criteria of knowledge they embrace but which contradict God's truth. The project entails truly believing God's word, God's revelation, firstly, above all else that we may believe and then expressing God's revelation and mind in the disciplines and general life duties that are ours. Philosopher Alvin Plantinga put it this way in his "Advice to Christian Philosophers" (intended for Christian thinkers of all disciplines):[17]

> [M]y plea is for the Christian philosopher, the Christian philosophical community, to display, first, more independence and autonomy: we needn't take as our research projects just those projects that currently enjoy widespread popularity; we have our own questions to think about. Secondly, we must display more integrity. We must not automatically assimilate what is current or fashionable or popular by way of philosophical opinion and procedures; for much of it comports ill with Christian ways of thinking. And finally, we must display more Christian self-confidence or courage or boldness. We have a perfect right to our pre-philosophical views: why, therefore, should we be intimidated by what the rest of the philosophical world thinks plausible or implausible?

We best serve both our brothers and sisters in Christ and the rest of the world, especially the West, by possessing and confidently expressing a mind truly Christian.[18]

---

17 *Faith and Philosophy: Journal of the Society of Christian Philosophers*, vol. 1, permanently copyrighted October 1984. Journal web site: www.faithandphilosophy.com

18 See Harry Blamires, *The Christian Mind* (London: S.P.C.K., 1963).

5

BART EHRMAN'S *GOD'S PROBLEM:*
A BELIEVING NEW TESTAMENT SCHOLAR'S
RESPONSE

Edward P. Meadors

I will call those who were not my people, 'my people,' and her who was not beloved, 'beloved.' And it shall be that in the place where it was said to them, 'you are not my people,' there they shall be called sons of the living God" (Rom 9:25–26). The Apostle Paul's appeal to conversion as the hope of unbelieving Israel remains today at the heart of the Christian gospel. "If any man is in Christ, he is a new creature; the old things passed away; behold, new things have come" (2 Cor 5:17). In Christ one may be "born again" (Jhn 3:7). Affirming this basic Christian truth, testimonies of dramatic conversions have inspired Christians throughout the ages. Unlikely converts like Paul, C. S. Lewis, and contemporary geneticist Francis Collins, substantiate God's power to change lives in intellectually satisfying terms. Surely these intellectuals would not have converted to Christianity unless their encounters with God were real.

Conversion stories are not intellectually conclusive or experientially consistent, however. Sometimes the encounter is not Christ on the road to Damascus but brazen skepticism on the road to Princeton or Cambridge or Chapel Hill. How are we to assess conversions that go the other direction, as when a professing believer experiences doubt followed by disillusionment and then skepticism? Enter Professor Bart Ehrman.

Bart Ehrman is the James A. Gray Distinguished Professor and Chair of the Department of Religious Studies at the University of

Edward P. Meadors <edmeadors@taylor.edu> is professor of Biblical Studies at Taylor University. He is the author of articles, book reviews, and two books, *Jesus, the Herald of Salvation* and *Idolatry and the Hardening of the Heart*. He holds his BA and MA degrees from Wheaton College and his PhD from the University of Aberdeen.

North Carolina at Chapel Hill. He completed his M.Div and Ph.D. degrees at Princeton Seminary after receiving undergraduate degrees from Wheaton College and Moody Bible Institute. He has written or edited more than twenty books, including a widely distributed college-level survey of the New Testament published by Oxford University Press. On the popular level, Ehrman's influence permeates the acclaimed Teaching Company, which distributes eight of Ehrman's courses, promoting him as one of the top 100 professors in America today. Most recently, Ehrman has authored through Harper One two destructive criticisms of Christianity entitled *Misquoting Jesus* (2005) and *God's Problem* (2008). With uncommon distinction, Ehrman has achieved celebrity scholar status as evidenced by his appearances in *Time* and on NBC's *Dateline*, *The Daily Show with Jon Stewart*, CNN, The History Channel, and NPR.

And yet Ehrman's is a painful story. His personal testimony and professional scholarship aggressively step beyond the bounds of objective inquiry and intellectual doubt to expose what he views as defects that decisively discredit the truthfulness of the Christian faith. With books on the *New York Times* bestseller list, his dismantling of Christianity has been spectacularly popular. And it has provoked immediate response from the Christian scholarly community, which has produced at least three books to contest what might be dubbed Ehrmanianism.[19]

With respect to the mission of the International Institute for Christian Studies, Ehrman is an important subject for study because his minimalistic view of the Bible and his skeptical perspective of Christianity appeal to and persuade many in our society today. Valid or not, his books are popular best sellers. Hence, to win the university for Christ, it will be necessary for academic Christians to be informed of Ehrman's tenets and to be able to respond in a way that serves the truth. With this goal in mind, this paper addresses these subjects: Ehrman's testimony, perspective, weaknesses, and popularity, and his "deconversion," along with what IICS can learn from him.

I. Ehrman's Testimony

Ehrman's story begins with his upbringing by Christian parents. He learned Bible stories from his mother at bedtime, was baptized in a Congregational church, was reared Episcopalian, became an altar boy at age 12, eventually had what he describes as a "born-again"

---

19 Timothy Paul Jones, *Misquoting Truth: A Guide to the Fallacies of Bart Ehrman's Misquoting Jesus* (IVP, 2007); Dillon Burroughs, *Misquotes in* Misquoting Jesus: *Why You Can Still Believe* (Nimble Books, 2006); Darrell Bock and Daniel Wallace, *Dethroning Jesus: Exposing Popular Culture's Quest to Unseat the Biblical Christ* (Nelson, 2007).

experience at a youth rally, studied Scripture to the point that he could quote large portions of the Bible, and, as mentioned, eventually attended Moody, Wheaton, and Princeton, before pastoring Princeton Baptist Church for a year. But as he relates in *Misquoting Jesus* and *God's Problem*, in his early adulthood he became irreversibly disillusioned by the Bible and Christianity's inability to explain reality. His critical study led to the conclusion that "the Bible was a very human book with all the marks of having come from human hands: discrepancies, contradictions, errors, and different perspectives of different authors living at different times in different countries and writing for different reasons to different audiences with different needs" (*God's Problem* 3). With regard to reality, "I could no longer reconcile the claims of faith with the facts of life. . . . In particular, I could no longer explain how there can be a good and all-powerful God actively involved with this world, given the state of things. . . . The problem of suffering became for me the problem of faith" (*God's Problem* 3).

Disillusioned with the Bible and reality, Ehrman left the Christian faith: "I no longer go to church, no longer believe, no longer consider myself a Christian" (*God's Problem* 2). And although he calls himself an agnostic, Ehrman is hardly neutral. He is aggressively anti-Christian and anti-theism. For Ehrman, Jesus was a first-century apocalyptic Jew, but he was not the Messiah, he was not raised from the dead, and he is not coming back. The biblical view of God is mythical and obsolete. The reality of suffering in the world makes impossible the existence of an all-powerful and all-loving God. Suffering "is simply something that happens on earth, caused by circumstances we can't control and for reasons we can't understand. And what do we then do about it? We avoid it as much as we can, we try to relieve it in others whenever possible, and we go on with life, enjoying our time here on earth as much as we can, until the time comes for us to expire" (*God's Problem* 195–96). And so his latest book concludes, "What we have in the here and now is all that there is" (*God's Problem* 278).

II. EHRMAN'S PERSPECTIVE: EHRMANIANISM

For Ehrman two forms of biblical criticism undermine the credibility of the Bible. Each form is detrimental in his mind because each necessitates the conclusion that the Bible is a human book by human authors without supernatural influence whatsoever.

The first major form is text criticism, the discipline that attempts to reconstruct the original texts of the Bible from the thousands of ancient copies and fragments of copies kept today in museums and libraries around the world. Ehrman finds text criticism a discredit to biblical trustworthiness because the ancient scribes who copied and passed on the texts of Scripture made occasional mistakes, so that our oldest copies of the biblical documents are fraught with differences, embellishments, and subtle contradictions that evidence human error, not supernatural authorship. How could the Bible be historically reliable when the Gospel of Mark has three different endings and our current copies of the Gospel of John include a story that clearly was not in the original Gospel (the story of the woman caught in adultery: John 7:53—8:11)? For Ehrman these and other specific phenomena strike devastating blows against the believability of Scripture.[20] *Misquoting Jesus* thus has the subtitle *The Story Behind Who Changed the Bible and Why*.

The second major form of criticism undermining biblical credibility for Ehrman is redaction criticism, which is the critical method that attempts to identify where and how the biblical authors edited the sources they worked with and shaped them to express the biblical authors' distinctive views. Redaction criticism is particularly influential in Gospel studies, and redaction critics express confidence in their ability to identify where and how the Gospel writers added to, deleted from, embellished, and ultimately infused into the "real" history of Jesus their own personal biases, which Ehrman cannot perceive as the thoughts of God—because they too are human. He cites the differences among the Gospels as evidence of irreconcilable contradictions, which would not be present if one God were inspiring them all.[21]

Ehrman's disillusionment with biblical credibility extends much further into the nooks and crannies of biblical studies, down to isolated sayings and events that he finds obviously erroneous—most emphatically the mistaken early Christian expectation of the immanent coming of the kingdom of God (a fallacy he traces back to John the Baptist and Jesus).

These general views carry over to establish Ehrman's working presuppositions for appraising the problem of world suffering. In *God's Problem* he portrays the Bible as an eclectic body of disparate documents that offer at least five different explanations for the problem of

---

20 For a more detailed response to these criticisms, readers may consult James R. Edwards, *Is Jesus the Only Savior?* (Grand Rapids: Eerdmans, 2005). For a detailed critique of Ehrman's apologetic use of redaction criticism, see Daniel Wallace, "The Gospel According to Bart: A Review Article of *Misquoting Jesus* by Bart Ehrman," *JETS* 49 (2006), 327-49.

21 For a fuller introduction and critique of the strengths and weaknesses of redaction criticism, readers may consult Craig Blomberg, *The Historical Reliability of the Gospels* (Downers Grove: InterVarsity Press, 1987), 35-43.

suffering: (1) Suffering is caused by God as punishment for sin (what he calls the Classical View); (2) suffering is a consequence of the sins of others; (3) suffering brings about greater good (Redemptive Suffering); (4) suffering is a mystery impossible to explain (parts of Job and Ecclesiastes); (5) God will terminate evil and suffering in the future (the apocalyptic view). These mutually exclusive and incompatible views mirror different human perspectives on the problem of suffering. They all fail to account for reality for Ehrman, except for view (4), which he adopts as his own: "I have to admit that at the end of the day, I do have a biblical view of suffering. As it turns out, it is the view put forth in the book of Ecclesiastes" (*God's Problem* 276).

In reaching these conclusions, Ehrman maximizes the subjective hypotheses of skeptical higher criticism while minimizing the historicity of the Bible. In this respect, his popular books are not argumentative in the sense that they judiciously weigh evidence. Instead, in them he simply assumes as self-evident the correctness of his views before moving on as if his opinion is unqualified fact—as in, for example, his portrayal of Job as consisting of two competing theodicies written by two different authors.[22]

III. EHRMAN'S WEAKNESSES

Ehrman's criticisms strike receptive readers as revolutionary and historically astute. Publisher descriptions and endorsements on the dust jacket of God's Problem refer to it as a "serious inquiry," "eloquently told," "wonderful book" that is "riveting" and written with "energy": "Ehrman has done it again." The popular reader, impressed by Ehrman's scholarly credentials, gains the impression that Ehrman is a trustworthy academic version of John Grisham. In truth, however, God's Problem proves the accuracy of the famous proverb of Ecclesiastes, "There is nothing new under the sun."

For text criticism and redaction criticism are now generations old and are widely practiced by believing and unbelieving scholars alike. Ehrman's refusal to see either as complementary with the divine inspiration of Scripture is simply his opinion, which is not shared by others in the field who perceive Scripture as the product of God's inspiring his prophets and apostles to speak God's message through his human spokespersons' languages, vocabularies, figures of speech, genres, local illustrations, and individual personalities. That these messages had a historical context then does not eliminate their potential for validly informing believers today of God's will. Further, scribal

---

22 *God's Problem*, 162.

errors undercut Scripture no more than a random typo or transposed word would in an otherwise accurate document. Of course the Bible is a human book in the sense that it was written by humans to humans and copied and transmitted by humans to humans; such indeed is the Bible's own testimony. But the humanness of the Bible does not disprove its inspiration by God and its revelation of God as witnessed by the Bible's human authors. Ehrman's age-old observations simply fall short of disproving the biblical authors' revelation of God.

For the most part, Ehrman builds his skepticism within the safe confines of unknowns that cannot be proven (or disproven!). Who can prove or disprove that there were two authors of Job? Who can prove or disprove that the prophets predicted events after the fact (*ex eventu*)? Who can conclusively prove that Jesus did or didn't rise from the dead? No one can, of course, and that provides Ehrman a safety net constructed of untestable conjecture—not one of rigorous, exacting argumentation.

However, Ehrman's credibility falters surprisingly in the arena of scholarly competence, the very arena advertised so sensationally by his media spin. Indeed, there are times when he is categorically wrong. For example, he is simply mistaken when he claims that the view that "all will be made right in the afterlife" is "not found in the prophets but in other biblical authors" (*God's Problem* 9). Isn't Isaiah 25:8, the classic statement on this subject, prophetic? "He will swallow up death for all time, and the Lord God will wipe tears away from all faces, and He will remove the reproach of His people from all the earth." Again, Ehrman's simply wrong when he writes, "For ancient peoples, however, there was never, or almost never, a question of whether God (or the gods) actually existed" (*God's Problem* 26). To the contrary, the Psalms speak of disbelief as a common vice: "The wicked, in the haughtiness of his countenance, does not seek Him. All his thoughts are 'There is no God'" (Psalm 10:4; cf. Pss 14:1; 36:1; 53:1; Rom 3:18). Similarly, Ehrman's reduction of Job's poetry is categorically wrong: "Anyone who dares to challenge God will be withered on the spot, squashed into the dirt by his overpowering presence. The answer to suffering is that there is no answer, and we should not look for one" (*God's Problem* 188). Job indeed does repent in the presence of God, not because of his sin but because of his direct encounter with God that has resulted in new awareness of wonderful things previously unseen: "I know that you can do all things, and that no purpose of yours can be thwarted. 'Who is this that hides counsel without knowledge?' Therefore I have declared that which I did not understand, things too wonderful for me, which I did not know . . . . I have heard of you by the hearing of the ear; but now my eye sees you; therefore I retract, and I repent in dust and ashes" (Job 42:2–3, 5–6). The poetry of Job has a silver lining every bit as real as Job's prose. Finally, Ehrman's invention of an agnostic Ecclesiastes simply misrepresents biblical Ecclesiastes' total confidence in God's existence: "Do not be hasty in word or impulsive in thought to bring up a matter in the presence of God. For God is in heaven and you are on the earth; therefore let your words be few" (cf. Ecc 5:2; cf. 3:11, 14; 7:29).

Yet again the stark fallacy is Ehrman's when he boasts "But the view that Jesus was himself God is not a view shared by most of the writers of the New Testament. It is, in fact, a theological view that developed rather late in the early Christian movement: it is not to be found, for example, in the Gospels of Matthew, Mark, or Luke—let alone in the teachings of the historical Jesus" (*God's Problem* 273). *But found it is!* In Matthew Jesus is Immanuel, God with us (Matt 1:23). In Mark, after John prepares the way for the Lord, it is Jesus who comes as Lord, thereby equating Jesus with Yahweh on the basis of Isaiah 40:3. In Luke, Jesus performs a pattern of miracles (Luk 7:22) that fulfill expectations of what God would do on the day of the Lord (Isa 26:19; 29:18; 35:5–6). The resulting equation is that Jesus is Lord, which his ascension into heaven affirms (Acts 1:9–11). And, of course, Jesus' identity with God is explicit in John's Gospel (Jhn 1:1), as it is in Paul's letters: In Philippians 2:9–11, God bestows on Jesus the name that is above every name, which, of course, for the first-century Jew was none other than God's special name YHWH. How Ehrman can so baldly misrepresent these elementary truths I cannot explain, especially in light of Larry Hurtado's highly regarded, rigorous affirmation of early Christian worship of Jesus as God in *Lord Jesus Christ: Devotion to Jesus in Earliest Christianity* (Eerdmans, 2003).

Ehrman creates still more Christological misunderstanding when he appeals to the corporate and not individual identities of the Suffering Servant of Isaiah 53 and the "one like a son of man" of Daniel 7:13–14. In Ehrman's view, these names represented Israel in the Old Testament, and the first Christians wrongly projected them on the individual Jesus.

Of course Ehrman is right—the Suffering Servant and the "one like a son of man" were originally designations for the people of Israel—as also was the name Son of God (Exo 4:22). However, Ehrman does not introduce his readers to the explanation that the first Christians attributed these titles to Jesus expressly *because* of their corporate association with Israel. Just as Paul identified Jesus as a second Adam who represented all humanity in his obedience and sacrifice (Phi 2:6; 1 Cor 15:22, 44–49), so also did the Gospel writers identify Jesus as Servant, Son of Man, and Son of God, who represented all Israel in his obedience and death. Yes, Jesus was an individual, but he represented the entire nation of Israel. Hence, the placard over the cross—King of the Jews. This dimension of corporate solidarity has been recognized by generations of scholarship.

Elsewhere Ehrman adopts idiosyncratic views. Such is the case, for example, when he generalizes the apostle Paul: "It was Paul's apocalyptic assumptions about the world that most affected his theology" (*God's Problem* 237). Agreed, Paul certainly had an apocalyptic worldview (Eph 6!), and by definition his encounter with the risen Christ was a revelation (an apocalyptic vision). However, Paul's radical theology was not in truth the result of his contemplation of an established apocalyptic worldview. According to his own testimony, Paul's gospel was the direct consequence of his encounter with the risen Christ: "For I neither received it from man, nor was I taught it, but I received it through a revelation of Jesus Christ" (Gal 1:12).

In general Ehrman's preoccupation with theodicy is idiosyncratic in view of widespread scholarly caution against reading theodicy into books that do not really have as their intent the justification of God in the face of evil (perhaps especially Job in its notorious resistance to simplistic interpretation). In this regard, Ehrman's statement that "Apocalypticism is nothing so much as an ancient kind of theodicy" (*God's Problem* 25) is a gross oversimplification of a complex genre. Similarly simplistic is his sharp division of the Bible into disparate contradictory units. To the detriment of the popular reader, Ehrman doesn't even pay lip service to unity within the Bible, the systemic interplay among prophetic, wisdom, and apocalyptic writers, and the historical reality that theological unity served as a control for the canonization of the Bible. Ehrman's axiom that different means incompatible is simply untrue.

IV. Ehrman's Popularity

How do we explain Ehrman's popularity, if his scholarship is so obviously suspect? First, Ehrman has found a formula that works for the popular secular reader. His blend of emotive personal autobiography, negative caricatures of evangelicals, sensational statistics and anecdotes of world suffering, sweeping tongue-and-cheek Bible summaries on a college sophomore level, and bald, simplistic conclusions mirror to a degree the foreclosed stereotypes secular culture expresses toward evangelical Christianity. And so, Ehrman satisfies casual skeptics by reinforcing what they want to hear and already suspect. Christianity is a self-contradicting fairy tale. Second, Ehrman's is a feel-good agnosticism:

> By all means, and most emphatically, I think we should work hard to make the world—the one we live in—the most pleasing place it can be for ourselves. We should love and be loved. We should cultivate our friendships, enjoy our intimate relationships, cherish our family lives. We should make money and spend money. The more the better. We should enjoy good food and drink. We should eat out and order unhealthy desserts, and we should cook steaks on the grill and drink Bordeaux. We should walk around the block, work in the garden, watch basketball, and drink beer. We should travel and read books and go to museums and look at art and listen to music. We should drive nice cars and have nice homes. We should make love, have babies, and raise families. We should do what we can to love life—it's a gift and it will not be with us for long (*God's Problem* 277, emphasis his).

'Drink beer, have sex, watch basketball'—is it surprising that Ehrman's lectures are popular with college students at Chapel Hill? 'Make money, spend money, cook steaks, drink Bordeaux, eat unhealthy desserts'—is it surprising that Ehrman is popular with the airport crowd? He makes people feel good about what they're already doing—living an agnosticized wealthy gospel of self-centered capitalism.

V. Why the "Deconversion" and What Christians Can Learn from Bart Ehrman

How can we explain Ehrman's disillusionment with Christianity? I would argue that the Christianity that Ehrman refutes is a false, convoluted Christianity configured upon Ehrman's caricatures, his dismissal of God's work in the world through the church, his own intellectually altered construction of the Bible, and his own image of what God must be like, if God exists in this world of suffering. In truth, like a contemporary version of Ivan Karamozov, Ehrman doesn't want to believe in God—"he rejects the idea that there can be a divine resolution that makes all the suffering worthwhile" (*God's Problem* 269). As a Bible scholar with an education very similar to Ehrman's, I can only say that I see things very differently.

What can Christians learn from Bart Ehrman? First, Ehrmanianism reaffirms the critical importance of informed, accurate, engaging Christian scholarship. To win the authentic seeker of truth, Christianity must present a message that meets head on the big issues, like suffering and evil, with honest, comprehensively informed responses that are clothed in winsome, reader friendly language. Books like Os Guinness's *Unthinkable* are model achievements in this respect. And the contributions of William Lane Craig, N. T. Wright, Darrel Bock, and other Christian scholars in debates such as this are honorable and in keeping with the Great Commission. We should surpass the Ehrmans of our world on their own terms. Second, Ehrman reminds us that academic scholarship is often heavily influenced by subjective bias and selective representation of truth. When Ehrman represents the truth, he does not represent the whole truth or nothing but the truth. His arguments are often simply false and should be identified as such. Criticism of false teaching head on is a responsibility Christians inherit from the apostolic authors John, Paul, Peter, and Jude and is fully compatible with Christian charity and agape love. For love separate from truth is not love.

Third, Christian scholars should also learn from Ehrman's foibles. Though a celebrated academic celebrity, Ehrman's *God's Problem* is fraught with lazy caricatures, unsupported generalizations, and gross errors in substance. While openly critical of Ehrman's scholarship, we have our own Christian "academic celebrities" whose books gain publication on the basis of name and not always substance. Christian publishers beware. Elton Trueblood's adage has never been more true: "Christian shoddy is still shoddy." Christian authors and publishers must do better to maintain the highest standards of scholarly excellence. In catering purely to what sells, the Christian publishing industry runs the risk of gaining the world at the expense of selling its soul. Fourth, Ehrman's blindness to the reality of God's presence in our world must be met with still more aggressive sacrificial Christian ministry to the poor and suffering. The church is doing this in amazing ways by the power of God, but as Paul challenges the Thessalonians in 1 Thessalonians 4:1 and 10, we must "excel still more" as the light of the world. And finally, at the end of our rigorous efforts, Christians shouldn't be surprised by secular culture's skepticism: "For the message of the cross is foolishness to those who are perishing, but to us who are being saved it is the power of God" (1 Cor 1:18).

6

RELIGION OF THE HEART: EXPELLED FROM THE AMERICAN UNIVERSITY

Reggies Wenyika & William Adrian

INTRODUCTION

This paper describes how "religion of the heart" has been systematically removed from the development of higher education in the United States, and with it the Judeo/Christian heritage of faith. The eminent historian of higher education, Richard Hofstadter, claimed in his Pulitzer-Prize-winning book, *Anti-Intellectualism in American Life,* that "religion of the heart" as expressed by evangelical Christians was the most pervasive "anti-intellectual" movement in 20th century America, and he viewed the Great Awakening in 1720 as the beginning of the evangelical movement, which he later described as "the most powerful carrier of . . . religious anti-intellectualism, and its antinomian impulse" (Hofstadter, 1962, 47). It was the beginning of what

Reggies Wenyika <reggies@swcu.edu> is the Vice President for Academic Affairs at Southwestern Christian University in Bethany, Oklahoma. Before, he served as the Assistant Director of the Veritas Worldview Institute at Oklahoma Wesleyan University. His general research interests are in Christian higher education; anti-intellectualism and Pentecostalism; and the impact of the Bible translation movement on global intellectualism. He did his undergraduate work at the University of Zimbabwe and received his MA and EdD from Oral Roberts University.
William B. Adrian <wadrian@okwu.edu> is Director and Fellow of the Veritas Worldview Institute at Oklahoma Wesleyan University. His professional career has been in university planning, reform and development in the U.S. and abroad, encompassing public and private universities, state and federal agencies and ministries of education abroad. He has served as a Fulbright scholar in Brazil, Poland, and Slovakia, and co-edited (with Richard Hughes) *Models for Christian Higher Education: Strategies for Success in the Twenty-First Century.* He received his PhD from the University of Denver and his BS and MS from Abilene Christian University.

ultimately led to the removal of traditional religion and morality from the American university. Ironically, "religion of the heart" is a fundamental descriptor of both Judaism and Christianity and found clearly in the Old and New Testament Scriptures.

The widening gap between the university and the general public in American society or, as Hofstadter stated, the intellect and "philistinism" (Hofstadter, 1962, 4), is an indication that religion is viewed as anti-intellectual and thus generally ignored or trashed in the academy. The religious heritage of the university has been subsumed under the rubric of culture and replaced by the notion of multiculturalism. It has raised questions and debates over whether the American university has been an ideal or model for emerging universities in the developing world that seek to be global in nature and function. Likewise, the European Union and its universities have mirrored this perspective and also sought to erase the memory of their own Judeo-Christian heritage. This omission may lead to a tragic end.

In the past twenty years a growing number of scholars have recognized a crisis in the modern university, and there has been an increasing "jeremiad against the universities and the professoriate," (Levine, 1996, 3). One major clash can be described by the titles of two books of radically opposing views, *The Closing of the American Mind: How Higher Education Has Failed Democracy and Impoverished the Souls of Today's Students*, by Allan Bloom, and *The Opening of the American Mind: Canons, Culture, and History*, by Lawrence Levine. Bloom's principal complaint against the university was that the classical curriculum and the Western intellectual tradition have been trashed and removed from the core of liberal education, while Levine defended the modern university as opening the minds of American students to myriad traditions and cultures while challenging the "arrogance" of those who saw the Western tradition as superior. It is the thesis of this paper, however, that scholars such as Hofstadter, Levine, and others have actually contributed to closing the American mind and distorted the principles of truth and freedom in the university.

Profound changes occurred in the ideals and functions of higher education in the 19th and early 20th centuries. Hofstadter described the emergence of the American university in the 19th century as nothing short of an educational revolution and summarized briefly the reason: "The methods and concepts of science displaced the authority of religion" (Hofstadter, 1961, viii). This statement reflected a fundamental change in authority from the church (religion) to the university (science), and it occurred by the slow and systematic removal of the Judeo-Christian heritage of faith and traditional morality from the modern university.

The initial separation of faith and reason was followed by a separation of science and religion, even "warfare" between the two. Since the emergence of Darwinism, growing hostility toward religion has been increasingly evident, to the extent that it is now common in the academy to hear that religion is the source of problems and conflicts in the world today. Thus, while religion is one of the major issues in the global environment, it has generally been dismissed or vilified in the modern university.

With the loss of the Judeo-Christian heritage of faith, no purpose now unifies the university. Nor do university educators agree on any course of general or liberal education for university students. In 1977, the Carnegie Commission for the Advancement of Teaching described general education as a "disaster area," and there was "no agreement about the meaning of a college education" (Boyer & Levine, 1981, 20). How did these things happen, and why were religion and morality removed from the modern university? Further, how should religion and morality be addressed in the new global universities to expand understanding of religious issues affecting all cultures? After addressing these questions, this paper concludes with a critique of "multiculturalism" that includes the urgent need to restore the Judeo-Christian heritage in the university.

RELIGION OF THE HEART: EXPELLED

Removal of religion from the university began with a fundamental split within the colonial religious community itself during the Great Awakening of the early 1700s:

> Puritanism had always required a delicate balance between intellect, which was esteemed as essential to true religion in New England, and emotion, which was necessary to the strength and durability of Puritan piety. This balance proved to be precarious, and there developed a tendency toward a split in the religious community itself. One side of the church tended to be socially correct, and sophisticated, liberal and latitudinarian in its intellectual outlook, but religiously cold and formal. The other side which was to prove vulnerable to revivalism, was moved by ideas and by religious fervor; but its partisans, in their most fervent moments turned antinomian and anti-intellectual. (Hofstadter, 1962, 64)

Sectarianism was a major cause of divisions within the religious community, but the split over religion of the heart was not a sectarian issue. It was over an attempt to separate intellect from emotion or expression of feelings and a denial that these expressions could be from the Spirit of God. Such was the case in 1744 with the condemnation of revivalist George Whitefield, recorded in *The Testimony of the President, Professors, Tutors and Hebrew Instructor of Harvard College in Cambridge against the Reverend Mr. George Whitefield, and His Conduct*:

> First then, we charge him, with Enthusiasm. Now that we may speak clearly upon this Head, we mean by an Enthusiast, one that acts, either according to Dreams, or some sudden Impulses and Impressions upon his mind, which he fondly imagines to be from the Spirit of God,…and if such Impulses and Impressions be not agreeable to our Reason, or to the Revelation of the Mind of God to us, in his Word, nothing can be more dangerous than conducting ourselves according to them. (Hofstadter & Smith, 1961, 62)

What were the specific actions that justified the banishment of *Enthusiasts* from the colleges? The most serious charge in the case of Whitefield, was, "the reproachful Reflections upon the Society which is immediately under our Care…What a deplorable State of Immorality and Irreligion has he hereby represented Us to be in!" (Hofstadter & Smith, 1961, 63). His strong criticisms of the College and the established clergy were the principal reasons for his dismissal. Yet, in his own defense he says, "I am determined to know nothing among you but Jesus Christ and him crucified. —I have no Intention of setting up a Party for my self, or to stir up People against their Pastors . . ." (66).

While there were many abuses of the *Enthusiasts*, it is clear that the principal reason they were removed from the colleges was their criticism of the religious establishment. Even religious leaders like Jonathan Edwards, who recognized the abuses and advocated "testing the spirits," were banned from Boston churches. Hofstadter (1964) recognized that Edwards was ". . . almost alone among the leading clergymen as exemplifying the old intellectualism and piety of New England and combining with them the ability to deal creatively with new ideas" (64). However, he still classified Edwards as anti-intellectual because he believed ". . . that discipline of the heart, and the old-fashioned principles of religion and morality, are more reliable guides to life than an education which aims to produce minds responsive to new trends in thought and art" (19). To Hofstadter, the "new" was intellectual, the "old" was not, and to presume character was more important than intellect was "anti-intellectual." The result was to pit evangelical religion (or religion of the heart) against intellect and, ultimately, to disconnect intellect from traditional morality.

The effects of the Great Awakening were mixed, but the major impact on higher education was the rapid development of denominational colleges in the movement west prior to the Civil War. Most of these were "anti-intellectual" in Hofstadter's view, and many failed to survive. He called this period in higher education the "great retrogression," and claimed that these institutions were hardly deserving of college status (Hofstadter & Metzger, 1955, 209–222). To be sure, most of these intellectual "backwater" colleges had meager resources compared to the more established colleges in the East, and religion of the heart was a major motivation in most, but they led the cause of democratization of higher education in the West and opened their doors to women and blacks decades before their wealthy intellectual cousins did in the East.

The Capstone Course on Moral Philosophy

The separation of faith and reason in the colonial colleges in the 19th century was played out through the decline and disappearance of the capstone course on Moral Philosophy taught by the presidents of the colleges. The climax of the college curriculum through and beyond the Civil War was the course taught by the presidents, who were the religious and academic leaders of the schools. The course typically focused on the Aristotelian virtues of temperance, prudence, justice and fortitude, and the challenge of the president was to bring the curriculum together by harmonizing science, reason, and revelation. It was clearly designed to integrate intellect and the Christian faith and viewed Scripture as the principal criterion of moral action. Material for the course came from biology, psychology, politics, economics, religion and ethics, principally the last two (Schmidt, 1930, 110).

Wilson Smith attributed the decline of the moral philosophy course to its transformation into "moral theology" that assumed a clear and exclusive dichotomy between faith and reason. On one side was intuition, clerical interest, piety, and faith, while on the other was scholarship, reason and rational knowledge:

> The assumption underlying the distinction between moral philosophy and moral theology is that while they both may be a system of ethics, moral theology clearly is founded upon religious motives and principles and its proper and exclusive field is that of truths which cannot be discovered by human reason. (Smith, 1956, 186)

The capstone course slowly disintegrated into its component parts as the scientific courses emerged into specialized disciplines. Eliot's initiation of the elective system at Harvard was the beginning of the revolution in higher education that replaced the classical curriculum and the presidents' capstone course with courses in science. The presidents as moral philosophers ultimately lost their influence and leadership in harmonizing faith and reason, and the colleges lost the unifying story of God found in the Judeo-Christian heritage of faith. The *ante bellum* presidents and professors were increasingly viewed as old fogeys, but it is important to note that the list of presidents who taught the moral philosophy course was a "Who's Who" of intellectual leadership in the colonial colleges (Smith, 211–214).

Even James Walker, President of Harvard College, along with other Unitarians, believed in theological and social progress, yet focused on Scripture as the final authority in religion and morals: "Unitarians are for the Bible, and the Bible only,…(but) they are among the very few Christian sects, who…recognize and respect…the sufficiency of the scriptures, and the right of private judgment in the interpretation of Scripture" (Smith, 1956, 154). It is interesting that Newman et al. (2004), inserted a brief comment about the moral philosophy course in his book on the future of modern higher education, "Unfortunately, presidents are no longer expected to teach moral philosophy" (215).

THE GERMAN UNIVERSITY: DEIFYING THE SECULAR MIND

The influence of the German university idea on the development of the American university cannot be overstated. The rise of the German university to the pinnacle of higher education in the world began in 1810 with the founding of the University of Berlin. It was to become the greatest intellectual center the world had ever known, proving that Germans were first in intellect if not in war (after the fall of Prussia to Napoleon). Johann Gottlieb Fichte was the leader and founding rector of the university. He claimed to be a Christian, but was accused of atheism and dismissed from the University of Jena in 1799. Following the opposition of the German Enlightenment to supernaturalism, Fichte conceived God as the "world order" and the human mind as the final arbiter of truth, arriving at absolute knowledge through reason. Fichte and other German philosophers attempted to "deify" the human mind, ultimately leading to Nietzsche's famous declaration that "God is dead," obviously killed by his own prophets. Unlimited individual freedom led to the arrogance of intellect that became a common characteristic in the German university, driven by the German Enlightenment, nationalism, and Darwinism.

Notice how the German university and its faculty were described by James Morgan Hart, an American scholar who had studied at several German universities, in his 1874 publication that became popular among other American scholars who were considering studying in Germany, *German Universities: A Narrative of Personal Experience* (as cited in Hofstadter & Smith, 1961):

- . . . a world in itself, existing for itself (573).
- . . . the university is an "end," not a means (574).
- . . . a world in and for itself (whose aim) is to engender culture (576).
- . . . The professor has but one aim in life: scholarly renown (577).
- (The professor) . . . is accountable only to his own conscience of what is true and what is false (578).

These quotes about the German university and its faculty describe what Paul Tillich viewed as the "secular mind." Coles recalled Tillich's basic understanding of the secular mind:

> For Tillich, . . . a secular person was one who looked within himself or herself, within our species, for whatever comprehension of the world is to be found, whereas the sacred mind . . . looked toward the beyond, toward that "Another," that "God" so often mentioned in our daily lives. (Coles, 1999, 4)

The German university described above reflected the ultimate and absolute "inwardness" of both individual faculty and the university itself.

John Henry Newman was prophetic in his brief comments on the German University of his day in the mid-1800s. Pelikan refers to his views:

> Here in his "Idea of a University" the German university as a model is significantly absent, except perhaps for the comment about "the open development of unbelief in Germany." . . . This is paralleled by a comment in Apologia pro Vita Sua about 'the perils to England which lay in the biblical and theological speculations of Germany'" (Newman as cited in Pelikan, 1992, 84)

Newman recognized that "'Knowledge Its Own End,' was liable to corruption." Pelikan continues:

> But if knowledge is defined as this chief good and end in itself, "everything else being desired for the sake of this," the moral

consequences can be frightening. . . . But during the twentieth century—partly, it is obvious, as a consequence of the Holocaust, but also as a consequence of more general reflection—it has become clear to all of us that such a definition is both simplistic and dangerous . . ." (43).

Newman's distinction between knowledge and faith was fundamental. "It was a distinction, not an identity; but it was also a distinction, not a separation" (Pelikan, 1992, 39):

> With a clarity that the secularist academic mind sometimes finds disturbing, Newman recognized that learning and scholarship must have a moral dimension or they can become demonic. Long before the moral crisis of the German universities in the 1930s and 1940s—which indelibly impressed that insight on some scholars of that generation and of those that have followed —he saw that the academic community is as liable to corruption as is the state or the marketplace or even the church. (114)

DISCARDING THE "OLD" RELIGION: DARWINISM AND DEWEY

"The rise of science was the most impressive aspect of curricular changes in the 18th century" (Hofstadter, 1962, 194), but science and religion were not initially at odds. "Science advanced as part of faith itself. No undermining of religion by scientists" (199). It was not until Darwin's theory was accepted early by American scholars and intellectuals and promoted as the "new" truth to replace outmoded views of religion that the Judeo-Christian heritage lost intellectual credibility. "The methods and concepts of science displaced the authority of religion" in 19th-century higher education (Hofstadter, 1955, viii).

Religion and morality soon became alienated from higher education, principally because of the twin D's of Darwinism and Dewey that pushed the alienation into warfare. Dewey, an early and militant adoptee of Darwinism, may have been the first who popularized the clash when he stated, "What took place in the earlier history of science was serious enough to be named the 'warfare of science and religion'" (Dewey, 1948, xx). He stated that "a deep and impassable gulf [exists] . . . between the natural subjectmatter of science and the extra—if not supra-natural subjectmatter of morals" (xiv) and declared that the "old" knowledge must be destroyed before the "new" moral order can be created, based on the scientific method. He admitted that the science of morals was in an "inchoate" state, but assumed as a true believer that the scientific method would lead to utopia.

While Dewey lauded the scientific method, his own writing was often vague, imprecise, and inconsistent. Statements such as "Growth itself is the only moral 'end'" (177) were so vague that even Hofstadter viewed the effects of his philosophy as "anti-intellectual." The notion of education as "growth" became "one of the most mischievous metaphors in the history of modern education" (Hofstadter, 1962, 373). "In the abstract," said Dewey, "there is no such thing as degrees or order of value." Therefore, "We cannot establish a hierarchy of values among studies" (376). Hofstadter evaluates Dewey thus: "The effect of Dewey's philosophy on the design of curricular systems was devastating" (377). These are very strong words from a fellow scholar with similar assumptions about religion and morality.

The American philosophy of pragmatism that emerged from the ideas and writings of James, Dewey, and Peirce, was convenient for many Darwinists, who were searching for rational ways to relate Darwin's theory to societies. It became the dominant American philosophy and the spirit of the Progressive era.

> Although profoundly influenced by Darwinism, the pragmatists soon departed sharply from prevailing evolutionary thought. . . . The pragmatist viewed the environment as something that could be manipulated. . . . As Spencer had stood for determinism and the control of man by the environment, the pragmatists stood for freedom and control of the environment by man. (Hofstadter, 1955, 124-125)

It is likely many pragmatists departed from Darwin after his prediction in the *Descent of Man* the year following the census of 1870 regarding immigrants: "At some future period, not very distant . . . the civilized races of man will almost certainly exterminate, and replace, the savage races throughout the world" (as cited in Levine, 1996, 130).

Social Darwinism was a secularist philosophy that had both conservative and liberal adherents. Herbert Spencer's *Synthetic Philosophy* (1864) became one of the first and most widely read and accepted books in America after Darwin's *The Origin of Species* (1859), and his most prominent disciple was Andrew Carnegie, who reflected on his new faith:

> I remember that light came as in a flood and all was clear. Not only had I got rid of theology and the supernatural, but I had found the truth of evolution. "All is well since all grows better," became my motto, my true source of comfort. Man was not created with an

instinct for his own degradation, but from the lower he had risen to the higher forms. Nor is there any conceivable end to his march to perfection. His face is turned to the light; he stands in the sun and looks upward. (as cited in Hofstadter, 1955, 45)

Carnegie was not unlike most scholars and prominent thinkers who saw in social Darwinism support for their own views of natural progress. Hofstadter admitted that a great many "intellectual gaucheries" were committed in the search for the social consequences of Darwinism but that it was necessary for a great many thinkers to "have groped about, stumbled, and perhaps fallen in the dark . . . to learn to live with and accommodate to startling revelations of possibly sweeping import. . ."(4). What Hofstadter called "gaucheries" others would call disasters, but his studied conclusion was that the biological ideas of Darwinism, "whatever their doubtful value in natural science, are utterly useless in attempting to understand society" (204). The Social Darwinists, regardless of their widely divergent political views, shared three common assumptions: 1) a naïve expectation of progress; 2) a denigration of antiquity; and 3) faith in the scientific method in forecasting the future.

According to R. M. Hutchins, Dewey's faith in science (Darwinism) discarded philosophy and religion.

> The faith of John Dewey leaves no place for philosophy or religion. . . . We do not say you must give up science if you believe in God. Mr. Dewey says you must give up philosophy and religion or you cannot truly believe in science. He requires us not merely to have faith in science, but to have faith in nothing else. (Hutchins, 1995, xxv)

Under the guise of academic freedom, John Dewey's philosophy of education prohibited any religious explanation of meaning in life, and denied values based on religion. This philosophy has permeated the public schools and universities in the U.S.

CHRISTIAN AID TO SECULARISM

One major issue often overlooked, especially by Christians, in describing the demise of religion in the academy is the support secularism has received from spokespersons for religion and the Christian faith. In some cases the support was unintentional and misinterpreted, while in other cases, it resulted from ignorance and arrogance. The cause of secularism has been supported by believers in at least three ways: by (1) being misinterpreted; (2) being sectarian; and (3) being anti-intellectual.

Misinterpretation and Unbelief

The object of the university is "intellectual, not moral." This claim by Newman made his work "intellectually accessible to readers of every religious faith and of none" (Pelikan, 1992, 9). This claim and another by Newman—"knowledge [is] its own end"—have been used by some to support the further claim that intellect is the final arbiter of truth without reference to God. Nothing could have been further from Newman's mind, but his quotes have been used to support self-indulgence, greed, and an "intellectualism" that "exerts a subtle influence in throwing us back on ourselves, and making us our own centre, and our minds the measure of all things" (Newman, quoted in Pelikan, 1992, 59). Anyone who cites Newman as support for unbelief is reflecting a serious misunderstanding of Newman or dishonesty.

Sectarianism

Henry Tappan, forward-looking President of the University of Michigan, specifically cited Fichte and the University of Berlin as the great model for the American university, but notice how he viewed religion:

> It will be remarked that we have omitted a Faculty of Theology in the constitution of this University. As each denomination of Christians has its peculiar Theological views and interests, it would be impossible to unite them harmoniously in one Faculty. It is most expedient, therefore, to leave this branch to the Theological Institutions already established by the several denominations. (Hofstadter and Smith, 1955, 506)

Sectarianism was rampant during Tappan's period, and he viewed the only way to avoid division and maintain some semblance of unity among the sects was to remove religion or theology from the university. Still, he viewed Christianity and Scripture as providing "everything that relates to human welfare:"

> With respect to its religious and moral character it should embody in its constitution: First, an entire separation from ecclesiastical control and a renunciation of all sectarian partialities. Secondly, but as every thing that relates to human welfare, needs to be taken under the protecting and nurturing wings of Christianity, it

should acknowledge Christianity to be the only true religion, the Bible to be of Divine inspiration, and the supreme rule of Faith and Duty, given freely to all men to be read and received with entire freedom of conscience and opinion. (507)

Tappan's attitude toward American colleges is also reflected in the following, "We have multiplied colleges so as to place them at every one's door . . . we have cheapened education so as to place it within the reach of every one" (491).

Anti-Intellectualism

Persisting notions that originated with the Puritans fueled the flames of anti-intellectualism in some religious circles of colonial America. Emerging from the Puritan Revolution of the 1600s in England was the misguided belief that education was an agent for perpetuating social injustices and that the role of the Holy Spirit in the affairs of man was diminishing (Solt, 1956). This notion arose from a theology that "stressed the direct manifestation of the Holy Spirit in the human conscience rather than reliance upon professional groups" (313) such as the educated clergy, the university teachers, and the lawyers. Carried over to the American colonies, it inadvertently aided the spread of secularism by arousing suspicion and contempt of everything religious among the academics. These perceived the antinomianism that had characterized Puritan Revolution as a threat to civilization, and they also reacted decisively to the excesses that occurred during the Great Awakening revivals, which they judged irrational and primitive.

THE SECULAR NARRATIVE OF REALITY: MULTICULTURALISM

Arthur Levine, a former student of Richard Hofstadter, best represents the modern view of religion in the academy when he defends American higher education. He lumps all of its critics together as wrongly attempting to resurrect, in some form, the Western classical curriculum as a foundation of "rational order" in the university and in the culture. He faults critics for having nothing positive to say about the American university, but it appears he finds nothing negative to say. Note the following:

I certainly have not seen as much progress as I had hoped in most aspects of American life, and I have seen almost none in far too many, but higher education has been a happy exception.

. . . [M]odern universities are performing precisely the functions institutions of higher learning should perform: to stretch the boundaries of our understanding; to teach the young to value our intellectual heritage not by rote but through comprehension and examination; to continually and perpetually subject the "wisdom" of our society to thorough and thoughtful scrutiny while making the "wisdom" of other societies and other cultures accessible and subject to comparable scrutiny; to refuse to simplify our culture beyond recognition by limiting our focus to only one segment of American society and instead to open up the entire society to thoughtful examination. . . .

The major consequences of the new heterogeneity on campuses, however, has not been repression but the very opposite—a flowering of ideas and scholarly innovation unmatched in our history. . . .

On the contrary, today's universities with their diverse student bodies, faculties, and curricula have done more to free us from the confines of self-absorption than Hutchins could have imagined. . . .

There is fragmentation in the United States; there is distrust; there is deep anger—and much of this is reflected in and acted out in universities, but none of it is caused by the universities or by professors or by young people. (Levine, 1996, 18, 21, 28, 29, 31)

Levine's exaggerated statements about the openness of the American university are hollow because he excluded religion as a narrative of reality. He rejected the Western intellectual tradition as an essential "core" of a liberal education and with it a Judeo-Christian worldview. He argued against the arrogance of assuming a "superior" culture, equating Western ways and thought with "civilization" itself (Levine, 1996, 20). However, he subsumed religion as a characteristic of culture rather than a transcendent reality. By denying the validity of the Judeo-Christian story of God, Levine assumed a secular view of reality, and the species of secularism that has come to be known as multiculturalism has replaced any sense of transcendent religious values. Levine described openness as accommodating all cultures without a basis for comparing or contrasting cultures as there is no hierarchy of values and there is no "core" knowledge that should be required of all students. His notion that fragmentation in the United States has not been caused by the universities, the professors or the students is pure nonsense. The lack of freedom and openness is clearly evident in Levine's omissions.

The opening statement in chapter two of his book is, "The best response to critics of the modern American university is the history of the university itself" (Levine, 1996, 37). Indeed, knowledge of the history of higher education is essential to understand the modern American university, but Levine idealized its history and neglected profound incidents in its development. For example, it is impossible to understand the history of the American university without reference to the German university from whence it came. He omitted reference to John Henry Newman's, *Idea of a University,* the first profound philosophy of higher education written in 1854 and still recognized as a classic. In his discussion of canons, Levine completely ignored religious canons. If religion is a crucial dimension of culture, especially in today's global environment, the Bible and the Koran are two essential canons for understanding major cultures. Levine believed no canon transcended the real world to "some ideal universe where pure values and eternal verities are free to assert themselves" (99). Yet Scriptures point to eternal verities, and the search for these truths has been a major purpose of the university for centuries. Levine paid scant attention or recognition to the Judeo-Christian heritage of faith and its influence on Western and other cultures. His "opening" of the American mind excluded faith and the Judeo-Christian heritage. This same exclusion was common in the German universities in the late 19th and early 20th centuries. They were lauded by American scholars as centers of intellectual freedom, but they were never free. The same is true of the American university, when it omits the study of religion in the search for truth.

When the university becomes, as in the history of the German university, an "end" and not a means, faith and authority rest ultimately in the community of scholars. What brings the community together is the search for those truths that transcend cultures and institutions, but if the community is an end and not a means, it cannot be transcended. William James recognized the problem of putting faith and authority in institutions when he stated

> We "intellectuals" in America must all work to keep our precious birthright of individualism, and freedom from these institutions (church, army, aristocracy, royalty). Every great institution is perforce a means of corruption— whatever good it may also do. (cited in Hofstadter, 1962, 39)

James could have included the university in his list of institutions that are susceptible to corruption.

One irony in Levine's book is the discussion of his own personal background to show how two different cultures (Jewish and American) could be accommodated, thus how all cultures could be accommodated in the university:

> I could have both Moses and Lincoln for forefathers, both the Hebrew Torah and the United States Constitution for moral and legal touchstones, both Joshua and Joe Louis for warrior heroes, both the Jewish shul and the American public school for houses of learning. (Levine, 1996, 135)

Levine recognized the value of his Jewish heritage—the importance of family, of education, of community; and he recognized freedom as the fundamental characteristic of his American identity. Yet he failed to mention that the roots of both of these cultures are found in the Judeo-Christian heritage of faith. In fact, his description of his own upbringing in a Jewish immigrant family (132ff) is an impressive account of transcendent religious values.

RESTORING THE STORY OF THE JUDEO-CHRISTIAN HERITAGE

The excising of religion of the heart from higher education was the beginning of an intellectual process that culminated in the removal of the Judeo-Christian heritage as the foundation for liberal education and common learning in the academy. Further, the role of the heritage in the development of Western civilization has been denied, if not grossly distorted. Arthur Holmes recognized that "religion and morality are closely linked" and that "the Judeo-Christian tradition is one of the main historical sources of the moral heritage of the West" (Holmes, 2007, 12–13).

Webber (2008) supported this notion, suggesting that the extent of Christianity's influence on Western civilization had "resulted in convictions that, until recently, dominated Western society" (65). How? By giving "an ordered understanding of the world"; by "forming the convictions of basic rationality" that gave rise to "education and the comprehensibility of the world"; and by "giving rise to the arts and the understanding of the role and place of the church in the world" (65).

At a time when religion is the most significant issue confronting our increasingly diverse global environments, it is a tragedy of society, from the academy, that the typical university graduate in the United States has little knowledge or understanding of the Judeo-Christian heritage of faith. The university's historic commitment to truth, freedom, and moral integrity have been undermined and replaced by a multiculturalism that denies the validity of the Judeo-Christian story of God or of any other religious narrative of history. The study of language, culture, religion, and history should be integral parts of the undergraduate experience in the university, but when viewed only through the secular lens of multiculturalism, the experience leads to fragmentation of knowledge with no basis for value judgments in the search for truth. Denying a religious explanation for reality makes freedom a mockery and encourages intellectual arrogance.

The difference between viewing reality from a secular lens (or worldview) and a religious lens (a Judeo-Christian worldview) can be seen in Richard Dawkins' book, *The God Delusion*. In the tradition of Dewey, Dawkins attacked not only religion generally, but his own Jewish heritage when he stated:

> The God of the Old Testament is arguably the most unpleasant character in all fiction: jealous and proud of it; a petty, unjust, unforgiving control-freak; a vindictive, bloodthirsty ethnic cleanser; a misogynistic, homophobic, racist, infanticidal, genocidal, filicidal, pestilential, megalomaniacal, sadomasochistic, capriciously malevolent bully. (51)

Needless to say, he dismissed as hopelessly ignorant a host of scholars, historical and present, who have spent a lifetime of study of the Judeo-Christian heritage and who view the God of the Old Testament very differently. (See *Jewish Literacy: The Most Important Things to Know about the Jewish Religion, Its People and Its History*, by Rabbi Joseph Telushkin [2008]; or *The Christian Tradition: A History of the Development of Doctrine* and *Jesus Through the Centuries*, by Jaroslav Pelikan [1971; 1997]; or *Great is the Lord: Theology for the Praise of God*, by Ron Highfield [2008].)

These scholars' views of the Judeo-Christian heritage are totally at odds with those of Dawkins, and the crux of the differences focuses on religion (or worldview). Dawkins has assumed an intellectual gulf between science and religion and views all believers in God as ignorant. Thus, it is easy to dismiss them as irrelevant or to deny them a place in the academy on the basis of their ignorance or anti-intellectualism. Without a public hearing and discussion in the academy, religion easily becomes a convenient scapegoat for problems besetting the globe, and the hallmark of academic freedom becomes a sham.

It is unlikely that the Judeo-Christian heritage will become a foundational study in the modern university, but if it is disregarded or abolished, it will again suffer the consequences of being dominated and compromised by intellectual arrogance, as were the great German universities of the 19th century. Global universities that aspire to freedom and truth should learn from the tragic history of the German university prior to World War II. It was generally recognized as the greatest university system in the world in the 19th and early 20th century. In the 19th century it was hailed by residents and thousands of visiting American faculty as the freest university on the globe and became the model for the modern American university, but it was never really free. Leading German scholars steeped in Darwinism and the scientific method provided the intellectual foundation for the Third Reich while dissenters in the universities were silenced or removed. The Holocaust remains a powerful condemnation of the intellectual arrogance that pervaded the academy. Academic freedom can be easily manipulated with ultimately devastating consequences.

For the modern university to remain viable as an institution and true to its own heritage of truth and freedom, the story of the Judeo-Christian heritage of faith (religion of the heart) must be restored. As long as there is freedom to pursue truth wherever it leads, and the opportunity to discuss, debate, and test values in a free, open and civil environment, there is hope for the university.

REFERENCES

Barclay, W. (1959). *Educational ideals in the ancient world.* Grand Rapids, Michigan: Baker Book House.

Bloom, A. (1987). *The closing of the American mind: How higher education has failed democracy and impoverished the souls of today's students.* New York: Simon and Schuster.

Boyer, E. & Levine, A. (1981). *A quest for common learning: The aims of general education.* Washington, D.C.: The Carnegie Foundation for the Advancement of Teaching.

Brubacher, J. S. (1982). *On the philosophy of higher education (Revised Edition).* San Francisco and London: Jossey-Bass Publishers.

Coles, R. (1999). *The Secular Mind.* Princeton, New Jersey: Princeton University Press.

Dawkins, Richard (2006). *The God Delusion.* New York: A Mariner Book, Houghton Mifflin Company.

Dewey, J. (1916). *Democracy and education.* New York: Macmillan, Inc.

Dewey, J. (1948). Paperback Edition (1957). *Reconstruction in philosophy.* Boston: Beacon Press.

Evans, C. Stephen (Ed.). *Ethics: Approaching moral decisions (2nd ed.). Contours of Christian Philosophy.* Downers Grove, Ill.: InterVarsity Press.

Highfield, Ron (2008). *Great is the Lord: Theology for the praise of God.* Grand Rapids, Michigan: William B. Eerdmans Publishing Company.

Hofstadter, R. (1964). *Anti-Intellectualism in American life.* New York: Alfred A. Knopf.

Hofstadter, R. (1955). *Academic freedom in the age of the college.* New York: Columbia University Press.

Hofstadter, R. (1955). *Social Darwinism in American thought.* (Revised Edition). Boston: Beacon Press.

Hofstadter, R. & Metzger, W. (1955). *The development of academic freedom in the United States.* New York: Columbia University Press.

Hofstadter, R. & Smith, W. (Eds). (1961). *American higher education: A documentary history.* Vols. 1 and 2. Chicago: University of Chicago Press.

Hutchins, R. M. (1995). *The higher learning in America* (with a new Introduction by Harry S. Ashmore, Originally Published in 1936.). New Brunswick, New Jersey: Transaction Publishers.

Hutchins, R. M. (1968). *The learning society* (reprint). New York: The New American Library

Kamm, R. (2001). *The best of mind and spirit (coping with America's moral and spiritual decline: An educator's vision for our beloved nation in the years ahead).* Atlanta, Georgia: Wisdom Press.

Kerr, C. (1964). *The uses of the university.* Cambridge, MA: Harvard University Press.

Levine, L. W. (1996). *The opening of the American mind: Canons, culture, and history.* Boston: Beacon Press.

Menand, L. (2001). *The metaphysical club: A story of ideas in America.* New York: Farrar, Straus and Giroux.

Metzger, W. (1955). *Academic freedom in the age of the university.* New York: Columbia University Press.

Newman, F., Couturier, L., & Scurry, J. (2004). *The future of higher education: Rhetoric, reality and the risks of the market.* San Francisco: Jossey-Bass Publishers.

Newman, J. H.. (1959). *The idea of a university.* New York: Image Books.

Oden, Thomas C. (2007). *How Africa shaped the Christian mind: Rediscovering the African seedbed of western Christianity.* Downers Grove, Ill.: InterVarsity Press.

Pelikan, J. (1992). *The idea of the university: A reexamination.* New Haven and London: Yale University Press.

Pike, K. L. (1996). Originally Published in 1962. *With heart and mind: A personal synthesis of scholarship and devotion.* Duncanville, Texas: Adult Learning Systems.

Schmidt, G. P. (1930). *The old time college president.* New York: Columbia University Press.

Smith, W. (1956). *Professors and public ethics: Studies of northern moral philosophers before the civil war.* Ithaca, New York: Cornell University Press.

Sommerville, C. J. (2006). *The decline of the secular university.* New York: Oxford University Press.

Thelin, John R. (2004). *A history of American higher education.* Baltimore: The Johns Hopkins University Press.

Webber, R. E. (2008). *Who gets to narrate the world? Contending for the Christian story in an age of rivals.* Downers Grove, Ill.: InterVarsity Press.

7

THE INTEGRATION OF FAITH AND PROFESSION IN THE ENGINEERING DISCIPLINE

Kenneth Van Treuren & Steven Eisenbarth

INTRODUCTION

The ascendancy of science and the secularization of society have so extensively transformed the modern educational system that only a schizophrenic relationship exists between work (profession) and faith in the minds of most scientists and technologists. An open question now exists: should this situation be considered normative or is there a pathway to the integration of faith and profession? If a pathway exists, how might academicians, in an act of integrating their faith and profession, stimulate and support this integration in students through curricular and pedagogical measures?

Kenneth Van Treuren <Kenneth_Van_Treuren@baylor.edu> is professor of Mechanical Engineering at Baylor University. He is currently Associate Dean of Research and Faculty Development in the School of Engineering and Computer Science. He served in the U.S. Air Force as a pilot and an instructor at the Academy prior to joining the engineering faculty at Baylor University in 1998. His research interests are in gas turbine heat transfer and renewable energy. He holds a BS degree in Aeronautical Engineering from the United States Air Force Academy, a MS in Engineering from Princeton, and a DPhil in Engineering Science from Oxford. **Steven Eisenbarth** <S_Eisenbarth@baylor.edu> is professor of Electrical and Computer Engineering at Baylor University. His teaching career of nearly 30 years spans the computer science and computer engineering fields. He is a registered professional engineer in the State of Texas and consults as an expert witness in patent-related intellectual property cases. His current research interests focus on wireless sensor networks and intelligent agent systems. He holds a BS degree in Mathematics from the College of Idaho and an MS and a PhD in Physics from Baylor University.

Most academicians (Christian and non-Christian) would agree that there should be little difference in the educational content and processes for scientists and technologists at religiously affiliated or secular campuses. On further reflection, this agreement may mirror a common set of shared values or a common worldview that promotes a profession/faith dichotomy, which is transmitted and reinforced by curricular selection and pedagogy.

On the other hand, a small minority of scientists and engineers see faith as integral to professional practice. They assert that there is a significant and profound difference between their professional practice as Christians and that of their colleagues who choose to ignore the interaction of faith and work. These differences range from the internal motivation generated from a faith-based humanitarian worldview to their selection of problems to address and knowledge to pursue. Faith-informed engineers may be in a unique position to tackle the multifaceted and endemic problems that challenge humanity today. If this be the case, then it may be incumbent on faithful Christians within academia to develop curricula and educational processes that help their students reject a false dichotomy and embrace an integration of their faith with their chosen profession.

Faculty members within Baylor University's School of Engineering and Computer Science have been engaged in issues related to the integration of faith and learning over the last decade. Their successes and failures provide unique insights into the resistance that face academicians from colleagues within their disciplines as well as across the campus.

WORKING DEFINITIONS—ENGINEER

The general populace would have little difficulty defining or describing the work product of a scientist; however, this is not the case when asked to describe the work product of an engineer. Much of this disparity can be explained by the ascendancy of the modern scientific method and our society's focus on science education. Only in the last 10 years have engineering curricula appeared in secondary school systems.[1] Nearly half of freshman engineering students select engineering as a major because they are "good at math and science"; however, it is quite common for these students to drop out of engineering and seek a business degree rather than continue in math or science.

Merriam-Webster's New Collegiate Dictionary[2] defines *science* as "knowledge attained through study or practice," or "knowledge covering general truths of the operation of general laws, esp. as obtained and tested through the scientific method [and] concerned with the physical world and its phenomena." A scientist discovers a fact, publishes a paper disclosing the fact, and then moves to discover the next fact. For an engineer, the facts are given and of interest, but the primary work focus is on the application of facts to the solution of an identified problem. Engineers are preeminently problem solvers and not scientists.

Engineering praxis dates from the earliest recorded history, and its artifacts include the pyramids of Egypt, the aqueducts of Rome, the Parthenon, the Appian Way, the Colossus of Rhodes, siege weapons, cannon, and other military hardware from the ancient world. Modern engineered artifacts include radio and television, air conditioning, the Apollo Moon Lander, the Sydney Opera House, the Bilbao Guggenheim Museum, the Golden Gate Bridge, the power grid, the interstate highway system, the New Orleans and Mississippi flood levees, the microprocessor and the cell phone. Clearly, the engineering disciplines produce an overwhelming percentage of the "space" that embodies our culture, and their work products help form societies and cultures.

Engineers employ the scientific method and mathematics to address a range of ill- or even well-defined problems and create solutions or design artifacts, unlike the craftsmen or artists who use well- understood and -mastered techniques to produce or manufacture artifacts of value and quality. To form a more concrete example: the construction of the Three Gorges Dam in China employs a large number of craftsmen to pour and form the dam's concrete structure; however, it is the engineers who determine where and in what shape that concrete must be formed to withstand the force of the water behind the dam. The modern engineer is definitely not a craftsman or tradesman.

WORKING DEFINITIONS—TECHNOLOGY AND DESIGN

Technology is the product of the engineering design process. Monsma, et al. define *technology* as "a distinct human cultural activity in which human beings exercise freedom and responsibility . . . by forming and transforming the natural creation, with the aid of tools and procedures, for practical ends or purposes."[3] These authors further assert that "doing technology [engineering] is not a [morally or ethically] neutral activity but one that involves valuing of a profound, fundamental nature."[4] The philosophical basis for asserting that valuing is inherent in the engineering design process [technology] is that "any set of standards for determining what does or does not constitute a solution to a problem must clearly lie outside the problem itself."[5] In other words, the evaluation of whether a particular design is a "good" or "bad" solution is not self-determined by a particular solution. Therefore, the presuppositions and pre-commitments of the designer [engineer] must play the central role in alternative design evaluation. In particular, one's personal perspectives, ethics, and moral commitments become important factors in determining the final design solution.

Monsma, et al. also define *design* as a structured "innovative activity whereby people [engineers] creatively use theoretical and practical knowledge and available energy and material in order to specify the size, shape, function, and material content of a technological object."[6] Furthermore, "design results in a blueprint or set of detailed instructions for the physical characteristics of a technological object— either a product or a tool. Instructions for facilities and procedures needed to fabricate the object are included in these specifications."[7] This definition describes the design process as the quest for a solution to a problem that is intrinsic or inherent in the resultant object itself. However, the design solution [object or artifact] must exist in a real world context, which defines the extrinsic interactions or externalities of the artifact. These externalities include elements of aesthetics, environmental, social, political and economic impact, safety and risk, reliability, maintainability, sustainability, cultural, gender and age appropriateness, ergonomics, energy efficiency, and end-of-life resource recovery, among others. It is within the realm of a design's externalities that cultural valuing is most intensely focused and therefore the area where an engineer's ethical and moral commitments may have the largest impact on the design process.

Monsma, et al. proposes a set of "eight normative principles," under the headings of cultural appropriateness, openness, communication, stewardship, delightful harmony, justice, caring and trust, for regulating the design outcome.[8] These normative principles are underpinned by the moral law, which is summarized in the two great commandments: 'Love the Lord your God with all your heart, and with all your soul, and with all your strength, and with all your mind; and your neighbor as yourself."[9] Although these two commandments are central to the Christian faith and extremely rich compared to all secular and non-Christian moral codes, many of their practical aspects are present in the Codes of Ethics promulgated by engineering societies.[10]

Occasionally, the term technologist is used to refer to an engineer, although its use must be carefully regulated by the context. A medical technologist is a specialist in medical arts but this specialization is not considered one of the branches of engineering. Alternatively, a computer engineer may be considered a technologist in the computer arts as she practices in her field.

For the most part, instruction in the formalism of engineering focuses on the artifacts that form the solution to a stated problem. The design of an object or artifact usually involves the application of mathematical and scientific principles that bound the artifact's functional parameters or intrinsic properties. Environmental inputs to the artifact and output into the environment are generally formalized and limited in scope so the problem is solvable within the timeframe of a class or weekly assignment. The nature of the teaching enterprise is such that precise quantitative results are rewarding to both students and teachers alike. The student knows when she has arrived at a correct answer and the instructor is assured he is able to teach because the student arrived at the correct answer. Many instructors also avoid the "hard problems" that are more open-ended because students tend to mete out punishment on faculty evaluations.

In the academic setting, students infrequently encounter ill-defined problems or problems that require sustained engagement for long periods. Rarely do students encounter problems that require the consideration of an artifact's extrinsic properties. At both the intrinsic and extrinsic level, the engineering design process requires choices and the application of values. Seldom is a design artifact a precise solution to the stated problem or design specification. The design artifact is generally the result of compromises because the mathematical and scientific principles used in design processes are imprecise or approximations at best. Engineers are not omniscient; their knowledge of nature and the future is limited and finite. Engineers are not capable of foreseeing all the possible environments that a design artifact might experience, many of which will cause an artifact's failure and possible bodily injury or loss of life for its user. It is precisely at this point that a Christian perspective and its commitment to biblically-based moral values and ethics can make a significant contribution to the engineering process.

The purpose for dwelling on vocational definitions is to isolate an area of practice in which there is a nexus of creativity and decision making. At this point, the qualities of engineered artifacts can be maximally impacted by the application of Christian ethics and values. Politicians may pass legislation for the construction of a hydroelectric project, lawyers may exercise considerable influence in where the dam is actually placed, but engineers are ultimately responsible for its design, construction, and operation. If engineers are important to a modern culture's development, then the production of engineers in an era of global competition should raise concerns.

Researchers at Duke's Pratt School of Engineering have studied the impact of globalization on the engineering profession. Their study focused on the quality of undergraduate engineering programs in the U.S. and China and India, two of our greatest competitors in the world market. For the 2004–05 academic year, their study shows that U.S. institutions awarded 134,854 four-year bachelor's degrees in engineering, computer science, and information technology, compared to 170,000 in India and 517,225 in China. Although there are reservations about the accuracy of graduation numbers in China, it is readily apparent that the numbers have dramatically increased over the past eight years because of government policy directives to increase the sciences and engineering workforce. Increasing undergraduate numbers also feeds post-graduate programs, so it appears that "China is racing ahead of the United States and India in its production of engineering and technology PhD's and in its ability to perform basic research." [11]

WORKING DEFINITION—WORLDVIEW

A worldview is an intellectual framework that interprets our experiences and guides our activities. As will be discussed below, all humans possess the genesis of a worldview. The human need for a worldview is "fourfold: the need to unify thought and life; the need to define the good life and find hope and meaning in life; the need to guide thought; the need to guide action." [12]

From the authors' point-of-view, the ability to articulate a worldview is an important outcome of the post-secondary educational process. The first and open question is whether it is possible and, if so, how is it possible to help students understand, develop, and adopt a worldview that is compatible with their engineering profession? The second and corollary question is whether worldview formation or re-formation can be explicitly directed by the engineering education process to the end that a Christian worldview, integrated with an engineering perspective, is the ultimate result?

A fundamental component to the educational process is a body of knowledge that must be inculcated by a teacher and mastered by the student. The particular content is dependent on the goals and objectives of a social institution that collects and codifies the knowledge and delivers it to its students. The social nature of education was a central tenant of the educational philosophy of John Dewey, who was, arguably, one of the most influential education reformers of the first half of the 20th century. Dewey, a representative of the progressive movement in U.S. education, published a "pedagogic creed" that delineated his personal convictions about the nature of the education process. He begins his creed by defining education:

> I believe that all education proceeds by the participation of the individual in the social consciousness of the race. This process begins unconsciously almost at birth, and is continually shaping the individual's powers, saturating his consciousness, forming his habits, training his ideas, and arousing his feelings and emotions. Through this unconscious education the individual gradually comes to share in the intellectual and moral resources which humanity has succeeded in getting together. He becomes an inheritor of the funded capital of civilization. The most formal and technical education in the world cannot safely depart from this general process. It can only organize it or differentiate it in some particular direction. [13]

Although Dewey may never have used the term "worldview," the opening paragraph of his creed certainly provides evidence for a worldview analysis and an indication of how one might impact the development of a worldview through the educational process.

Arthur F. Holmes parallels Dewey's statement: "The genesis of a world view is at the pre-philosophical level. It begins, without either systematic planning or theoretical intentions, but with the beliefs and attitudes and values on which people act." [14] For Holmes, a worldview rests upon a set of unanalyzed and un-systematized beliefs (pre-philosophical) and only upon reflection, examination and systematization (i.e., educational processes) does one's worldview take shape. A discussion of how a worldview is formed must consider the materials from which a worldview is constructed.

As one considers worldview construction, an important starting place may be the human use of language. Through language we categorize what we observe and do and give meaning to our world. The acquisition of language is a social process and it is in the community setting that language conveys values to its members. Through the acquisition of language, the process of forming habits, training ideas, and arousing feelings and emotions starts and ultimately saturates our consciousness. As per Dewey, through this process the "individual gradually comes to share in the intellectual and moral resources" of the community. Our use of community suggests the existence of small social units that can be differentiated on the basis of particular belief systems. When taken in the aggregate, communities naturally become submerged in the broader, more widely held belief systems of society.

The community resources are linguistically constrained by the stories or narrative held by the community. These narratives form the basis of models that allow a community to extend its intellectual processes from the practical into the theoretical. Without an adequate set of models it may be impossible for a community to support philosophical inquiries that would produce a comprehensive worldview. For example, the absence of words and patterns for logical analysis may make it difficult to construct philosophical statements, in much the same manner as the absence of zero makes some mathematical analysis impossible.

Because the community is a central repository of the intellectual and moral resources that an individual acquires, there are several aspects of community that should be considered. First, communities are bound to a communal history. In Dewey's terms, this is the "funded capital" of the community. This history sets limits on what is acceptable and even theoretically possible from the perspective of the community. For example, the medieval Europeans "knew" that by sailing west they would eventually fall off the edge of the earth, so any suggestion to the contrary was met with incredulity. Similarly, Ptolemaic astronomy and astrology locked medieval minds into a geocentric view of the universe.

Second, communities are characteristically religious in nature. Religion is a significant source of worldview building materials because religion is a wellspring of community values and attempts to understand and integrate human perspectives concerning the meaning of life. Because religion is a community differentiator, it is possible to categorize particular worldviews in terms of underlying or supporting religious perspectives (theology). Some of these religious elements are part of the pre-philosophical level, while elements that are derived through intellectual reflection and doctrinal studies can be the essence of a worldview. Because religion plays a part in both the pre-philosophical as well as the actual intellectual work of worldview development, there can be Christian worldviews or Islamic worldviews or Buddhist worldviews.

Even though we use the common religious discriminators, within any particular religious tradition, there is pluralism and finer distinctions can be made. Hence, within the Christian religion, these distinctions include Catholic, Reformed, Lutheran, Orthodox, non-conformist, and Coptic perspectives, or within Islam, Shiite or Sunni perspectives. Each of these religious distinctions could also be subdivided further into smaller denominational groups with similar, yet subtly different values. There are also communities that are not overtly religious in an institutional sense, although there are usually religious substitutes present, such as naturalism, scientism, romanticism, or Marxism; to name a few.

Although social forces are fundamental in shaping individuals, there are also other, more personal, forces at work. The rise of psychology in the eighteenth century provided key insights into the internal life of the mind. One key discovery was the nature of human sensory perception and the limits that both our sensory system and the brain's ability to process and correctly interpret sensory inputs imposed. Limits on human perception raised deeper concerns as to our ability to observe reality. Psychology was also able to study the wide range of human personal behavior and emotional states. These studies revealed particular patterns of behavior and mental activity that color individual life responses, e.g. paranoia, neurosis, schizophrenia, phobias, etc. Certainly, a limit on our ability to perceive and interpret reality also limits our ability to construct coherent and consistent worldviews.

Post-modern philosophy has asserted that it is impossible to generate a comprehensive worldview. This is necessarily the result of human limitations, i.e. humans are not all-knowing, omnipresent or omniscience. These limitations force human-generated knowledge to be perspectival and anthropocentric. However, on the positive side, philosophy, in general, provides a collection of "ideas and arguments about virtually every subject and virtually every type of worldview." [15]

James W. Sire takes the position that a worldview is essentially pre-theoretical (or pre-philosophical) rather than a set of propositions or a web of beliefs (philosophical). He states:

> A worldview is a commitment, a fundamental orientation of the heart, that can be expressed as a story or in a set of presuppositions (assumptions which may be true, partially true or entirely false) which we hold (consciously or subconsciously, consistently or inconsistently) about the basic constitution of reality, and that provides the foundation on which we live and move and have our being. [16]

Sire considers a worldview to be "a matter of the soul. . . represented more as a spiritual orientation or perhaps a disposition" rather than an intellectual endeavor.[17] For Sire, his worldview analysis has shifted from propositions and stories (intellectual engagement) to the "heart that grasps and understands them." [18] His methodology would reduce worldview analysis to two categories, Christian versus non-Christian;

or believer versus non-believer, because of the radical and fundamental difference between the core commitments of the human soul, which is the result of conversion and regeneration. Sire's worldview analysis does not imply that philosophic thinking about one's worldview is without merit, but that the results of such reflection is for the most part already determined by one's core religious (pre-philosophical/pre-theoretical) beliefs and commitments. Although Sire's position has merit and much that is commendable, it does not necessarily explain the diversity that is evident among Christians. Sire's and Holmes' position are not intrinsically incompatible. Without doubt the Christian conversion experience has a fundamental and profound impact on one's worldview. As per Holmes, following conversion there is renewed motivation for reflection, examination and systematization (i.e. educational processes) by which the nascent worldview generated by conversion can blossom.

If John Dewey's assertion that communities are the central repository of intellectual and moral resources is correct, the straight-forward implication should be that communities are of central importance in the formation of an individual's worldview. For Christians, the community is not only the connections between the individual and his immediate worship or study group, but in a much broader context, a connection between the individual and the cultural legacy of the Bible plus two millennia of Christian community expression. The larger Christian community supplies a staggering number of theological works, scriptural commentaries, devotional materials, and histories from which an individual can draw inspiration and capital in his worldview development quest. As we consider how an academic institution can create an environment that fosters worldview development, the focus would naturally turn to how the institution might cultivate communities that promote Biblically-based inquiry concerning the need to unify thought and life; the need to define the good life and find hope and meaning in life; the need to guide thought; the need to guide action.

WORLDVIEW DEVELOPMENT AND THE ACADEMIC SETTING

We now return to the first of the two questions posed at the beginning of this paper: is it possible to help students develop a worldview that informs their engineering praxis? To this question we must answer in the affirmative, however, in a much broader manner than might be expected. Let us assume for the sake of argument, that many entering undergraduate students are only at the pre-philosophical level with respect of a worldview; they possess the materials out of which a worldview can be constructed; but they have not reflected, analyzed or integrated this material using biblically informed philosophical processes. If worldview construction is a desired outcome, then the curriculum, in some part, must provide the setting, opportunities and encouragement for students to begin the process. In typical undergraduate programs, it is the liberal arts component of a curriculum where these opportunities are most often encountered; particularly in courses that deal with human values, e.g. literature, philosophy and ethics, art, religion, anthropology, etc. Much of the balance of the curriculum either expands the pre-philosophical building material or might be considered minimally worldview oriented, e.g., mathematics, physics, chemistry and many engineering topics.

On the other hand, if worldview construction is possible, is it possible for worldview formation to be explicitly directed by the engineering education process to the end that a coherent Christian worldview is the ultimate result? The answer to this question must be carefully crafted, but in general, the answer is negative. Typical engineering curricula provide few opportunities for the reflection and analysis needed for the worldview generation process to be successful. An analysis of the Baylor University engineering program will provide some insight into the challenges faced by those attempting intentional Christian worldview development within an engineering community.

First, it should be said that students who major in engineering possess perspectives that are compatible with many elements of a Christian worldview. These students have a positive outlook on life, even possibly bordering on hubris. They believe the world to be rational, that problems are amenable to analysis, that events can be predicted and that solutions can always be developed to solve problems. Secondly, Baylor attracts a high percentage of students who are culturally and religiously tied to the Christian faith, a result of "Bible Belt" geography. Baylor also attracts students with non-Christian backgrounds, many who believe that the institution provides a greater level of religious toleration than is normally available at state institutions.

Baylor publicly promotes its Baptist heritage and the faith commitments of its faculty, although the depth of these commitments varies significantly across the institution. Baylor hires Christians (with one minor caveat), giving preference to Baptists and members of other mainline protestant denominations. In his spring 2003 State of the University Address, ex-president Sloan stated, "I believe our commitment to the recruitment and retention of faculty who proclaim the confession 'Jesus Christ is Lord' does not inevitably lead to narrowness, mediocrity, or parochialism."[19] Sloan took an active role in hiring each new faculty member to ensure candidates had the spiritual and academic credentials essential to Baylor's historic mission. Sloan's focus on a candidate's faith profession alienated many tenured faculty members especially when he vetoed prospects with weak faith statements. Hiring practices under the current Provost and President have relaxed somewhat with the primary burden for vetting a candidate's faith commitments being shifted to the departmental level.

Many older faculty members are reluctant to engage in worldview discussions either because they were ill-prepared intellectually to do so or they considered the endeavor of little value to their discipline. Other faculty members are not convinced that the Christian faith has any relevance to the physical or natural sciences. All to say, the very essence and nature of a Christian university is being hotly debated and has spilled into national prominence in Ben Stein's academic critique, "Expelled, No Intelligence Allowed." Stein amply demonstrates that academic freedom does not apply when widely held scientific "truths" are appropriately challenged.

Even within the School of Engineering and Computer Science, a rather homogenous group of faculty in terms of discipline perspectives, divisions arose when the University administration requested a policy statement from the School that would articulate how it was intentional in its Christian mission. Divisions surfaced over explicit references to the Triune God and personal redemption through Jesus Christ. However, one sentiment that the engineering faculty shares is that the intentional discussion of faith and worldview perspectives should be limited to those academic activities where it is most natural and appropriate.

Given the absence of a consensus among both the engineering faculty and the larger University academic community, is there any reason to hope that worldview development can be directly influenced? The authors believe that a qualified yes can be given. Using Sire's viewpoint, a Christian worldview must start with the central gospel message, the presence of sin and the need for a savior. Even though some members of the engineering faculty are uncomfortable sharing their faith in the open classroom, most students will hear a clear message of redemption at more than once in their undergraduate tenure. They will most likely hear similar messages from their Christian classmates. Obviously, if they embrace the message, a worldview change will naturally occur. For those students who already embrace the Christian faith, the occasional classroom discussion that connects faith with the subject at hand only serves to broaden their understanding of the world and of God's gracious and creative nature. Although the class-room setting provides opportunities for worldview formation, the opportunities are sufficiently sparse that intentionality is questionable.

From a biblically-based Christian worldview we understand that "all knowledge is God's knowledge" and that our quest to understand God's creation (his general revelation) is also a quest to understand Him more completely. Therefore, even though there may not be a specific application of principles of the Christian faith in every engineering problem, students can often be reminded to take a step back and look at the big picture of his presence and sustaining activity in the world. As an engineer works through the extrinsic elements of a design artifact, a Christian worldview can provide a basis on which to consider and make the necessary value judgments and choices required by the engineering design process. An understanding of the sinful and fallen nature of human beings and our need for redemption can supply insights to the misuses of an artifact as well as how a particular design choice might provide added value because it has beneficial side-effects.

If the engineering classroom setting lacks intentionality, it is certainly possible that the extracurricular setting might be more fruitful, particularly if these activities are directed toward the development of student-led community groups that are either focused on spiritual development and growth or promote such activities as a secondary effect. The faculty should encourage and support these communities and, where appropriate, serve as advisors and mentors for the student leadership. Although the specific activities of these groups should be controlled by the students themselves, faculty mentors can provide enough influence to insure that content and conduct are bounded within Christian norms.

In an attempt to promote community among students, Baylor has moved to significantly increase the percentage of students who reside on-campus. In the past, most freshmen lived on-campus, but non-freshman students were forced to move off-campus for lack of residential space. In 2003, the first residence facility to be built in 30 years was sited next to the engineering building. A portion of this facility was subsequently reserved for engineering and computer science students and a "living and learning" center (LLC) was developed and staffed to promote student community activities. The existence of this residential community is now a major recruiting tool for the School. Freshman engineering enrollments have grown from just under 100 in 2003 to the current enrollment of over 200 for fall 2008, largely due to the LLC's presence. A second residential complex, Brooks College, was added in 2007. These community learning centers provide rich opportunities for students to interact with their peers as well as assigned faculty mentors "by providing an atmosphere that fosters serious intellectual pursuits."

Baylor has a number of academic resources that engage students at the pre-philosophical and philosophical level of worldview development. All students are required to take two religion classes, usually in their freshman year. The first class, an introduction to the Old and New Testaments, emphasizes "appropriate strategies for interpretation of the Bible."[20] The second class, an introduction to Christian life and thought from the early church to the present, emphasizes "Christian doctrine, ethics, witness and institutions."[21] Many see religion courses as a framework where there can be serious intellectual wrestling with literary philosophical, scientific, technological, and worldview issues,[22] although it is not obvious that either of Baylor's courses attempt to systematically engage the student in terms of worldview formation.

The core curriculum for engineering students differs in some respect from the more prevalent liberal arts version across campus. In a core curriculum review, the engineering faculty chose to replace the six-semester-hour English literature requirement with two courses on the intellectual traditions of the ancient and medieval worlds. The first course, Intellectual Tradition of the Ancient World, engages students in the reading and discussion of "foundational texts that establish the parameters of morality, aesthetic, religion, and philosophy."[23] The second course, Medieval Intellectual Tradition, focuses on the "development of thought from the medieval to the modern period, with particular attention paid to the Christian intellectual tradition."[24] Both of these courses could play a significant role in the worldview development of students. However, at this time, little is done within the engineering curriculum to capitalize on the foundation laid by these courses.

Junior-level engineering students must complete one course in the field of ethics. Students can choose between a number of courses taught by the religion faculty, a business ethics course, or recently added, a course taught by the engineering faculty, Social and Ethical Issues in Engineering. This latter course investigates the relationships between engineering, technology, and society. Topics studied include: philosophical perspectives on engineering and technology, technological values, social and ethical responsibilities of engineers, public technology policy, and Christian perspectives and responses. This course provides an excellent opportunity for students to consider how faith impacts engineering practice.

In the extra-curricular religious area, the Baylor community is currently not as rich and diverse as might be desired. Until recently, on-campus religious activities were constrained by a policy that restricted campus access for parachurch groups such as Inter-Varsity Fellowship and denominational groups such as the Catholic Student Association and the Reformed University Fellowship, although Campus Crusade for Christ has been a recognized on-campus group for many years. Many of these parachurch organizations could provide excellent opportunities for student community formation and thereby worldview development.

Numerous student professional organizations, such as the ASME, IEEE, SWE, and NSBE chapters provide opportunities for professional service, many of which specifically target humanitarian endeavors. Service can be organized in many venues, including to the University community as well as the surrounding city and county through the University's broad-based Stepping Out Program or more focused activities such as the local Girl Scouts Day Camp program. The faculty sponsors for these student organizations are a critical resource and their presence provides opportunities for students to discuss the motivations and rationale for their humanitarian service and activities.

Individual faculty members as well as the student service organization, Engineers with a Mission (EWAM), have organized engineering projects in developing third-world countries. During the normal school year students develop strategies to build and deliver appropriate technology artifacts which are installed during summer on-site visits. These projects have included the development of a school and community computer lab in Belize, bridge design and construction in rural Kenya, installation of wind turbines and lighting for a small Kenyan village, and the design and installation of a water filtration system for a Kenyan orphanage. This summer's project is a micro-hydroelectric power installation near small villages in Honduras. This project also provides the local community with a sustainable means to generate income as well as a means for improving the local quality of life. Each project has given students the opportunity to interact with individuals in the local culture and to team with them to solve a problem that has been locally identified. The completion of these humanitarian projects gives students a sense of accomplishments and professional self-worth. Faculty sponsors have many teachable moments as the local field conditions often overwhelm students and the work naturally raises larger questions about God and our purpose in life. Most students return from these trips with a new perspective on the nature of our world and an appreciation for the hardships and deprivations that many face in their daily lives.

SUMMARY

What has the Baylor experience taught us about Christian worldview development within the context of an academic institution? Foremost, the presence of Christian faculty, especially those that are willing to engage students in the exploration of their faith commitments and the integration of faith and praxis is a given and essential element. Unless there are faculty who have the necessary faith and practice commitments, commensurate worldview development among students will be self-driven with faculty providing little or no guidance or mentorship.

Committed faculty members may be able to identify a number of opportunities for student worldview development even where the curriculum appears to provide few resources. For example, projects in engineering design courses can be selected that focus on the extrinsic rather than intrinsic design elements of an artifact. Of particular interest would be projects that require students to design products that provide utility to persons of disability or that support appropriate technology development in poor third-world countries. The humanitarian nature of these projects can provide a springboard for worldview discussions about life motivations and the nature of God's providence.

Even if committed faculty members are present, their discipline (e.g. sciences, mathematics and engineering) may not provide the settings needed for curriculum-based intentional worldview development. However, at a minimum, the curriculum can play a significant supportive role through the careful selection of a set of humanities-based general education requirements. This set could include courses in religion, history, literature, philosophy and social science.

Even in the absence of a supportive curriculum, worldview formation can still flourish in student-led community learning groups and Bible studies where committed faculty members serve as advisors and mentors. Some of these may be humanitarian service organizations that engage students in extracurricular projects focused on community development or that involve more complicated international humanitarian relief. A key theme and motivation in these organizations can be faith-informed humanitarianism.

By working to integrate faith and praxis in the profession of engineering, it is hoped that our students will be aware of the challenges facing the world, thereby encouraging them to apply faith-informed values and their profession in a deep humanitarianism. The events of the last decade have clearly pointed to the growing social and economic interdependence of previously independent societies. This fact is clear when one considers the impact of health issues related to HIV, SARS, and H5N1 in the presence of inadequate third-world health systems or the impact of rising energy prices on the green revolution. A significant percentage of the world's food production is underpinned by agricultural mechanization and the use of fertilizers and chemicals, all of which are energy intensive. One implication of this situation is that rising energy prices may soon translate into growing and endemic famine in many parts of the world.[25]

There is evidence[26, 27] that within a decade there will be urgent global issues that, by comparison, may trivialize the arms and space race, which absorbed a large percentage of the U.S. engineering efforts at the end of the 20th century. It is hard these days to discuss energy without the subject of global warming being raised. The National Academy of Engineering identifies the following additional technical challenges: physical infrastructures in urban settings, information and communications infrastructures, the environment, and technology for an aging population[28].

The complexity of these global issues will require greater and more sustained efforts by the global engineering community than it has been able to muster in the past. The U.S. engineering community could make significant contributions if we train young engineers to connect with their counterparts around the world to generate the ideas, vision and leadership needed to meet the future's challenges. A Christian worldview and faith-informed engineering praxis could provide an enormous reservoir of humanitarian values-oriented engineered products that would significantly impact the quality of life in this world.

CITED REFERENCES

1. Project Lead the Way, online at http://www.pltw.org

2. *Merriam-Webster's Online Dictionary*, <http://www.merriam-webster.com/dictionary/science>.

3. Monsma, et al., *Responsible Technology, A Christian Perspective*, Eerdmans, 1986, p.19.

4. Monsma, preface.

5. Monsma, p. 28.

6. Monsma, p. 165.

7. Monsma, pp. 165–166.

8. Monsma, pp. 170–177.

9. Luke 10:27; Revised English Bible (REB), Oxford University Press, 1996.

10. IEEE Code of Ethics, online at http://www.ieee.org.

11. Wadhwa, et al., "Where the Engineers Are", online at http//:ssrn.com/abstract=1015843, (Spring 2007).

12. Holmes, Arthur F., *Contours of a World View*, Eerdmans, Grand Rapids, 1983, p. 5.

13. Dewey, John, "My Pedagogic Creed," *School Journal* vol. 54 (January 1897) pp. 77–80 http://dewey.pragmatism.org/creed.htm, accessed April 15, 2009.

14. Holmes, pp. 31–32.

15. Holmes, p. 39.

16. Sire, James W., *Naming the Elephant: Worldview as a Concept*, p. 122.

17. Sire, p. 123.

18. Sire, p. 135.

19. President Robert Sloan, Spring 2003 State of the University Address, Baylor University, Waco, Texas.

20. Baylor University, 2008 Undergraduate Catalog, p. 559.

21. Baylor, p. 559.

22. Dockery, David, "Integrating Faith & Learning in Higher Education," http://www.cccu.org/resourcecenter/printerfriendly.asp?resID=2242 accessed April 13, 2008.

23. Baylor, p. 451.

24. Baylor, p. 451.

25. Williams, James H., David von Hippel, and Peter Hayes, "Fuel and Famine: Rural Energy Crisis in the Democratic People's Republic of Korea," *Institute on Global Conflict and Cooperation*, March 1, 2000.

26. Savinar, Matt, "Life after the Oil Crash", http://www.lifeaftertheoilcrash.net/ accessed on March 7, 2006.

27. Deffeyes, Kenneth S., *Beyond Oil*, Hill and Wang, 2005

28. National Academy of Engineering, "The Engineer of 2020: Visions of Engineering in the New Century," The National Academies Press, Washington, DC, 2004, pp. 17–22.

8

Application of the "Engineering Mindset" for Worldview Evaluation

Dominic M. Halsmer

Connections between Worldview and Engineering

A major aspect of engineering education deals with the appropriate application of available resources for the solution of human problems. This aspect has become increasingly more important as the finitude and possible fragility of once abundant natural resources has become clear in light of current discussions on sustainability. Engineers have the important task of applying their knowledge, skills, creativity, and wisdom to make the best use of these resources. Thus, the fundamental assets that each engineer brings to the table in the solution of any problem are the personal resources of his or her own time, energy, technical abilities, and understanding. How these personal resources are applied, and if they will be applied to a particular problem, depends on the worldview of the engineer.

Worldview, or how a person sees life and the world at large, plays a part in determining motivations and behaviors. This is particularly true of young people when they are deciding on a career path. Earning a four-year degree in engineering requires a significant amount of very hard work for an extended length of time and can cost a lot of money. Why would someone make such an investment? What are the

Dominic M. Halsmer <dhalsmer@oru.edu> is dean of the School of Science and Engineering at Oral Roberts University, where he has taught engineering for 17 years. His current research involves the potential for reverse engineering studies to contribute to natural and systematic theologies. He has recently written several articles on the role of Christian engineers in the current science and theology dialogue. He received his PhD in Mechanical Engineering from UCLA and his BS and MS in Aeronautical and Astronautical Engineering from Purdue University. He is currently working toward an MA in Biblical Literature at Oral Roberts University.

motivating factors? Of course, there are the enticements of high sala-
ries and prestige. But with lower percentages of American students
currently choosing science and engineering than in other major nations of the world, maybe it's time to rethink the adequacy of such
motivations. A recent *New York Times* editorial by Columbia University
physicist and author, Brian Greene, strongly advocates teaching science in a way that includes its dramatic implications for worldview.
He emphasizes "the powerful role science can play in giving life context and meaning." He suggests that instead of just focusing on the
technical details, "science needs to be taught to the young and communicated to the mature in a manner that captures this drama. We
must embark on a cultural shift that places science in its rightful place
alongside music, art, and literature as an indispensable part of what
makes life worth living."[1] As a whole, American youth enjoy a level of
prosperity and comfort that is considerably higher than nearly all the
rest of the world. Is it possible that they are already so comfortable that
they would rather not put forth the effort needed for the successful
completion of a degree in science or engineering? Perhaps worldview
considerations might provide additional and more effective motivation for such endeavors.

Everyone has a worldview, which typically takes shape based on
various life experiences such as formal education and personal relationships. But people generally don't think much about their worldview. They tend to lose sight of the forest for the trees. That is, they get
so bogged down in the details of their lives that they tend to ignore
the big questions involving overall worldview. Sometimes they establish a particular worldview early in their lives and try to force-fit any
newly learned information into an old and outdated worldview. Many
peoples' worldviews are established, or significantly modified, during
their higher education experience because this is when they receive a
huge influx of information from diverse fields and meet many new and
interesting people. Thus, the university setting is an excellent place to
investigate issues related to worldview. This paper gives a taste of the
content of a university course for engineers on evaluating worldview,
but does not discuss the pedagogy or assessment of such a course.

The purpose of this paper is to discuss the value and method of
testing one's worldview to see how well it matches with reality. A further purpose is to propose and support the idea that an "engineering
mindset" is particularly applicable to the accurate formation and testing of a worldview. Engineers are in the business of gathering diverse
pieces of information and trying to make some practical sense of it

all. Typically, this results in the synthesis of some complex device or system that makes extensive use of the laws of nature. That is, engineers understand how the world works to a substantial degree, and they make use of this knowledge in an attempt to improve the human condition. Furthermore, engineers often find themselves engaged in the reverse process, in which they carefully dissect an existing device or system in order to learn its secrets or discover how it is supposed to work. This process, which is known as reverse engineering, is actually a microcosm of our ongoing effort to understand all that we can about ourselves and the universe in which we live. This idea was introduced by the author at the 2008 ASEE Annual Conference in a paper entitled "The Applicability of Engineering Design Principles in Formulating a Coherent Cosmology and Worldview." [2] This paper continues that theme by describing how engineering students at Oral Roberts University are encouraged to investigate the evidence and think critically regarding the components of their worldviews by using appropriate tests. These tests, along with the standard components of worldview, are discussed in the next section.

WORLDVIEW COMPONENTS AND TESTS

According to philosopher Kenneth Samples' book, *A World of Difference*, six major components make up the conceptual heart of any worldview:

1. Theology— Concept of **God**, or absence of such
2. Metaphysics— View of external **reality**, especially the cosmos
3. Epistemology— Study of the origin, nature, limits, and validity of **knowledge**
4. Axiology— Study of the origin, nature, meaning, and criteria of **values**
5. Anthropology— Study of the origin, nature, problems, and destiny of **human beings**
6. History— Study of the nature, direction, and purpose of unfolding **historical events**[3]

These are the most important categories of knowledge for thinking about the world, its meaning, and basically how it works. A person's collection of beliefs in these areas will determine thinking, motivation, and behavior, making it of critical importance for living a successful life. For the purpose of evaluating worldview, Samples also suggests the following nine tests:

1. **Coherence**—Is it logically consistent?
2. **Balance**—Is it appropriately balanced between simplicity and complexity?
3. **Power & Scope**—How well does it explain and how wide is the range of explanation?
4. **Correspondence**—Does it correspond to empirical facts and human experience?
5. **Verification**—Can the central truth-claims be verified or falsified?
6. **Pragmatic**—Does it promote relevant, practical, and workable results?
7. **Existential**—Does it address the internal needs, desires, and aspirations of humanity?
8. **Cumulative**—Is it supported by multiple lines of converging evidence?
9. **Competitive**—Can it successfully compete in the marketplace of ideas?[4]

Scientists and engineers typically have a very high regard for truth because they daily experience the value, indeed the profitability, of having an accurate representation of physical reality. However, they also understand that their representations are probably not perfect. Engineers are especially in tune to the idea that full and complete knowledge of all aspects of a project need not be attained before decisions are made to finalize a "good-enough" design and get the product "out the door". Samples confirm this same idea with regard to worldview decisions when he writes, "No worldview is perfect in explaining reality. Instead, a worldview functions much like a scientific model in its attempt to provide a broad and general explanatory theory about reality. Lack of perfection should not prevent anyone from evaluating various positions and embracing the one that scores highest on the nine critical tests."[5] Students evaluate their own worldviews using these tests, while keeping in mind the dangers of egocentric and sociocentric thinking to the process of critical thinking.[6] Since most of the students that attend Oral Roberts University profess a belief in the historic Christian worldview, it will be used as an example in the next section by applying the nine tests listed above.

EVALUATION OF THE HISTORIC CHRISTIAN WORLDVIEW

Before evaluating the worldview known as Christian Theism, it may be helpful to summarize its perspectives on each of the major worldview components. Samples provides the following:

1. **Theology**— God is an infinite, eternal, immutable, morally perfect, and tri-personal spiritual being (Triune); the transcendent Creator and sovereign Sustainer of all things.
2. **Metaphysics**— The time-space-matter universe was created by God ex nihilo and thus has a real existence, yet is dependent upon God's providential power, control, and guidance.
3. **Epistemology**— Authentic knowledge (of God, the self, and the world) is available to man through God's general and special revelation (via the created order and redemptive actions).
4. **Axiology**— Objective, universal, unchanging and prescriptive moral values exist (absolutes) and find their source and ground in God's perfect and immutable moral character.
5. **Anthropology**— Human beings were created in the image of God (as rational, moral, and spiritual beings) but have misused their freedom in order to sin and thus need redemption in Christ.
6. **History**— The linear direction of historical events is ordained by God and unfolds according to his sovereign will (including creation, fall, redemption, glorification and new creation).[7]

In applying each of the nine tests to this worldview, the application of the "engineering mindset" will be briefly demonstrated with varying degrees of effectiveness. This is obviously not intended to be an exhaustive evaluation, but simply an example demonstrating the usefulness of engineering principles in this regard. Objective evaluation is facilitated by keeping an ever-vigilant lookout for egocentric thinking (exemplified in sentiments such as these: "It's true because I believe it, or because I want to believe it, or because it's in my selfish interest to believe it.") and sociocentric thinking (e.g., "It's true because my family, culture, nation, society, or religious group believes it."). Let's now apply each of the tests.

1. Coherence—Is it logically consistent?

Most of the training that engineers receive in school is based on systems of mathematical or scientific thought. In order to achieve successful engineering outcomes, it is vital that these systems be logically consistent. Thus, engineers generally have a profound appreciation for the value and utility of logically consistent systems of thought. This is recognized at the university level in the maturation of engineering students who may not have liked math in high school but later acknowledge its inherent power and beauty in describing the physical world. How is it that humans are able to engage in such coherent reasoning?

How is it that these systems of thought even exist in the first place? Scientist Eugene Wigner discusses this enigma in a famous paper entitled "The Unreasonable Effectiveness of Mathematics in the Natural Sciences," where he concludes, "The miracle of the appropriateness of the language of mathematics for the formulation of the laws of physics is a wonderful gift which we neither understand nor deserve."[8]

Christian theism provides a sufficient and meaningful basis for rationality. It also supplies an adequate explanation for why reason and rationality exist in the universe. It holds that a perfectly rational being, God, is the ontological ground and source of reason. Therefore such conceptual realities as logic, mathematics, knowledge, and truth flow from a supremely intelligent divine mind. And because God made human beings in his image with rational faculties and sensory organs that generally function properly, humans are able to discover the world's basic intelligible and empirical order. The omniscient and wise Creator (working like a transcendent cosmic computer engineer) networked the intelligibility of the world with the minds of human beings. In addition, while the great revealed truths of historic Christianity cannot be fully comprehended or fathomed by human reason, they do not violate reason. Mystery always accompanies divinely revealed truths, but those truths are not formally at odds with the laws of logic, for God is the source of both.[9]

However, some Christian doctrines face charges of alleged incoherence. One of the most troubling is how God can be all-powerful and all-good in the midst of such extensive evil, pain, and suffering as is daily observed and experienced in our world. At first, this issue may seem to be well out of reach of the engineering mindset, but actually the required analysis involves considerations of purpose, requirements, constraints, and the associated tradeoffs that are common to the practice of engineering. First of all, the acknowledgement of evil presupposes an ultimate standard of goodness, which appears to be beyond the mere conventions of humans and yet is clearly understood by everyone. Love is universally understood to be one of the greatest goods that humans are able to demonstrate. This appears to be consistent with God's purpose to establish eternal love relationships with people. However, it seems that love is a pretty tricky business to engineer, even for God. As far as we know, only spiritual beings with free will are capable of real love. The necessity of free will imposes a constraint that restricts the systems that God can use to accomplish his purposes. It is plausible that such a system would necessarily involve the introduction of evil and hence pain and suffering. This situation then appears to be a failure on God's part, or at least a defamation of his character.

Engineer and author Henry Petroski has written multiple books investigating the key role of failure in successful engineering designs. In his latest book, *Success through Failure: The Paradox of Design*, he writes "Failure is thus a unifying principle in the design of things large and small, hard and soft, real and imagined. . . . Whatever is being designed, success is achieved by properly anticipating and obviating failure."[10] This idea may help to shed light on the story of fall and redemption that is central to the Christian worldview. Engineering educators know that failure is an important part of gaining knowledge. Matt Green and Paul Leiffer, Engineering Professors at LeTourneau University, call this "Flearning" as described in a recent conference paper, "Failure is often how students realize that some things work better than others, and some do not work at all. Failure clearly and eloquently demonstrates the real world phenomena [that] computer simulations or pencil-and-paper calculations fail to capture. Milestone-driven prototyping with specific goals in mind encourages 'Flearning,' learning catalyzed by failure, which is critical to the design process."[11] Thus, we can see how God uses our failures to teach us important truths, causing good to come out of seemingly bad situations. In this way, God literally "makes the Devil work for him." This concept is recognized as an important part of the inventive process of creative problem solving as described in Semyon Savransky's book entitled *Engineering of Creativity: Introduction to TRIZ Methodology of Inventive Problem Solving*.[12]

2. Balance—Is it appropriately balanced between simplicity and complexity?

With regard to understanding and explaining how the universe works, Einstein once said that everything should be made a simple as possible, but not simpler. This is the idea with the balance test. An accurate worldview should be sophisticated enough to account for all the subtleties of reality, but not more complicated than it needs to be. This idea is reminiscent of a famous principle that is often used in science called "Ockham's Razor," which states that the simplest explanation that fits the data is most likely the correct one. Christian theism has the necessary metaphysical complexity to account for both the material and immaterial aspects of reality. In contrast, naturalism strains to account for nonempirical abstract entities such as logic, propositions, universals, mathematics, values, and so forth.[13]

Studies in quantum mechanics and cosmology now suggest that there are more dimensions of space, and possibly time, than the four that we experience every day. The implication is that our universe resides in a much larger space-time reality that may include many other universes or a transcendent being who is responsible for engineering our universe. If these extra dimensions truly exist, this would help to explain difficult doctrines of the Christian worldview, such as the Trinity and free will vs. predestination. It would also help to explain some of the miraculous accounts surrounding the life of Jesus that are central to the Christian worldview.[14] From an engineering perspective, it is not unusual that God would choose to engineer us in a space-time realm with fewer dimensions than he resides in. Isn't that exactly what human engineers do when they get an idea, and they need to work out its details? They pull out a two-dimensional sheet of paper, or make use of a 2-D computer screen, and begin to sketch out the design. Often this process culminates in very detailed and complex two-dimensional blueprints before the final three-dimensional prototype is approved and produced. Perhaps humans exercise this kind of creativity and this method of engineering simply because they're made in God's image.

3. Power & Scope—How well does it explain, and how wide is the range of explanation?

According to philosopher William Wainwright, "Metaphysical theories are better when they explain a wider range of phenomena. A system that illuminates humanity's scientific, moral, aesthetic, and religious experience, for example, is superior to one that only illuminates science."[15] The historic Christian viewpoint accounts for the vast array of realities in nature and in human experience, including the universe, abstract entities, ethics, human beings, and religious phenomena.[16] Systems engineering is the synthesis of diverse information and resources into a combination of complex subsystems that work together as a unified whole to solve some problem or accomplish some purpose. A systems engineering mindset is useful in thinking about the power and scope of a worldview because diverse elements of the worldview must come together to form a unified explanation that makes sense. Engineers who have experience with complex systems are better able to engage in this kind of analysis.

4. Correspondence—Does it correspond to empirical facts and human experience?

Throughout history, Christianity has generally demonstrated respect for the empirical findings from nature. The fact that the origin of modern science is due to the strong influence of Christian theism has been well documented.[17] However, this does not mean that occasional contradictions will not arise between science and Christian theology. But such occurrences should not be surprising or troubling for the Christian. It is helpful to remember that neither science nor theology hold complete and inerrant truth. Science is our best interpretation of the facts about nature, but it is still a human interpretation of the facts, and thus subject to error. Likewise, theology is mankind's best interpretation of the facts about God, based largely on the Bible. As such, it is also subject to errors of interpretation. Therefore, contradictions between current science and theology do not necessarily imply that the facts regarding nature and the divine do not correspond. An example of such a controversy is the young-earth interpretation of the Genesis account, which holds that the earth and the rest of the universe have only been in existence for a few thousands of years. This may or may not turn out to be true, but it is helpful to realize that there are other valid and scholarly interpretations of Genesis that align very closely with our current understanding of nature and its history.

5. Verification—Can the central truth-claims be verified or falsified?

The value and profitability of the fields of science and engineering are due largely to the fact that their hypotheses, theories, and practices are continually subjected to appropriate testing. In this way, errors and deficiencies can be corrected and the body of knowledge is further refined. Likewise, it is important that the central truth-claims of a worldview be verifiable or falsifiable since claims that lack this characteristic cannot be investigated, evaluated, and critiqued, thus carrying little rational weight. "Testability increases a worldview's intellectual credibility. The concept of 'testable truth' contains persuasive power."[18] Engineers use several different methods for testing reality, such as theoretical calculations, computer simulations, and experimental testing in the laboratory. They typically look for good agreement among such methods before proceeding with a design-related decision.

However, the approach to verification or falsification of worldview truth-claims can be somewhat different from that of verifying the material properties of a specimen in the engineering laboratory. The major truth-claims of Christianity are rooted in historical fact. This is an area where engineering principles may not be as useful, but that does not mean that such claims are not open to the rigors of historical investigation. The key historical event of the Christian worldview is Jesus' resurrection. Christianity could theoretically be falsified by providing convincing evidence that this event never occurred. The apostle Paul admits as much in his first letter to the Corinthians. On the other hand, overwhelming evidence for Jesus' resurrection can also verify the truth of Christianity. On the surface, this may appear to be a totally unbelievable event because it does not conform to our normal experiences of life and death. But there are many examples of unusual historical events that don't correspond to our everyday experience. Nevertheless, we have significant evidence that events like the Big Bang, total solar eclipses, the first moon landing, and major earthquakes have actually occurred. Careful research has resulted in six primary strands of evidence to support the historical and factual nature of Jesus' bodily resurrection:

1. the empty tomb
2. Jesus' post-crucifixion appearances
3. the transformation of the apostles
4. the conversion and transformation of Saul of Tarsus into the apostle Paul
5. the emergence of the Christian church
6. the shifting of the day of worship from the seventh to the first day of the week[19]

In addition to this kind of evidence, philosopher Richard Swinburne, in his book *The Resurrection of God Incarnate*, presents the evidence from natural theology for the existence of a God who has some reason to miraculously intervene on Jesus' behalf, his being uniquely the kind of person whom God would have raised. Swinburne argues that God has reason to interfere in history by becoming incarnate and that it is highly improbable that we would find the evidence we do for the life and teaching of Jesus, as well as the evidence from witnesses to his empty tomb and later appearances, if Jesus was not God incarnate and did not rise from the dead.[20] These streams of evidence from history and philosophy combine to increase the plausibility of Jesus' resurrection, but there is yet another kind of evidence that is readily available and may be quite powerful, although somewhat mysterious. If Jesus really is alive and desiring to have an intimate relationship with all those who are willing, then one should be able to conduct a kind of "devotional experiment"[21] by seeking such relationship with a sincere and contrite heart. Christians readily testify to the reality of this relationship and the ways it has positively and dramatically impacted their lives. This internal reality is probably the most convincing evidence of all, but alas, it arrives after the fact. Could it be that God has engineered things to work this way, being consistent with the non-compelling nature of love relationships and the necessary involvement of an element of faith?

6. Pragmatic—Does it promote relevant, practical, and workable results?

Engineers make their living by developing relevant, practical, and workable products and systems. If they do not continually tend to such essential pragmatism, they will quickly go out of business. Likewise, a worldview that is not relevant, practical, and workable may not be in business for long. Engineers are trained to conduct a broad range of problem solving activities. But like everyone else, they can sometimes be at a loss for how to solve problems in their own personal lives, such as character flaws, immorality, broken relationships, and guilt. The Christian worldview has been found by many people to provide an extremely effective solution to these kinds of problems. It provides the educational, economic, legal, political, moral, and spiritual framework and incentives (as well as safeguards) necessary to promote a healthy and thriving culture. By virtue of the high value placed on human beings, it is not surprising that Christians have led the way in establishing many of the world's charitable organizations.[22] It has become popular in some circles to emphasize abuses that have occurred under the guise of Christianity, but these must be weighed against all the good for which it has been responsible over the past two millennia. Engineers evaluate the utility of various scientific truths for potential use in the development of new technologies. This ability should also assist in their evaluation of the utility of various worldviews in solving the problem of life's meaning and purpose. It seems clear that the Christian worldview, if true, offers an extremely relevant, practical, and workable form of truth that provides value to humans that far exceeds anything in this world. This alone should be reason enough to investigate it thoroughly and test it extensively before dismissing it.

7. Existential—Does it address the internal needs, desires, and aspirations of humanity?

A worldview should address humanity's desire for meaning, purpose, and significance, but only if such existential satisfaction really exists. It should also help to explain why human beings are the way they are. Engineers survey natural resources and determine their best uses for the good of mankind. From a reverse engineering point of view, it seems that the best use of humans would have something to do with our innate capacity to love and our strong desire to receive love. That is one good and satisfying thing that humans are capable of, which can't be obtained from other sources in the universe. Yet this is an area of our lives that is so challenging to get right. We sense our great potential as loving beings but are confronted with the realities of selfishness, apathy, and broken relationships. As famous blues guitarist Eric Clapton once wrote, "Why does love got to be so sad?" Love is a mystery that may be unraveled only through fully engaging in the relationships of our lives. The Christian worldview has a lot to say about love as the pinnacle and purpose of the human experience. But it also explains the need for our hearts to be restored to their original working condition through the loving sacrifice of Jesus. In fact, Christianity claims a defining revelation that, "This is how we know what love is: Jesus Christ laid down his life for us."[23] Apparently, the engineering of eternal love relationships inevitably involves the acquisition of wisdom that comes through the process of rebellion, repentance, and redemption of the human heart. Again, a powerful evidence for the truth of Christian Theism can be found in the readily available testimonies that such existential satisfaction is currently being experienced.

8. Cumulative—Is it supported by multiple lines of converging evidence?

During my days as an undergraduate engineering student at Purdue, I enjoyed participating in their cooperative work-study program in the aerospace industry. It was there that I first interacted with experienced engineers on a daily basis. And it was there that I learned the importance of striving for absolute reliability in engineering solutions. Good engineers use redundancy and multiple lines of evidence and reasoning to avoid failure. This was vividly brought to my attention as a co-op student when I was introduced to the concept of a "belt and suspenders" design. This kind of design includes built-in redundancy mechanisms for additional confidence of success. What made the lesson especially memorable was when, upon completion of our meeting, as my mentor was leaving the office, I noticed that he really was wearing both a belt and suspenders to keep his pants up. Thus, engineers understand the importance of a cumulative case of supporting evidence and may require more than the average amount of evidence, and possibly from a broader range of sources, to be convinced of any particular proposition.[24]

C.S. Lewis nicely described the cumulative nature of the evidence for Christian Theism when he wrote about the basis for his belief, "I believe in Christianity as I believe the sun has risen, not only because I see it, but because by it I see everything else."[25] Virtually every field of study contributes to the veracity of the Christian worldview, as illustrated by the following brief list:

1. **Cosmology**— The universe had a singular beginning (Big Bang cosmology); there was a beginning of time.
2. **Astrophysics**— Nature's laws appear to be engineered (fine-tuned) to allow for human life (anthropic principle); so do the universe's content and systems (galaxies, stars, planets, chemical elements, etc.).
3. **Biology/Chemistry**— Life systems and ecosystems yield evidence of having been intelligently engineered.
4. **Engineering**— The fact that all of nature is so readily and profitably reverse engineered by human beings suggests that it was somehow engineered for our provision and education.
5. **Anthropology/Psychology**— Human beings are richly endowed intellectually but morally flawed.
6. **Neuroscience**— Humans possess consciousness and a capacity for intentionality and rational reflection.
7. **Mathematics**— Mathematical theories correspond with physical reality.
8. **Logic**— As abstract entities, the laws of logic are universal, invariant, and independent of human conventions.
9. **Ethics**— Moral absolutes seem intuitively authentic, and moral relativism is self-defeating.
10. **Religion**— Belief in the divine is a universal phenomenon and religious experience seems intuitively real and consistent with biblical revelation.
11. **History**— Credible historical reports corroborate the life, death, and resurrection of Jesus Christ.
12. **Philosophy**— Human beings crave meaning purpose and immortality.[26]

Philosopher Douglas Geivett, in his article "David Hume and a Cumulative Case Argument,"[27] makes this evidence even more compelling by suggesting a particular order of presentation which adds to its explanatory power. This is especially important for scientists and engineers since it begins with natural theology based on the general revelation, which then serves as a rational basis for the special revelation found in the Bible. It begins with cosmological and design evidence and then moves to a study of the human condition as a means of establishing the need for additional revelation. This revelation is assumed to reside in the arena of religious traditions, where evidence of miracles, especially surrounding the life, death, and resurrection of Jesus are significant. This then naturally leads to the execution of a devotional experiment, as mentioned earlier, to test the validity of these ideas. According to the Christian worldview, all sincere seekers of truth will then enjoy a genuine religious experience of reconciliation to their creator, which will be evidenced by a changed life and an assurance of salvation. It is interesting to note the importance of scientific evidence and engineering concepts in the development of this case.

9. Competitive—Can it successfully compete in the market-place of ideas?

Engineers know that the long-term success of a product in the market place is driven by how well it has been engineered to meet people's needs, hopes, and desires. Such a well-engineered product will persuade new customers of its value, even as repeat customers spread the word about their satisfaction. Something very much like this has happened over the history of Christian Theism. Philosophers J.P. Moreland and William Lane Craig illustrate in *Philosophical Foundations for a Christian Worldview*[28] that the ratio of non-Christians to committed Christians has been decreasing steadily ever since the first century. The following table presents the numbers published by the Lausanne Statistics Task Force of the U.S. Center for World Mission:

Date	Non-Christians (millions)	Committed Christians (millions)	Column 2 divided by Column 3
AD 100	180	0.5	360
1000	220	1	220
1500	344	5	69
1900	1,062	40	27
1950	1,650	80	21
1980	3,025	275	11
1989	3,438	500	7

The obvious trend which has persisted from the beginning of Christianity tells a striking tale of customer satisfaction. If "the proof is in the pudding," then it's no wonder that the Bible encourages its readers to "Taste and see that the Lord is good; blessed is the man who takes refuge in him."[29]

CONCLUSIONS

A portion of the content of a course dealing with worldview evaluation for undergraduate engineering students is discussed and reasons are given for why engineers are well-equipped for such an exercise. Additional information on this course was presented at the 2008 Christian Engineering Education Conference.[30] As an example, the Christian worldview is evaluated based on a comprehensive set of nine tests, in which it fares pretty well. Perhaps the reason why the engineering mindset is so helpful in this pursuit is because the Christian worldview presents a picture of a transcendent engineer who has designed this universe as a laboratory where humans can gain the wisdom needed to participate in eternal love relationships.[31] Anecdotal evidence suggests that engineering students who participate in this course find inspiration and motivation for a fulfilling life, infused with purpose, and marked by service and mission.

BIBLIOGRAPHY

1. Brian Greene, "Put a Little Science in Your Life," *New York Times*, June 1, 2008.

2. Dominic Halsmer, "The Applicability of Engineering Design Principles in Formulating a Coherent Cosmology and Worldview," presented at the ASEE Annual Conference, Pittsburgh, PA, June 25, 2008.

3. Kenneth Samples, *A World of Difference*, Baker Books, Grand Rapids, MI, 2007, pp. 23–28.

4. *A World of Difference*, pp. 33–37.

5. *A World of Difference*, p. 37.

6. Richard Paul and Linda Elder, *The Miniature Guide to Critical Thinking*, 5th Edition, Foundation for Critical Thinking Press, Dillon Beach, CA, 2008, pp. 21–22.

7. *A World of Difference*, p. 277.

8. Eugene Wigner, "The Unreasonable Effectiveness of Mathematics in the Natural Sciences," *Communications in Pure and Applied Mathematics*, Vol. 13, No. I (February 1960). New York: John Wiley & Sons

9. *A World of Difference*, p. 267.

10. Henry Petroski, *Success through Failure: The Paradox of Design*, Princeton, NJ, Princeton University Press, 2006, p. 5.

11. Matthew Green and Paul Leiffer, "Enhancing International Humanitarian

Design Projects: a Contextual Needs Assessment Case Study of Remote Power for Faith-Based Organizations," presented at the Christian Engineering Education Conference, Geneva College, Beaver Falls, PA, June 26, 2008.

12. Semyon Savransky, Engineering of Creativity: Introduction to TRIZ Methodology of Inventive Problem Solving, CRC Press, 2000.

13. *A World of Difference*, p. 270.

14. Hugh Ross, *Beyond the Cosmos: What Recent Discoveries in Astrophysics Reveal about the Glory and Love of God*, NavPress, Colorado Springs, CO, 1999.

15. William Wainwright, *Philosophy of Religion*, Belmont, CA, Wadsworth Publishing, 1998, p. 172.

16. *A World of Difference*, pp. 270–271.

17. Nancy Pearcey and Charles Thaxton, *The Soul of Science: Christian Faith and Natural Philosophy*, Wheaton, IL, Crossway, 1994.

18. *A World of Difference*, p. 35.

19. William Lane Craig, *Reasonable Faith: Christian Truth and Apologetics*, Wheaton, IL, Crossway, 2008.

20. Richard Swinburne, *The Resurrection of God Incarnate*, New York, Oxford University Press, 2003, back cover.

21. Carolyn Franks Davis, *The Evidential Force of Religious Experience*, Oxford, Clarendon, 1989.

22. *A World of Difference*, p. 273.

23. *Holy Bible*, New International Version, 1 John 3:16.

24. Dominic Halsmer, "Multidiciplinary Cross-cultural University Outreach to Secular Scientists and Engineers (Why Engineers Make Good Apologists)," International Conference on Engineering Education, San Juan, Puerto Rico, July 23–28, 2006.

25. C.S. Lewis, *The Weight of Glory and Other Addresses*, New York, Macmillan, 1965, p. 92.

26. *A World of Difference*, pp. 274–275.

27. Douglas Geivett, "David Hume and a Cumulative Case Argument" (Chapter 14), *In Defense of Natural Theology*, ed. James F. Sennett & Douglas Groothuis, Downers Grove, IL, Intervarsity Press, 2006, pp. 297–315.

28. J.P. Moreland and William Lane Craig, *Philosophical Foundations for a Christian Worldview*, Downers Grove, IL, Intervarsity Press, 2003, p. 546.

29. *Holy Bible*, New International Version, Psalm 34:8

30. Dominic Halsmer, Jon Marc Asper, and Benjamin Zigrang, "Enhancing Science and Engineering Programs to Equip and Inspire Missionaries to Technical Communities," presented at the Christian Engineering Education Conference, Geneva College, Beaver Falls, PA, June 26, 2008.

31. Dominic Halsmer, Jon Marc Asper, Nate Roman, and Tyler Todd, "The Coherence of an Engineered World," presented at the Design and Nature Conference, The Algarve, Portugal, June 25, 2008.

9

IS THERE ONE CRITERION OF TRUTH IN HIGHER EDUCATION?

David A. Ross

INTRODUCTION

Most North American universities were established with a strong sense that their purpose was to integrate scientific and moral education. In the early colonial colleges in the US, presidents often taught a capstone course entitled "Moral Philosophy" or "Moral Science" or "Science of Mind and Morals" (Schmidt 1930:108). Such courses were designed to connect and integrate the learning from all the disciplines and to focus on the "ultimate in morals." Many have pointed to the spiritual assumptions under which such venerable institutions as Harvard University were founded, but Laney (1990:52) links this well with the search for truth:

> No small part of that founding vision was an understanding of the extraordinary intertwining of the finest learning, the most exalted and loftiest communal vision, and religious-ethical virtue. . . . Along with this understanding of education went an awareness that the academy was committed to truth in the most general sense—the truth that makes one free.

This tradition continued until after the Civil War, but gradually this capstone course "disintegrated into its component parts, as the

David A. Ross <david_ross@gial.edu> is President of the Graduate Institute of Applied Linguistics in Dallas, an institution focused on preparing students to communicate effectively across language and culture boundaries, especially in the areas of Bible translation, linguistics, and literacy. He has had careers in civil engineering, Bible translation, and higher education administration, and has published scholarly papers in all three areas of service. He received his PhD from Lehigh University, holds an MA degree from University of Texas at Arlington, and the Bachelor of Engineering and Master of Engineering degrees from the University of Auckland.

advance in scientific knowledge raised its subdivisions to the dignity of separate subjects worth studying for their own sakes" (Schmidt 1930:110). This change did not occur in isolation (Laney 1990:53–54):

> Two changes . . . have made it more difficult to hear anew the central moral note in the charge to higher education. The first is the rise of scholarly guilds and the concurrent breakup of knowledge into disciplines. The second is the loosening of institutional ties between the academy and the external entities of church and state. (emphasis original)

Cox (2004:1, 2) has an interesting and thoughtful commentary on this situation:

> Higher education, even in schools that had been founded by churches, had become more secular and more specialized. Science, rather than theology, had become the queen of the disciplines. Religion was consigned to seminaries and divinity schools. Harvard, which had been founded by pious Puritans, had long since left its religious purpose behind. The Divinity School had been pushed to a remote corner. . . . "Objectivity" was believed to be the only legitimate approach to teaching anything, and religion—it was thought—could never be taught objectively.

The result of this change in perspective has been that the study of religion is peripheral at most institutions, if it exists at all. Some feel moral education of students no longer needs reference to biblical standards of truth (Schmidt 1930:115):

> Their entire argument is based on the rationalistic assumption that man is competent to evolve standards of right and wrong and even to discover the nature of the deity by applying rational judgments to the phenomena of nature and of his own consciousness. No external authority is required to determine these "laws of nature", for every man contains within himself the means of recognizing them.

HYPOTHESIS FOR STANDARDS OF TRUTH

If it is true that science has become the "queen of the disciplines", and that "objectivity" is the only legitimate approach to teaching and learning, we should be able to conclude that objective, scientific criteria will always lead us to "truth". Furthermore, if higher educational institutions are committed to a search for truth, then we should be able to show that (a) institutions of higher education that seek the truth through scientific techniques are making progress on solving pressing problems, and (b) that the educational disciplines committed to a scientific approach are making progress on producing standards which are both international and independent of time.

It is the opinion of the author that these hypotheses are false and that scientific techniques will not inevitably lead to discovery of the principles of "truth". Many of the issues we will discuss in this paper are ethical or moral issues, for which we must look beyond science to faith-based and, in particular, Christian values.

Before beginning this discussion, however, we must understand the difference between "natural truth" and "spiritual truth" (see Ross, 2008). By allowing this distinction, and introducing the concept of the "hourglass of truth", Ross shows that a faith conviction is essential to understanding truth in its entirety. In particular, the Christian perspective claims that the only connection between the worlds of "natural truth" and "spiritual truth" is in the acknowledgement that Jesus is Divine. This worldview maintains that Jesus alone reveals God completely, and thus is the only person who has ever expressed full moral truth.

This distinction between natural truth and spiritual truth is helpful in confronting the claim that "science is the queen of the disciplines" (Cox 2004:5). In the world of natural truth the scientific method may indeed lead to accuracy of observation and even to the legitimate prediction of events as an extension of observed phenomena. (The principles of many of the disciplines of academia, including engineering, are built on the assumption that phenomena observed in small-scale experiments may be extrapolated into larger-scale situations where it is impractical, or even dangerous, to test by experimentation.) However the scientific method cannot interpret events beyond its basic assumptions, even in its narrow segment of the world of natural truth, nor can it make any worthwhile statement about the world of spiritual truth. If we insist on scientific objectivity as the ultimate standard of truth, this precludes any approach to issues of ethics and morality, since science is not equipped to make observations or deductions about the world of spiritual truth. The scientific technique was developed for the world of natural truth, and it is unreasonable to expect it to be able to function in the world of spiritual truth.

Rather than rely on the scientific technique, if we are to make any meaningful observations in the world of spiritual truth, or if we are to make any value judgments in the world of natural truth, as ethics attempts to do, we are forced to adopt a framework of assumptions about the nature of spiritual truth. Further, if we agree (perhaps reluctantly) that the university has become atomized into its component disciplines, then we are forced to consider each discipline independently, as we search for spiritual truth.

This paper first of all illustrates some of the contemporary ethical dilemmas facing higher education in general. It is the opinion of the author that these problems are sufficient indicators of a need to re-introduce an explicit spiritual basis for higher education. However, allowing that some might dispute this conclusion, this paper also provides an introduction to the topic of ethics in two different academic disciplines—medicine and engineering.

These disciplines were chosen carefully, since each has a strong basis in the natural sciences, and could be expected to exhibit relatively little need of an ethical basis other than that which it is claimed "science" could provide. Furthermore, each discipline has a strong professional guild, each of which attempts to consider ethical issues specific to the discipline. We could thus expect a wide variety of professionals to have developed a relatively stable ethical basis for the practice of the profession. To the extent, then, that we can illustrate either the changing nature of ethical standards within the profession or the confusion within the discipline about permissible activities for professionals within the discipline (or both of these), we will have illustrated the inadequacy of leaving the elucidation of spiritual truth to such disciplines.

CONTEMPORARY TRUTH-RELATED ISSUES IN HIGHER EDUCATION

We begin this search for truth in higher education by noting that universities are retreating from instruction in ethical and moral values just at a time when students are apparently seeking such input. Results of the "Spirituality in Higher Education" project, undertaken on a large sampling of students by the Graduate School of Education and Information Studies, University of California, Los Angeles (see 2008 report), indicate that three-fourths of students say they are "searching for meaning/purpose in life" or that they have meaningful discussion about the meaning of life with friends. Perhaps even more significant, about the same proportion of students have high expectations that their college experience will help them develop emotionally and spiritually.

As further indication of student interest in this topic, Cox (2004) created a stir when he reported on a course entitled "Jesus and the Moral Life", which he had taught at Harvard University for twenty years, beginning in 1982. After noting that there had not been a course taught at Harvard with Jesus in the title or with contents specifically about Jesus for the previous seventy years, Cox comments on the popularity of the course among students (Cox, 2004:5):

> The burgeoning enrollment came as a surprise to the people both inside and outside of Harvard who had considered the university to be a bastion of secularism. Why were so many students crowding into a course that had the words moral and Jesus in the title? Those who were so surprised had obviously misjudged both the mood of the current student generation and the changing temper of the times. (emphasis original)

A survey released in April 2008 by the Association of American Colleges and Universities suggests that students may be disappointed at the lack of attention to ethics and moral issues in their education. Reporting on this survey (involving 23,000 undergraduates and 9,000 faculty) in the *Chronicle of Higher Education*, Wasley (2008) notes:

> The results show that while most students felt that developing personal and social responsibility should be a major focus of their college education, many felt that such instruction was not a priority on their campuses. Only 30 percent of the respondents, for example, said they "strongly agree" that their campuses emphasized refining ethical and moral reasoning.

For the purposes of this paper, we shall illustrate the ethical issues confronting higher education primarily with three examples—the issues of "tolerance", "plagiarism", and "responsibilities of citizenship". However, we shall also use this discussion as a transition into our disciplinary examination of ethics, by mentioning the issue of "truth" as it arises in higher education.

Tolerance

One of the issues addressed by Cox is "tolerance", which has become a watchword within the academy. Cox notes that tolerance, while a commendable virtue in many respects, has the inherent danger to the stability of society (Cox, 2004:9)

> In a society as mixed as ours, without tolerance we would be constantly at each other's throats. It is a sine qua non. But a thoughtful and mature approach to the moral life requires something more than tolerance. It pushes us from insisting on the "right to decide"

to considering what is the right thing to decide. . . . a nation with 250 million separate moral codes is an impossibility, and a world with 6 billion individuals each doing his or her own thing would be unlivable. (emphasis original)

Herein lies the first of our ethical dilemmas currently facing higher education. It is held by many to be a moral imperative to promote tolerance, even in situations where there is clearly biblically defined sin involved. However, the very promotion of tolerance leads inexorably to instability in the culture that allowed higher education to flourish—a case of eventual self-destruction. Without a moral code superseding "tolerance", higher education is doomed to promote its own demise.

Corruption

Many studies have chronicled incidences of plagiarism in institutions of higher education, and it is not the intent of this paper to belabor the obvious. Citing industry reports, well-publicized instances of ethical lapses in universities and colleges, and various poll results, Jennings (2008) documents the increasing incidence of plagiarism by college students as follows:

a. in 1963, 11% of college students acknowledged they had cheated in college
b. in 1993, 49% of college students acknowledged they had cheated in college
c. by 2003 & 2007 surveys, 76% of college students acknowledged they had cheated in college.

Reporting on this situation, Labi (2007) cites a UNESCO report (entitled "Corrupt Schools, Corrupt Universities: What Can Be Done?") and notes an international "weakening of ethical norms" that threatens the integrity of the entire academic system. The study's authors say

[I]n many former Soviet countries . . . bypassing the law has become the general rule . . . to obtain admission to universities. . . . Academic fraud in the United States is so widespread . . . that the problem is undermining the validity of American degrees. The United States is especially susceptible to Internet-related academic fraud because it is at the forefront of many of the technological developments taking place in higher education. . . .

In some places in India, cheating is now so well established that when universities try to resist, students protest and demand their traditional "right to cheat". . . .

Perhaps this increasing incidence of plagiarism is related to an unwillingness of faculty and university administrations to actively pursue reported instances of plagiarism. Jennings reports that only 44% of faculty say they will typically pursue cases of academic integrity. The reasons for this lack of interest include (2006 data):

a. 96% of faculty fear that, if they pursue such cases, they will be accused of "not being a team player";
b. 81% of faculty fear that, if they pursue such cases, corrective action will NOT be taken by their institution;
c. 68% of faculty fear that, if they pursue such cases, they will suffer retribution from their supervisors.

Leaving aside the general problem with plagiarism, however, it is frightening to accept Jennings' claim that, in 2006, 50% of all graduate students acknowledged cheating in their programs. These students, on whom we depend for academic advance during the foreseeable future, are subject to great peer pressure to "short-cut" their research.

Reporting in the *Chronicle of Higher Education* on efforts to teach graduate students "scientific ethics", Brainard (2006) lists some of the more egregious, recent examples of lack of integrity in research:

Last December [2005] allegations broke that a South Korean stem-cell researcher had fabricated parts of a landmark study published in 2004. This year Eric T. Poehlman, a former medical researcher at the University of Vermont, was sentenced to one year in prison for making up data in numerous grant applications and studies in what federal regulators called the worst research-misconduct case in 20 years. . . .

In 2005 a study in the journal *Nature* reported that one-third of scientists surveyed admitted engaging in at least one of 10 practices that were potentially sanctionable by university compliance officers.

The way that the secular academy seems to want to deal with this situation is through courses or programs teaching "research ethics". Unfortunately, it is not at all clear that students who have graduated from such courses benefit from them. Brainard notes a study which concluded that "those who received training in research ethics engaged in most of the questionable behaviors at the same rates as those who did not get training" (Source: "Graduate Education for the Responsible Conduct of Research," Council of Graduate Schools). Assuming this conclusion to be accurate, we have yet another indicator of the fact that the discovery of "truth" cannot be assured, apart from a faith-based commitment to both "spiritual truth" and "natural truth".

Responsibilities of Citizenship

For most of the 1960s and 1970s, universities in North America were the center of activism, sometimes also the center of activities promoting civil disobedience. Much of this activity centered on opposition to the Vietnam War. This illustrates another ethical dilemma which higher education could not avoid and yet for which, having relegated spiritual discussions to the periphery, it was ill equipped. Geisler (1989: 237) summarizes the various approaches to the issue of the responsibilities of citizenship, especially as they relate to war:

> There are three basic views on war: activism, pacifism, and selectivisim. Activism claims it is always right to go to war in obedience to one's country. Pacifism claims it is never right, and selectivism holds that it is sometimes right—when the war is a just war. . . . The activists are right in pointing out that God has ordained government and given it the sword. They are correct in insisting on human obedience to government, even at times to the point of taking life. . . . [T]he pacifists are right that we should pursue peace and try to live peaceably with all men. We should be peacemakers, not warmakers. . . . Selectivism . . . correctly points to the need to put God over government and to encourage obedience to government but to preserve the right of conscience to dissent from oppressive commands.

The fact that not all Christians would agree with Geisler's conclusion (that the correct approach is selectivism) merely underlines the fact that this issue is one on which even Christians will have difficulty speaking with a united voice. Institutions of higher education are uniquely equipped to provide a forum in which this sort of issue can be discussed, with the aim of explicating a truth. However, when a Christian perspective is not permitted at the table, then there is little, if any, prospect of reaching a lasting conclusion.

Truth and the Academy

Before considering the topic of truth in various academic disciplines, we need to discuss briefly the nature of truth from a philosophical viewpoint. We shall see that, even on this topic, higher education is unable to speak with any convincing unanimity.

Singer (2002:37) gives two of the formal properties of truth.

1. "Deduction, or entailment, is truth-preserving—from true propositions only true propositions are deducible. No true proposition entails a false proposition"; and
2. "Truth is timeless—if a proposition is true then it is always true, and it makes no difference whether the proposition is one of fact or of logic or of morality"

It is the second of these properties that is of primary concern for us here. As we delve into the ethical issues of various academic disciplines we shall be looking for a quality of timelessness, by which to indicate that the ethical statements produced by practitioners of the disciplines have produced something which is true.

Somewhat tangential to this discussion, we note that there has been considerable discussion among philosophers about the question of whether moral judgments may ever be determined to be true. Bertrand Russell is among the more famous of those who have expressed skepticism about this (1946:723).

> A judgment of fact is capable of a Property called "truth", which it has or does not have quite independently of what one may think about it. . . . But . . . I see no property, analogous to "truth", that belongs or does not belong to an ethical judgment. This, it must be admitted, puts ethics in a different category from science.

It is interesting to note that Russell tried to draw a parallel between the worlds of natural truth and spiritual truth and discovered correctly that this is impossible. However, rather than allowing these two worlds to have different properties, Russell ended up denying the validity of the world of spiritual truth.

While agreeing that ethics is different from science, Singer disagrees with Russell's doubts about whether moral judgments can ever be judged as true. He adds (Singer 2002:38–39):

> One of the reasons Russell espoused scepticism about truth in ethics is that there is so much controversy about (certain) ethical and of course political matters. . . . But that there are differences of opinion on some matter does not show that the matter is incapable of truth or falsity; and that the differences of opinion may be ineradicable has no such tendency either. It is true that on

many moral matters there are deep-seated differences of opinion. This does not show that the differences of opinion are on matters incapable of truth, hence really matters of preference, not opinion.

By way of illustrating this claim, Singer quotes examples of historical fact in which there is a truth, but that truth may not be ever discovered, because of the political climate—for example, the answer to the question "Who killed President John F. Kennedy?" The fact that the true answer to this question may never be established does not negate the fact that a true answer does, indeed, exist.

For the purposes of this paper, therefore, we shall assume that it is possible for moral judgments to have a quality of truth and that one of the indicators of truth is that these judgments do not change with time.

Before leaving this topic of truth and the academy, we should consider briefly the claim of May (1990:15,16) that the processes of institutional self-assessment and accreditation provide good opportunities for "self-understanding as a moral community". He claims that

> Accreditation is a process through which ethical reflection is initiated. It is also a process involving ethical issues reflecting such matters as the seriousness with which the process is taken, the extent to which various constituencies are involved, and the extent to which the purposes of the institution are fully addressed.

In view of this surprising assertion, it is worthwhile to examine whether this is, in fact, claimed to be an element of the accreditation process. The accreditation process for higher education in the United States involves many different agencies. For the purposes of this investigation, however, reference will be made to only one of the six regional accrediting agencies, the Southern Association of Colleges and Schools (SACS). Its *Principles of accreditation: foundations for quality enhancement* states:

> Integrity, essential to the purpose of higher education, functions as the basic contract defining the relationship between the Commission and each of its member and candidate institutions. It is a relationship in which all parties agree to deal honestly and openly with their constituencies and with one another. Without this commitment, no relationship can exist or be sustained between the Commission and its accredited and candidate institutions.
>
> ...
>
> The Commission on Colleges expects integrity to govern the operation of institutions and for institutions to make reasonable and

responsible decisions consistent with the spirit of integrity in all matters. . . . Failure of an institution to adhere to the integrity principle may result in a loss of accreditation or candidacy. (SACS: 2008,11)

Certainly, the principle of integrity is an essential part of higher education, as it is to the effective functioning of society, and this statement from SACS attempts to explain this principle for higher education accreditation purposes.. Beyond this it is difficult to find references to ethical values in the Principles of Accreditation for SACS. Nothing directly addresses any of the issues mentioned above that face higher education today. Therefore, if this is all there is to the topic of ethics in higher education, then we would need to conclude that contemporary higher education has little to offer in terms of promoting ethical values.

DISCIPLINARY SEARCH FOR TRUTH—MEDICINE AND ENGINEERING

If the assumptions of this paper are correct, we should be able to demonstrate that the treatment of ethics, or morality, on a disciplinary basis has led to an inconsistent and relative treatment of truth. In other words, it should be obvious that confining the discussions to the issues of each specific discipline, largely independent of other disciplines, has led to different solutions. Such solutions could vary over time, or be different in different cultures, and still illustrate the inadequacy of a discipline-specific search for truth in that particular academic discipline.

It would also be helpful if we could show that even secular proponents of ethics in specific disciplines are forced to resort to scriptural principles, as this would further validate the hypothesis that Scripture can provide a uniting force to the academic endeavors of higher education.

Ethics in the Medical Discipline

The Hippocratic oath, or "Oath of Hippocrates", has survived for many centuries as a moral guide to physicians, exhorting them to maintain the privacy of clients, practice their profession to the best of their ability, etc. We might expect, then, that the medical discipline would have relatively few problems gaining acceptance of its practitioners for an unchanging standard of ethical behavior.

We begin by noting that, whereas in 1928, only 24 percent of graduating medical-school students swore by some form of the Hippocratic oath, the practice is almost universal in the US today (Orr, Pang,

Pellegrino, and Seigler, 1997). Noting that there are a considerable number of modern versions of the Hippocratic oath in use, Orr, Pang, Pellegrino, and Siegler surveyed them and discovered that "only 43% vow to be accountable for their actions, only 14% include a prohibition against euthanasia, only 11% invoke a deity, only 8% forswear abortion, and only 3% retain a proscription against sexual contact with patients". The modern versions of the oath have thus shown a steady drift away from the moral strictures espoused in the classical form of the Hippocratic Oath. (See Table 1, beginning next page.)

An excellent discussion of the Hippocratic oath and of how a popular modern version differs from the classical version is available on the Public Broadcasting Service website (http://www.pbs.org/wgbh/nova/doctors/oath_today.html). This article notes several significant contrastive features of the classical and modern versions of the oath, including these:

a. the classical version has clear pagan origins;
b. the classical version makes no mention of such contemporary issues as the ethics of experimentation, team care or a doctor's responsibilities to society;
c. few modern versions prohibit euthanasia, abortion, or sexual contact with patients —all specifically prohibited in the classical version; and
d. few modern versions invoke any deity, or contain any accountability for keeping the pledge.

These types of challenges have led many to question whether the Hippocratic Oath is even still relevant for the medical profession. For a discussion of this, see Orr 1998.

The inescapable conclusion of this is that the ethics of the medical profession are clearly changing. While we might expect changing emphases as new technologies become available, we cannot claim (for example) that technological change accounts for a modern lack of accountability nor that technology accounts for deletion of a prohibition on abortion (since this practice is clearly proscribed in the classical version). Rather, we must conclude that, irrespective of scientific "advances", the ethics, and therefore the definition of truth, in the profession are changeable.

In an effort to restore credibility to the Hippocratic Oath, the Christian Medical and Dental Society adopted a Christian Physician's Oath in 1991. The goal was to retain the valid principles and precepts of medical tradition, but to re-cast them in a Christian context.

	HIPPOCRATIC OATH – CLASSICAL	HIPPOCRATIC OATH – MODERN
	Translation from Harvard Classics, vol. 38, Francis Adams, translator; copyright 1910 by P.F. Collier and Son. This text entered the public domain June 1993. Accessed 23 June 2009 at <http://classics.mit.edu/Hippocrates/hippooath.html>	Written in 1964 by Louis Lasagna, Academic Dean of the School of Medicine at Tufts University, and used in many medical schools today.
1	I swear by Apollo the physician, Aesculapius, and Health, and All-heal, and all the gods and goddesses, that, according to my ability and judgement, I will keep this Oath and this stipulation.	I swear to fulfill, to the best of my ability and judgment, this covenant:
2	To reckon him who taught me this Art equally dear to me as my parents, to share my substance with him, and relieve his necessities if required; to look up his offspring in the same footing as my own brothers, and to teach them this art, if they shall wish to learn it, without fee or stipulation; and that by precept, lecture, and every other mode of instruction, I will impart a knowledge of the Art to my own sons, and those of my teachers, and to disciples bound by a stipulation and oath according the law of medicine, but to none others.	I will respect the hard-won scientific gains of those physicians in whose steps I walk, and gladly share such knowledge as is mine with those who are to follow.
3	I will follow that system of regimen which, according to my ability and judgment, I consider for the benefit of my patients, and abstain from whatever is deleterious and mischievous	I will apply, for the benefit of the sick, all measures [that] are required, avoiding those twin traps of overtreatment and therapeutic nihilism.
4	I will give no deadly medicine to any one if asked, nor suggest any such counsel; and in like manner I will not give a woman a pessary to produce abortion. With purity and with holiness I will pass my life and practice my Art.	I will remember that there is art to medicine as well as science, and that warmth, sympathy, and understanding may outweigh the surgeon's knife or the chemist's drug.

165

	HIPPOCRATIC OATH – CLASSICAL	HIPPOCRATIC OATH – MODERN
5	I will not use the knife, not even on sufferers from stone, but will withdraw in favor of such men as are engaged in this work. I will not cut persons laboring under the stone, but will leave this to be done by men who are practitioners of this work. Into whatever houses I enter, I will go into them for the benefit of the sick, and will abstain from every voluntary act of mischief and corruption; and, further from the seduction of females or males, of freemen and slaves.	I will not be ashamed to say "I know not," nor will I fail to call in my colleagues when the skills of another are needed for a patient's recovery.
6	Whatever, in connection with my professional practice or not, in connection with it, I see or hear, in the life of men, which ought not to be spoken of abroad, I will not divulge, as reckoning that all such should be kept secret.	I will respect the privacy of my patients, for their problems are not disclosed to me that the world may know. Most especially must I tread with care in matters of life and death. If it is given me to save a life, all thanks. But it may also be within my power to take a life; this awesome responsibility must be faced with great humbleness and awareness of my own frailty. Above all, I must not play at God.
7		I will remember that I do not treat a fever chart, a cancerous growth, but a sick human being, whose illness may affect the person's family and economic stability. My responsibility includes these related problems, if I am to care adequately for the sick.
8		I will prevent disease whenever I can, for prevention is preferable to cure.
9		I will remember that I remain a member of society, with special obligations to all my fellow human beings, those sound of mind and body as well as the infirm.

	HIPPOCRATIC OATH – CLASSICAL	HIPPOCRATIC OATH – MODERN
10	While I continue to keep this Oath unviolated, may it be granted to me to enjoy life and the practice of the art, respected by all men, in all times! But should I trespass and violate this Oath, may the reverse be my lot!	If I do not violate this oath, may I enjoy life and art, respected while I live and remembered with affection thereafter. May I always act so as to preserve the finest traditions of my calling and may I long experience the joy of healing those who seek my help.

Table 1: Comparison of the classical and a modern version of the Hippocratic Oath

Trueblood (1988) went so far as to claim that the moral basis of the medical profession was to acknowledge that there is a "real right and a real wrong", and that, in reality, the spiritual life of a medical scientist is more important than his technical ability. This hardly sounds like the enthroning of science as queen of the disciplines.

Geisler (1989:192) summarizes the conflict over ethical issues in medicine as a conflict of world views:

Biomedical issues clutter the stage of crucial ethical decisions. The conflict in opinion on these issues arises out of two opposed world views, the secular humanist and the Christian perspectives. The former denies a Creator, that humans were created, and God-given moral obligations. Humans are merely higher animals with greater intelligence. This intelligence should be used to improve the human species. Hence, secular humanists favor abortion, euthanasia, and genetic engineering to do so.

By contrast with the humanist biomedical ethic, Christians believe that God specially created humans in his own likeness and gave moral imperatives to preserve the dignity and sanctity of human life. Hence, the Christian obligation is to serve God, not to play God. We are not the engineers of life, but merely its custodians. Medical intervention, therefore, should be corrective, not creative. We should repair life, not attempt to reconstruct it. Technology must serve morality, not the reverse.

It is far from clear that all Christians would entirely support Geisler's position, which was written before the potentials of stem cell research were envisaged. It is also unclear whether "secular humanists" would agree with his harsh characterization of their position. However, it is interesting that both Geisler and the modern version of the Hippocratic Oath (quoted above) forswear the intention to "play

God"—in other words, neither position intends to act in place of the Almighty or to usurp the rights and powers of a higher authority. Perhaps agreement on this issue will maintain an open dialogue between those of differing persuasions.

Ethics in the Engineering Discipline

We begin this brief survey of ethics in the profession of engineering by considering the contents of a contemporary textbook on the subject, as used in a secular, state-sponsored, major university (see Harris, Pritchard and Rabins, 2005)

According to these authors there are two basic questions to be answered for the engineering professional:

1. To whom does an engineer owe his/her primary allegiance?
2. On what basis should the profession establish its ethical standards?

In introducing the concepts of ethics in the engineering profession, Harris, Pritchard and Rabins (2005:11) claim:

Professional ethics should be distinguished from personal ethics and common morality. . . . Professional ethics is the set of standards adopted by professionals insofar as they see themselves acting as professionals. Personal ethics is the set of one's own ethical commitments, which are usually acquired in early home or religious training and often modified by later reflection. Common morality is the set of moral ideals shared by most members of a culture or society. (emphasis original)

It seems, therefore, that this textbook is following the common practice of trying to divorce one's personal morality from the objectives of the profession. The authors note, however, that the problem with separating "professional ethics" and "personal ethics" in this way is that we end up basing professional ethics on some changeable standards. They continue:

Professional codes have not always been the same. They have been modified in many areas as a result of changing perceptions of professional obligations. (p. 12)

The authors illustrate these "changing perceptions" by tracing the change in emphasis during the 20th century in the area of professional obligations: whereas early in the century it was held that the engineer's primary responsibility was the protection of the client's or employer's interests, more recent codes of ethics acknowledge also a responsibility to the public. The authors predict that there will be another change also in future such that codes of ethics also recognize a responsibility towards the environment.

If indeed the growing interest in the environment produces desire for change in engineering codes of ethics, there will still be a question of how such codes should be changed. Geisler (1989:294) points out that one's approach to the environment depends on one's worldview. He claims that some atheists show little regard for the preservation of the environment, preferring to "advance society" by means of technology, while others (whom he refers to as pantheists) seem to worship nature and oppose any human interventions that disturb the natural environment. In trying to find a Christian response to this challenge, Geisler (1989:294) notes that

> the Christian believes in the proper respect for and use of natural resources. This respectful utilization of our physical environment grows out of the Christian concept of creation and our divinely appointed obligation to be good stewards of what God has given us.

The problem with this statement is that it will be difficult to interpret for a profession that needs much more specific guidance than is supplied by this principle, accurate though it may be. If there is any desire for a Christian perspective to influence engineering codes of ethics on this topic of respect for the environment, there will need to be considerable Christ-centered inter-disciplinary input into the discussion.

Returning to the topic of "changing perceptions" within the profession, Harris, Pritchard, and Rabins claim that the challenge of this becomes even more acute in the world of international engineering endeavors. Since different cultures assume different ethical perspectives, there is a search for "culture-transcending norms" as a way of trying to ensure that those involved in international engineering projects have a base for communication. Even the authors note, however, that although there may be "norms for at least rudimentary fairness and procedural justice" independent of culture, "not all societies appear to adhere to even this rather restricted set of common values" (p. 247).

A major issue in the international practice of engineering has been the temptation to bribery. This temptation is particularly acute in Civil Engineering, since many international projects are very large, and there is thus a great deal of money being transferred to a variety of recipients. In fact, the Institution of Civil Engineers, in its journal *New*

Civil Engineer (4 November 2004), had this to say about the scale of the problem:

> The European Commission estimates that the global cost of corruption is equivalent to 5% of the world economy. And according to anti-corruption lobby group TI, construction and engineering is the most corrupt business sector in the world.

In response to this situation, the ASCE's Board of Direction, perhaps concerned about US-based engineering corporations becoming uncompetitive in the international arena, took a very pragmatic approach and voted in 1963 to add the following footnote to the Code of Ethics:

> On foreign engineering work, for which only United States engineering firms are to be considered, a member shall order his practice in accordance with the ASCE Code of Ethics. On other engineering works in a foreign country he may adapt his conduct according to the professional standards and customs of that country, but shall adhere as closely as practicable to the principles of the Code.

This footnote became known as the "When in Rome Clause" and clearly opened the possibility of engaging in practices internationally which would not have been permitted in the US. The footnote disappeared from the Code in 1977, which was also the year that the US Congress passed the Foreign Corrupt Practices Act prohibiting bribery by US corporations of foreign officials (Smith, 1999).

The purpose of this discussion of bribery is not to criticize the authors and promoters of any particular Code of Ethics. Rather, it is to highlight the ethical issues within the engineering profession and to illustrate again that Codes of Ethics are not "changeless" either in scope or through history and thus make an unstable and unreliable basis for establishing truth in the discipline.

Rather than attempt a historical study of the development of codes of ethics (or they are sometimes referred to as Rules of Professional Conduct) for the engineering profession, we will examine briefly the way such codes or rules differ internationally. If indeed, there is a truth expressed by these codes, we would expect there to be little difference between such codes in different nations. The comparison in Table 2 (pp. 174–176) is between the code adopted by the US-based American Society of Civil Engineers (ASCE) and that adopted by the Japan

Society of Civil Engineers (JSCE). The value of this comparison is that they were both adopted within about one year of each other.

A few comments on the ASCE code are in order here. First of all, the code makes high-level statements (given in Table 2) that are further explicated by many lower-level, explanatory statements (not presented here) in an attempt to provide greater specificity about (presumably) controversial topics. Further, the code (in contrast to most contemporary Hippocratic Oaths for the medical profession) attempts significant enforcement, specifying penalties for contravening the requirements of the codes and binding members to report violations of which they become aware.

Another observation about the ASCE codes is that there is some reason to believe that, in some respects, the code was written to restrict the practice of engineering rather than to promote ethical behavior of engineers. Why, for example, should the "dignity", "honor", and "prestige" of the engineering profession be promoted in a code of ethics (all of these words are important to the ASCE code)? Or why should a code of ethics delve into unfair competition, apart from a desire to restrict the practices of some members (specifically mentioned in the code)? This is further questioned by the observation of Smith (1999:3) that the ASCE Code of Ethics has sometimes come under scrutiny for antitrust violations by the US Department of Justice.

As we compare the ACSE and JSCE codes, we note first that the codes are addressed very differently. Whereas the ACSE code addresses "engineers" (largely referring to civil engineers as a group), the JSCE code is addressed to engineers as a group of individuals. Thus the JSCE code exhorts each individual to "live up to his/her own beliefs and conscience" and to contribute to society "through his/her knowledge and virtue with an emphasis upon his/her dignity and honor", whereas the ASCE code is more concerned with the integrity, prestige, and dignity of the engineering profession.

Beyond this, however, we note that the codes address different concerns. It is particularly noticeable that the JSCE code addresses issues omitted by the ASCE code, such as the consideration of cultural sensitivities (an interesting observation in a relatively homogeneous society), the comparison of traditional and advanced technologies, and the need to continue dialog between those of differing viewpoints.

The two societies have elevated some different concerns to the level of ethical concerns. While few would disagree with the principles stated, we have already discovered that ethics is an attempt to elucidate truth without resort to spiritual principles. It is helpful to note the

Japanese background to the teaching and promotion of moral values in the wider society, as this helps to understand some of the differences in the codes discussed above. Tomoda (1988:91) observes:

> In contemporary Japan no one would deny that some kind of moral education is necessary at school. . . . The term moral education is controversial, since it was once exploited as a means to realize political goals. There still exists a deep-rooted distrust of pre-war moral education . . . which was used for the indoctrination of ultranationalism and militarism. . . . Furthermore, even if everyone agrees that moral education is necessary, it is not easy to get a consensus about what its content should be. In this diversified society, moral principles supported by one sector of society are not necessarily encouraged by other sectors of society.

This fear of a nationalized moral code helps us understand the JSCE code emphasis on the individual and the need for the individual to live up to his/her own moral code. However, it also shows the impossibility of deriving an international standard of truth without a basis in a common spiritual foundation.

We discovered, during our discussion of medical ethics, that the various codes were inadequate guardians of truth because of their variability through time. (Engineering codes also exhibit this diachronic change, but that is not the object of this discussion.) In our discussion of engineering ethics, we have now discovered a variability of ethics based on nationality (or possibly, culture)—another indicator of the unreliability of such codes to embody truth.

Perhaps the most insightful observation, concerning the search for culture-transcending norms in engineering, returns the reader to Scripture. Even though Harris, Pritchard, and Rabins acknowledge no bias towards a Christian worldview, they make the following statement (pp. 248–249):

> One source [of culture-transcending norms] is the writings of major ethical philosophers and religious teachers. Probably the major guideline from this area is the Golden Rule. The Golden Rule is embraced in some form by most of the major ethical and religious traditions of the world. Using the Golden Rule, one can ask, "How would I want foreign engineers to act in my country if I were a host-country citizen?" This question is not always easy to answer, because it may be difficult to put yourself in the position of a host-country citizen. . . . It is difficult to imagine, for example, that anyone would want to be exploited, or that anyone would not want the traditions of her own country respected. . . .

While the assertion that all major religious traditions embrace some form of the Golden Rule is highly debatable, it is interesting that even the secular perspective of the authors returns them to the Christian Scriptures for a source of dependable authority. It is clear that they have not found any other reliable basis for asserting the basis of truth, even though they prefer not to cite Scripture directly.

CONCLUSION

We have now completed our introductory excursion through the ethical issues faced by higher education in general, as well as by the academic disciplines of medicine and engineering. In each case, the topic has merely been introduced, but sufficient evidence has been given that in no case has the discipline or institution, when approaching ethical issues from a secular perspective, been able to derive a satisfactory, unchanging, international ethical code, which could fairly be represented as a standard of truth. Indeed, in each case examined the opposite has happened—either the discipline has avoided the topic altogether, or it has discovered that such a standard of truth is impossible with the given assumptions. In the case of medicine, we have shown that, over time, the ethical oath taken by doctors has been diluted, so that, in many cases, it is no longer a gate-keeper of appropriate moral standards for practitioners. In the case of engineering, we have shown that codes of ethics have international variability based on cultural understandings of what is appropriate behavior, but they are insufficient in a global economy. These observations are consistent with the hypothesis that it is futile to attempt to use the scientific approach to problems originating in the world of spiritual truth.

We began this paper by noting that in the era prior to the Civil War it was common for university presidents to take an active role in the spiritual and moral education of students. It is perhaps appropriate that we return to this assertion as part of our conclusion. Perlman (1990:382) tries to place the ethical health of a contemporary institution of higher education squarely on the institution's president:

> The president should encourage and promote ethical behavior throughout the institution, both by discouraging bad behavior and [by] encouraging good deeds. The president should see to it that the college is helping to advance understanding about ethical theory and ethical growth. And the president should take pains to exhibit ethical behavior in his or her own affairs.

173

ASCE CODE OF ETHICS (1998) FUNDAMENTAL CANONS	JAPAN SOCIETY OF CIVIL ENGINEERS (1999; RE-ORDERED)
Engineers uphold and advance the integrity, honor and dignity of the engineering profession by: using their knowledge and skill for the enhancement of human welfare and the environment;	A Civil Engineer shall apply his/her technical skills to create, improve, and maintain "a beautiful national land", "a safe and comfortable life", and "a prosperous society", thus contributing to society through his/her knowledge and virtue with an emphasis upon his/her dignity and honor. A Civil Engineer shall respect nature while giving the highest priority to the safety, welfare and health of generations today and in the future, and shall endeavor to preserve and work with nature and the global environment for the sustainable development of mankind.
being honest and impartial and serving with fidelity the public, their employers and clients;	A Civil Engineer shall keep a fair and impartial attitude to the public, clients of civil engineering work, and himself/herself while performing work sincerely. A Civil Engineer shall treat everyone fairly and without any discrimination against race, religion, sex, or age.
striving to increase the competence and prestige of the engineering profession; and supporting the professional and technical societies of their disciplines.	A Civil Engineer shall live up to the Code of Ethics stipulated by the Society while continuously seeking to enhance the status of civil engineers. In particular, members of the Society shall take the initiative of professional dignity by observing this Code of Ethics.

ASCE CODE OF ETHICS (1998) FUNDAMENTAL CANONS	JAPAN SOCIETY OF CIVIL ENGINEERS (1999; RE-ORDERED)
Engineers shall hold paramount the safety, health and welfare of the public and shall strive to comply with the principles of sustainable development in the performance of their professional duties.	A Civil Engineer shall disclose all relevant information concerning public safety, health, welfare, and sustainable global development, in an effort to carry out irreversible civil engineering work that is of long-term and large-scale in nature.
Engineers shall perform services only in areas of their competence.	A Civil Engineer shall perform civil engineering work from a broad perspective based on his/her specialized expertise and experience regardless of his/her organizational affiliation.
Engineers shall issue public statements only in an objective and truthful manner.	A Civil Engineer shall act as an honest agent or trustee of the employer or client in regard to technical work.
Engineers shall act in professional matters for each employer or client as faithful agents or trustees, and shall avoid conflicts of interest.	
Engineers shall build their professional reputation on the merit of their services and shall not compete unfairly with others.	
Engineers shall act in such a manner as to uphold and enhance the honor, integrity, and dignity of the engineering profession and shall act with zero-tolerance for bribery, fraud, and corruption.	A Civil Engineer shall perform work in compliance with applicable laws, ordinances, rules and regulations, contracts, and other standards, and shall and shall not give, ask, nor receive directly or indirectly any undue compensation.
Engineers shall continue their professional development throughout their careers, and shall provide opportunities for the professional development of those engineers under their supervision.	A Civil Engineer shall strive to enhance his/her own expertise, study diligently concepts and engineering methods, and contribute to technological development through informing academic societies of results of these efforts. A Civil Engineer shall endeavor to cultivate human resources by effectively utilizing his/her own personality,

175

ASCE CODE OF ETHICS (1998) FUNDAMENTAL CANONS	JAPAN SOCIETY OF CIVIL ENGINEERS (1999; RE-ORDERED)
	knowledge and experience while providing support for others to enhance their professional proficiency. A Civil Engineer shall value traditional technology rooted in indigenous cultures, engage in research and development of advanced technology, promote international cooperation, deepen mutual understanding of other cultures, and enhance welfare and safety of human beings. A Civil Engineer shall publish reports and express opinions based on his/her accumulated expertise and experience, and live up to his/her own beliefs and conscience. A Civil Engineer shall understand the function, forms, and structural characteristics of civil engineering facilities and structures. In their planning, design, construction, maintenance, and disposal, apply not only advanced technology but traditional technology as well while preserving the ecosystem and the beauty it contains, while staying mindful to preserve historical heritage. A Civil Engineer shall actively explain the significance and role of his/her own work and respond sincerely to any criticism of such explanation. Further, he/she shall evaluate objectively the work completed by himself/herself and by others, and express positively individual opinions.

Table 2: Comparison of Codes of Ethics from American Society of Civil Engineers and Japan Society of Civil Engineers

Few would argue with the claim that the president serves as a role model for the institution and that the "tone at the top" is very important in any institution. However, Perlman gives few guidelines for determining the ethical values that should be promoted at an institution of higher education. It is thus unfair to expect a university president to be responsible for the ethical health of his or her institution, when the institution itself cannot determine the basis of its own ethical decisions.

It is the opinion of the author that biblical standards provide an adequate basis for developing a satisfactory criterion for truth and that no other standard will ultimately prove acceptable. In this they are joined by Laney (1990:59), who asserts that

> the wisdom of our forebears must guide the strategies and hopes of those of us in higher education today. We can begin by recalling that we are the heirs of a tradition that found in higher education a high moral calling. And we can remind ourselves that part of what we are called to is stewardship of our institutions as a dwelling place for the human spirit. . . .

In attempting to answer the question posed by this paper—Is there one criterion of truth in higher education?—we have been forced to acknowledge the atomizing of higher education into its constituent disciplines, even as the enterprise has remained organized as a series of institutions (usually organized by location rather than discipline). We have noted that, whether we consider the search for truth as an institutional imperative or an imperative for each academic discipline, the answer is the same: it is impossible to derive standards of truth from a secular perspective (i.e, without a faith-based set of assumptions), and yet it is entirely reasonable once we allow the distinction between natural truth and spiritual truth. To some this will be a surprising conclusion, since many expect science, as the queen of the disciplines, to be able to derive truth using the scientific technique.

On the basis of our investigation, we can go one step further than this to note that, in many cases, even secular investigators are forced back to a biblical standard, rather than merely to any standard with a religious basis. Sometimes this manifests itself as (for example) promotion of the Golden Rule, while at other times the reference might be to spiritual traditions. Whatever the precise reference, however, it seems clear that only a biblical standard shows promise for deriving an enduring criterion of truth in higher education.

REFERENCES

Brainard, Jeffrey, 2006. Universities experiment with classes in scientific ethics: pilot programs tackle a difficult topic amid questions about such education's efficacy. Chronicle of Higher Education, Vol 53, Issue 12, p A22, November 10, 2006. http://chronicle.com/weekly/v53/i12/12a02201.htm

Cox, Harvey G., 2004. When Jesus came to Harvard: making moral choices today. Houghton Mifflin: New York, NY.

Cummings, William K., Gopinathan, G., and Tomoda, Yasumasa (editors), 1988. The revival of values education in Asia and the West. Comparative and International Education Series, Volume 7. Permagon Press: Elmsford, NY.

Geisler, Norman L., 1989. Christian ethics: options and issues. Baker: Grand Rapids, MI.

Harris, Charles E., Jr, Pritchard, Michael S, Rabins, Michael J., 2005. Engineering ethics : concepts and cases, third ed. Thomson Wadsworth: Belmont, CA.

Jennings, Marianne, 2008. Overcoming the culture's influence in young people: a look at how we might realign post-modernist's progeny with the pursuit of virtue ethics. Presentation at AAPICU Conference, Scottsdale, AZ. Feb. 2008. http://www.aapicu.org/documents/AAPICU%20Feb%2021.ppt

Labi, Aisha, 2007. Corruption in education is growing worldwide, UNESCO reports. Chronicle of Higher Education, Vol 53, Issue 41, p A42, June 15, 2007.

http://chronicle.com/weekly/v53/i41/41a04202.htm

Laney, James T., Through thick and thin— two ways of talking about the academy and moral responsibility. In May, 1990:49–66.

May, William W. (ed.), 1990. Ethics and higher education. American Council on Education, and Macmillan: New York, NY.

Orr, R.D., 1998. The Hippocratic oath: is it still relevant? Loma Linda University. http://www.llu.edu/llu/bioethics/update/u141b.htm

Orr, R. D., N. Pang, E. D. Pellegrino, and M. Siegler. 1997. Use of the Hippocratic Oath: A Review of Twentieth Century Practice and a Content Analysis of Oaths Administered in Medical Schools in the U.S. and Canada in 1993. *The Journal of Clinical Ethics* 8 (Winter): 377–388

Perlman, Daniel H., 1990. Ethical challenges of the college and university presidency. In May, 1990: 364–385.

Ross, David A., 2008. Does "truth" exist?—a linguistic approach to the rationalism/postmodern debate. Journal of Christian Higher Education, Vol 7, No 3, July–August 2008: 253–269.

Russell, Bertrand, 1946. Reply to criticisms; in The Philosophy of Bertrand Russell, ed. Paul Arthur Schilpp. Library of Living Philosophers: Evanston, IL.

SACS, 2008. Principles of accreditation: foundations for quality enhancement. Southern Association of Colleges and Schools, Commission on Colleges: Decatur, GA.

Schmidt, George P.,1930. The old time college president. Columbia University Press: New York, NY.

Singer, M.G., 2002. The idea of a rational morality: philosophical compositions. Oxford University Press: Oxford.

Smith, Thomas W., 1999. ASCE ethics: edicts, enforcement and education. www.asce.org/files/pdf/global/asceethics.pdf

Tomoda, Yasumasa, 1988. Politics and moral education in Japan. Chapter 5, in Cummings, William, Gopinathan, and Tomoda, Yasumasa, 1988.

Trueblood, D. Elton, 1988. The moral basis for medical science. Christian Dental and Medical Society Journal, Winter/Spring 1988; XIX(1):5–7.

Wasley, Paula, 2008. Survey: Colleges fall short in teaching morals, ethics. Vol 54, Issue 34, p A21, May 2, 2008. http://chronicle.com/weekly/v54/i34/34a02101.htm

10

How to Think about Intelligent Design: Modern Science and the Christian Worldview

David H. Leonard

Introduction

While Intelligent Design (ID) proponents are eager to distance their hypothesis from the peculiarities of religious doctrine, much in their writings is congruent with a Christian worldview perspective. One can certainly endorse the conclusions of ID without being religiously oriented; but for those who gravitate toward some version of theism there is sufficient motivation for embracing this account of physical reality. Nevertheless, a fair number of scientists and philosophers have expressed doubts concerning the legitimacy of the intelligent design project.

The basis for many of these doubts is the perception that the design inference, though perhaps intelligible and reasonable from a certain perspective, fails to fall under the umbrella of *bona fide* scientific inquiry. Central to this criticism is a particular view concerning the nature of the scientific enterprise: that science deals exclusively with empirical data and direct observation and therefore cannot be expected to consider the existence of any supernatural entities. Indeed, even some Christian scientists have employed this attitude: God most probably

David H. Leonard <dleonard@uark.edu> is a philosophy lecturer at the University of Arkansas and the Northwest Arkansas Community College. He is completing a doctoral dissertation at the University of Arkansas that explores the connections between the intellectual virtues and contemporary theories of knowledge and has presented scholarly papers for the International Institute of Christian Studies, the Evangelical Philosophical Society, and the Baptist Association of Philosophy Teachers. David holds the BA from Iowa State University and the MA from Denver Seminary.

does exist, and the universe, as a result, is quite plausibly character-ized by order and purpose. Yet however sensible this perspective may be, it is not the job of modern science to explicate it, or so the argument often goes.

One of the purposes of this essay is to call into question this nar-row understanding of scientific method by highlighting the relative failure of philosophers of science to specify the conditions that are nec-essary and sufficient for an activity to qualify as science. In light of this failure, it is strikingly misleading for critics to thrust the "pseudo-science" label upon ID theory, as if scientists knew exactly which fea-tures distinguished science from non-science. Contrary to the popular criticisms, ID theorists do, in fact, derive their conclusions from ob-servations of the physical data, making their methodology every bit as scientific as the practices involved in forensic science as well as the various social sciences.

This lack of consensus regarding the true nature of the scientific enterprise provides an opportunity for Christians to incorporate their worldview into their understanding and practice of science. Given the fact that contemporary views concerning science are heavy laden with philosophical assumptions that cannot be confirmed by scientific method, it follows that there are sources of knowledge, known inde-pendently from empirical observation, which can serve to inform not only our understanding of the world, but also the nature of the meth-odologies employed in seeking that understanding. In short, within the details of the Christian worldview there exists the adequate impe-tus for constructing a holistic model of the scientific enterprise, and the current debate over intelligent design provides the fertile ground for developing such an approach.

Having reflected on this subject, it strikes me that hardly anyone can articulate, on purely philosophical grounds, why the ID hypoth-esis should be excluded from the marketplace of scientific ideas. One might wonder why it is necessary to use philosophical themes in at-tempting to meet this challenge; and the simple response is that the very act of claiming that ID represents pseudo-science is itself philo-sophical in orientation: the ability to effectively analyze the design in-ference inevitably appeals to philosophical discourse and reasoning. And it is precisely within the scope of philosophical speculation that a plausible argument can be marshaled for viewing ID as legitimate science.

Nevertheless, the common criticisms leveled against ID theory, while perhaps somewhat misguided and confused, do highlight the relative failure of the design inference to persuade most scientists and philosophers. While it is tempting to attribute this lack of success to brute prejudice and bias, the most insightful critical literature suggests there are additional concerns with ID that have little to do with dogmatic commitments to philosophical naturalism or *a priori* discomfort with notions of supernatural entities.

In light of these particular concerns, this essay will challenge the proponents of ID to incorporate the concept of design into their scientific methodology, but in a way that treats design as a guiding premise or presupposition, rather than a deduction or inference to the best explanation. In this way, Christian scientists and all practitioners who are sympathetic to the design inference can satisfy both the demands of their faith commitment and the established methodology of their discipline. In short, treating design as a guiding presupposition or meta-theory allows for science to be informed by religious doctrine, while at the same time remaining firmly entrenched in a naturalistic methodology.

THE DEMARCATION PROBLEM

How, then, are we to understand the nature of the scientific discipline? This question raises the so-called "demarcation problem," which involves the task of citing the conditions which must be satisfied for an activity to qualify as legitimate science. It goes without saying that this challenge is fundamental and is directly pertinent to the ID debate. If scientists are capable of specifying, in non-arbitrary fashion, the objective features of genuine scientific inquiry, and the methodology of ID fails to conform to those features, then it trivially follows that ID is unscientific, no matter how *prima facie* reasonable its conclusions might be. Such a consequence, of course, would represent the deathblow to ID theory, since its proponents are eager to insist that their methodology is perfectly compatible with currently accepted scientific practices.

Nevertheless, philosophers of science are virtually uniform in the conviction that no line of demarcation exists between science and non-science. Indeed, all attempts to solve the problem have resulted in conceptions of science that are either too restrictive or too permissive in their scope: the definition either excludes some intuitively legitimate scientific practice or includes a system that is obviously pseudo-scientific in its orientation. There is a strong sense of irony in this insight, and the well-known ID advocate Steven Meyer has pointed out that

> The use by evolutionary biologists of so-called demarcation arguments . . . is both ironic and problematic from the point of view

of philosophy of science. It is ironic because many of the demarcation criteria that have been used against non-naturalistic theories of origin can be deployed with equal warrant against strictly naturalistic evolutionary theories. Indeed, a corpus of literature now exists devoted to assessing whether neo-Darwinism . . . is scientific when measured against various conceptions of science.[1]

Attempts to solve the demarcation problem tend, invariably it seems, to produce counterintuitive results for the task of grounding our understanding of the scientific discipline. While it is important to possess at least a general comprehension of the various criteria that have been cited over the years, it is not within the scope of this essay to adequately describe and analyze the major options. At any rate, it is important to know that, from the verifiability criterion of the logical positivists to Karl Popper's influential theory of falsification and to the more contemporary deductive-nomological model, there is no single account of scientific inquiry that is widely accepted by practicing scientists and philosophers of science.

Thus, however science is to be understood, it must primarily be characterized as an organic methodology for discovering the truth—one that is rigorously sensitive to the insights of tradition, but intimately aware of the social factors that give rise to the endorsement of such tradition. The conclusions of current scientific practice, as well as the methodologies employed in arriving at these conclusions, are inherently tentative and open to reform and refutation. As the late chemist and economist Michael Polanyi has related, the conjectures embodied in natural science are not deductively inferred from any *a priori* rules concerning the data of experience. But rather, "they are first arrived at by a form of guessing based on premises which are by no means inescapable and cannot even be clearly defined."[2]

Of course, scientists are not infallible and their pronouncements must, therefore, be accepted with a grain of salt, particularly if 'guesswork' is as essential to scientific practice as Polanyi has suggested. The salient point is that even if there existed considerable agreement concerning the boundaries of scientific practice, this common understanding would lack the canonical status that most practitioners of the discipline think it should possess. Scientific inquiry is, first and foremost, a socially constructed approach to obtaining knowledge about

---

1 Steven Meyer, "The Scientific Status of Intelligent Design," in *Science and Evidence for Design in the Universe*, Michael Behe, William Dembski, and Steven Meyer, eds. (San Francisco: Ignatius Press, 2000), p. 153.

2 Michael Polanyi, *Science, Faith and Society* (Chicago: University of Chicago Press, 1946), p. 42.

the physical world. Now it is also an approach which has proven particularly successful over the years, and so there is considerable pragmatic impetus for championing its continued implementation. But its conclusions and methodologies are always subject to correction and modification, and this insight must be firmly kept in mind when considering the ID controversy.

SCIENCE AND PHILOSOPHY

Most contemporary scientists are unaware of the fact that their discipline rests on a number of key philosophical assumptions that, if false, would jeopardize the very scientific enterprise that they promote. For example, it is often taken for granted that the universe exhibits an orderly nature and, therefore, it is possible to know its physical character at some level. But this premise has been hotly debated in philosophical circles: Immanuel Kant, for example, posited a metaphysical distinction between the *noumenal* world (the world as it really is) and the *phenomenal* world (the world as it appears to us), with the consequence that one could never get beyond mere appearances to grasp the true nature of reality. Yet such a distinction proves absolutely fatal to the scientific realist, for the laws of science would not describe a mind-independent world, but merely the structure of our consciousness in the world we experience. That is, these laws would be "the way we must experience the *phenomenal* world, the way in which the categories of the knowing subject take the chaotic input from the *noumenal* world, subsume and classify it, and create an ordered world of experience."[3]

If the so-called "order of nature" is merely an appearance of reality and therefore not indicative of reality itself, then why believe that our scientific theories are accurate in describing the structures of the universe? And if we cannot be ultimately justified in believing in their overall accuracy, then it would follow that such theories are inherently empty and entirely unhelpful. To be clear, the point is not to defend or condemn this perspective, but merely to draw attention to the fact that a major assumption of science is based on a rather controversial metaphysical position. And the debate over epistemological realism represents just one arena for demonstrating the relevance of philosophy for scientific understanding.

What follows from this observation? At the very least, it suggests that there are sources of knowledge and insight that are available independent of the scientific method. To think otherwise is to implicitly endorse the doctrine known as "scientism": the view that only the natural

---

3 J. P. Moreland, *Christianity and the Nature of Science* (Grand Rapids: Baker Books, 1989), p. 112.

sciences can provide one with genuine knowledge about reality. In its strongest form, scientism employs a strict verifiability criterion, insisting that those items outside the scope of empirical investigation are not worthy of intellectual assent. To wit, a proposition or theory is true and rational only if it is empirically testable.

But if only empirically-based science can provide genuine knowledge, then this very position is false, since it clearly cannot be tested by an experiment nor scrutinized by scientific methodology. The statement itself implies its logical denial—that it is not the case that only science provides genuine knowledge—and is therefore self-referentially incoherent. The promoter of scientism may continue to maintain that the view is still true, but this entails her appealing to some criteria outside of science to justify that position. Scientism is not, strictly speaking, a scientific position but rather a philosophical position *about* science.

Given these arguments, it follows quite clearly that the fundamental criticism of ID, that it represents pseudo-science, is incorrect and misguided. Recall that the basis for this criticism is the view that science deals only with direct observation and experimentation, and therefore the alleged existence of any supernatural entities necessarily falls outside its proper domain. However, this criticism cannot account for the following facts: 1) that there are no universally accepted conditions for science, in which case such criticism appeals to a criterion which simply does not exist; and 2) that which currently passes as genuine science is ultimately grounded in philosophy, in which case such criticism assumes a methodology which is impossible to satisfy. In short, if ID theory is susceptible to any criticism at all, its weakness must lie in something other than the mere fact that it appeals to the existence of a supernatural entity.

Intelligent Design and Its Critics

With these specific points in mind, let us now consider their relevance for the theory of intelligent design. According to the leading ID proponent, William Dembski, the design inference is essentially the view that "only intelligent causes adequately explain the complex, information-rich structures of biology and that these causes are empirically detectable."[4] Dembski helpfully explains ID by comparing it to the strategies employed by the astronomers depicted in the film *Contact*. Just as these scientists were justified in attributing intelligence to the radio signal from outer space, so scientists, in general,

---

4 William Dembski, *The Design Revolution* (Downers Grove, Ill.: InterVarsity Press, 2004), p. 34.

are warranted to make a similar inference with respect to the specified complexity of biological entities and other facets of the universe.

Dembski, as well as other ID advocates, have been clear to distinguish between this theory and the traditional doctrine of creationism. It is argued that one can have creation without intelligent design, as well as intelligent design without creation. So it is simply unfair to portray ID as inherently religious in nature, since someone could hold to ID without believing in any transcendent deity. And one certainly could ascribe to ID without being a Christian committed to biblical creationism, although as mentioned earlier, there is much in the details of ID theory which is congruent with the Christian worldview. The central point, however, is that the overall merits of ID are independent from whatever motives generated its development. And what is more, ID theorists insist that their commitment to ID is derived from the empirical data, and is not evidentially grounded in any religious presuppositions. As Dembski carefully articulates,

> The opposition of design theorists to Darwinian theory rests in the first instance on strictly scientific grounds. Yes, we are interested in and frequently write about the theological and cultural implications of Darwinism's imminent demise and replacement by intelligent design. . . . But the only reason we take seriously such implications is because we are convinced that Darwinism is on its own terms an oversold and overreaching scientific theory.[5]

Of course, ID critics are typically unimpressed with this explanation and continue to maintain that ID, despite its initial appeal, fails to qualify as legitimate scientific inquiry. A common line of justification for this conviction is that ID is just a thinly veiled theological position, making use of scientific language to cloud its true purpose and identity. As Barbara Forrest, the influential critic of ID, has stated, science is merely the façade behind which ID proponents are attempting to stage what is primarily a cultural or social revolution. They are not presenting their work at conferences or in scholarly journals, but rather are focusing their efforts in the legal courts and through popularized forms of multi-media.[6]

But surely this is a most uncharitable interpretation of the motives and methodologies of ID proponents. Given the theory's relative

---

5 William Dembski, "What Intelligent Design is Not," in *Signs of Intelligence*, William Dembski and James Kushiner, eds. (Grand Rapids: Brazos Press, 2001), p. 12.

6 Barbara Forrest, "The Wedge at Work" in *Intelligent Design Creationism and Its Critics*, ed. Robert Pennock (Cambridge: Massachusetts Institute of Technology, 2001), p. 32.

novelty in scientific circles, it is only to be expected that significant opposition will be exercised from the pulpit of the scientific establishment, resulting in widespread difficulty to gain a hearing in the major academic journals and to receive invitations to speak at the most prestigious scientific conferences. Again, if the common perception among practitioners of science is that ID is a pseudo-scientific hypothesis and if these same practitioners are the individuals who exercise control over which views are allowed expression in the public life of the discipline, then it's hardly fair to point to ID's lack of visibility in the journals and conferences as evidence for its unscientific status.

To be fair to the critics, not all counterarguments leveled against ID take this misleading approach. Some scientists are careful to avoid both making claims about objective standards for scientific inquiry and pronouncing judgments about the personal motives of ID advocates. Instead, they focus on analyzing the claims of ID on their own terms. For example, the University of Wisconsin philosopher, Elliot Sober, has offered a penetrating critique of Michael Behe's theory of "irreducible complexity," which aims to show the weaknesses in his appeal to the bacterial flagellum as evidence of design.[7] Similarly, the Italian geneticist, Massimo Pigliucci, has effectively demonstrated the limitations of William Dembski's explanatory filter for detecting intelligent design.[8]

In these criticisms and others, the general consensus seems to be that ID, because of its implicit appeal to the supernatural to explain biological phenomena, represents a genuine "science stopper" by discouraging the search for further naturalistic causes to explain the phenomena in question. In other words, if some biological feature is to be explained by appeals to ID, then such explanation represents the final link in the causal chain, and there is no more work for science to do in pursuing an understanding of the material processes involved. But surely it is possible, with respect to any given biological entity, that a naturalistic explanation of its origin is forthcoming, despite initial appearances to the contrary. Scientists should, therefore, be encouraged to continue their various research projects in the hopes that such natural explanations are just around the corner.

Nevertheless, it is one thing to argue that ID, as a genuine scientific hypothesis, simply fails to convince that its conclusions are likely to be true or represent a legitimate alternative to evolutionary theory;

---

7 Elliot Sober, "What is Wrong with Intelligent Design?" *The Quarterly Review of Biology*, Vol. 82, No. 1, pp. 3–8.

8 Massimo Pigliucci, "Design Yes, Intelligent No," in *Darwinism, Design, and Public Education*, John Angus Campbell and Steven Meyer, eds. (East Lansing: Michigan State University, 2003), pp. 463–73.

it is another thing to claim that ID is nothing more than pseudo-science and is therefore not even worthy of scientific scrutiny. One of the points I wish to make is that insofar as the former claim is reasonable and worth considering, the latter assertion is, in an important sense, alarmingly close-minded and ignorant in light of the current state of the philosophy of science.

In short, that much of what currently passes as legitimate science is so tightly connected to questionable philosophical presuppositions and that scientists themselves cannot agree on which features constitute necessary and sufficient conditions for science suggests that there is virtually no foundation upon which to claim that ID fails to represent *bona fide* science. And this paves the way not only for a reconsideration of the plausibility of the design inference, but also a return to an understanding of science firmly rooted in the Christian worldview—perhaps despite the request of ID advocates that religion *not* play a motivating role in scientific inquiry.

MODERN SCIENCE AND THE CHRISTIAN WORLDVIEW

Much confusion exists regarding the relationship between science and religion. It is often argued that one cannot be both scientific and religious at the same time, since the conclusions of these two fields are inevitably in conflict. Though there may certainly be instances in which the conclusions of science come into conflict with Christianity, does it follow that these two fields are necessarily at odds? The first proponents of science would find such a conclusion shocking, as it was firmly believed that the purpose of science was to study and reflect on God's orderly creation. As Alfred North Whitehead has explained concerning the origin of modern science in Europe, "faith in the possibility of science, generated antecedently to the development of modern scientific theory, is an unconscious derivative from medieval theology."[9]

One of the central theses of this essay is that Christian faith, far from being antithetical to scientific endeavors, actually provides good justification for the practices and assumptions of science. In other words, science itself is very much at home within the framework of a Christian worldview, and it is seemingly peculiar and out of place with respect to a materialistic view of reality. For instance, the uniformity of nature is also presupposed by most scientists. As argued earlier, such a presupposition can only be justified by appealing to philosophical concepts and categories. And it is clear that Scripture tells us of God's

---

9 Alfred North Whitehead, *Science and the Modern World* (New York: Macmillan Company, 1925), pp. 12–13.

faithfulness in governing the cosmos. If such is the case, then we should only expect that nature is predictable and uniform, since it is presided over by a God who does not change. Science also assumes that nature is comprehensible; that is, that we can understand its intricate workings at some level. And of course, this would be well accounted for if God created our cognitive faculties, and that the reason by which we try to understand the world was also created by him.[10]

So if one is inclined to accept a realist understanding of science, then Christianity would certainly fit in well with such a position. In fact, if a decent argument for realism is forthcoming, then the Christian need not feel pressured to compartmentalize her faith with respect to scientific beliefs. The point is that Christianity and science seem to have much more in common than is typically assumed. Indeed, when one explores the various foundations of science it becomes clear that Christianity actually provides, at least at first glance, a better metaphysical foundation than the rival naturalistic system. How could a proponent of naturalism ever be confident that her sensory and cognitive abilities are working properly and accurately representing reality? It seems difficult to imagine how such confidence is possible. Yet for the Christian, the belief in God provides the ultimate justification for scientific pursuits—it is precisely because God exists that science represents a promising enterprise.

A Modest Proposal for Intelligent Design

But there is another way to incorporate the Christian worldview into the practice of scientific inquiry, and it is this insight which represents the primary thesis of this essay. The approach just described treats Christianity as an explanatory model for making sense of physical reality. But like any such model, the Christian account is subject to challenges and refutations. Why is that the case? Precisely because the facts which it attempts to clarify can, in theory, be explained by appeals to other competing systems. And this is true even if the Christian model seems best suited for explaining our experience of the world. Not surprising, the design inference suffers from a similar sort of weakness: the fact of biological complexity might, in theory, be better explained by mechanisms other than ID. In recent years, in spite of the best attempts to give the design inference a fair hearing, most practicing scientists remain unconvinced that ID theory represents a very compelling scientific hypothesis.

Perhaps the primary difficulty for the ID movement is that it treats the notion of design as the inference or conclusion of its argument,

---

10 See Del Ratzsch, *Science and Its Limits*, 2nd ed. (Downers Grove, Ill.: InterVarsity Press, 2000).

rather than as one of the supporting premises or presuppositions. If the universe is truly characterized by design, then we should expect the world and its inhabitants to be characterized by biological complexity. And so the possibility of design could represent a guiding principle in the practice of scientific inquiry. But we should not necessarily expect such design to manifest itself in the physical world, at least not in the manner preferred by ID theorists. The problem of induction is relevant at this point: any claims concerning the presence of design in the physical world will be unavoidably fragile in their epistemic strength and always capable of being explained away by various naturalistic features.

Again, let's suppose that the universe is, in fact, designed. Surely if that were the case, then biological entities would manifest such design in their various physical qualities. But the problem is that the antecedent of this hypothetical proposition, namely, that the universe is designed, is unavoidably difficult to demonstrate or prove. Why is that the case? Because such a proof would be required to show the designer's role as the *efficient* cause of the biological complexity of the universe, whereas the available evidence, being based on the empirical data, is limited merely to the *material* causes. It may be that an intelligent designer is responsible for the so-called irreducibly complex systems in our world, but that fact could never be sufficiently demonstrated by appeals to their natural features.

But the problem is not that arguments concerning the existence of supernatural entities are categorically inappropriate or somehow fail to satisfy the conditions for genuine scientific inquiry. Rather, the problem is that the material causes that are cited for explaining these phenomena are consistent with any number of alleged efficient causes. And furthermore, it might very well be the case that the material cause is identical to the efficient cause, in which case appealing to the efficient cause provides no new insight into the structure of the universe. In short, the primary difficulty facing ID is philosophical, rather than scientific in nature. And there is a bit of irony here: while it is philosophy that is needed to show that ID is genuine science, it is also philosophy that is sufficient for demonstrating that ID is inadequate science.

It seems the only way to avoid this epistemic handicap is to broaden the emphasis to highlight the general features of the world, rather than the specific qualities possessed by individual entities *in* the world. For instance, there is a difference between arguing, on the one hand, that complex biological structures exhibit signs of intelligent design and, on the other hand, that the fact of the universe's contingency requires a supernatural being to adequately explain its existence. Both arguments are, in an important sense, based on empirical observation. Yet the former argument is limited in ways the latter argument is not.

As already explained, an organism's physical features might be sufficiently accounted for by the material causes that contributed to its existence. But the same line of retreat is not available with respect to the typical argument from contingency. The goal here is not to explain a single part of the universe, but rather to explain the universe itself: why does something exist rather than nothing? To cite as an answer to this question the material causes that gave rise to the universe is to miss the point entirely, as the same question would be pushed back further to apply to these material entities as well. With this kind of argument, the efficient cause is distinct from the material cause, a fact that clearly does not necessarily obtain with respect to the design inference. One of the problems with the ID hypothesis, from a philosophical perspective, is that the mere possibility of a material cause for explaining biological complexity represents an adequate defeater for the view that the efficient cause must be non-material. But to be clear, it is not the positing of a supernatural entity, *tout court*, which renders ID philosophically problematic. Rather, the design inference is judged unsound because of where, in the physical realm, it specifies that the act of design took place.

It is this important distinction between material and efficient causes that, at least implicitly, drives some of the criticism leveled against ID. The bacterial flagellum, for instance, despite claims to the contrary, is really not irreducibly complex. Its impressive features can be adequately explained by appeals to naturalistic causes, and evolutionary biologists often take these causes to be efficient in orientation as well. This insight, however, doesn't necessarily suggest that design is not a related feature of biological systems. Rather, the conclusion is that established methods, whether philosophical or scientific, are simply incapable of demonstrating the presence of design in such systems.

But why should this conclusion be particularly surprising or troublesome? After all, it stands to reason that if design is present in the universe, then this fact will probably manifest itself in the complex structure of physical entities. But it doesn't follow that because these entities display such complex structure, it is therefore the case that they are designed. In other words, while specified complexity is a necessary condition for the presence of design, it is not a sufficient condition—the fact of biological complexity doesn't guarantee that design represents the best explanation.

So the order of inquiry ought to be inverted: rather than beginning with the raw physical data of experience and trying to infer design from its features, we ought to begin with the hypothesis that design is present in the universe and allow that starting point to guide our investigations accordingly. Philosopher of science Robin Collins, in an unpublished paper, employs a similar methodology when he suggests that design be treated as a "meta-scientific" theory. In his view, the design inference, when used in this fashion, "allows for a whole range of theories of life's origin and nature that would tend to be excluded . . . on a naturalistic metaphysics."[11] For instance, scientists point out that a large percentage of the human genome consists of so-called "junk DNA," which is, very simply, that portion of the genetic sequence for which no function seems to exist. From an evolutionary perspective, such junk DNA is perfectly unproblematic, since the blind mechanism of natural selection would not necessarily find all portions of the genome advantageous or useful. Nevertheless, the scientist who is guided by the design premise might be motivated to consider the matter further: if the world of microbiology is intimately guided by an intelligent designer, then all DNA sequences will be purposeful and capable of serving some function. The task of the scientist informed by this premise, therefore, would be to discover the nature of that function, despite present appearances that no such function exists.

While I'm certainly inclined to embrace Collins' suggestion here, I would also prefer to broaden his understanding of a "meta-scientific" theory to include, not only the theory of design, but the Christian worldview itself: if Christian theism were true, then of course the universe would be characterized by design, and it would be only natural to expect some measure of order and regularity in the cosmos. That expectation, in turn, could motivate the search for specific answers to questions regarding the regulation of physical events. But the implications of treating Christianity as a "meta-scientific" theory would not be limited to design, and its application would certainly extend beyond the fields of physics and biology.

Such an approach, no doubt, would model the practice of the first "natural philosophers," who were explicitly driven by their theological convictions to discover the underlying reality of the physical universe. But there was no reason, from their perspective, to defend that starting point. Again, Christianity wasn't the conclusion of an argument, but rather an initial premise or guiding hypothesis. And so the scientist would seek to validate that original presupposition in his ongoing analysis and experimentation. But at no point in this methodology was

---

11 Robin Collins, "A Critical Evaluation of the Intelligent Design Program: An Analysis and a Proposal," Unpublished paper, 1998.

there anything like an argument or defense for the Christian world-view—or at least such an argument was not necessary to adequately engage the discipline.

Roy Clouser, in his thought-provoking work *The Myth of Religious Neutrality*, argues for something along these lines when he considers the role that belief in God should play in shaping theories:

> Our belief in God as the sole divinity, exercises its most profound and pervasive influence by regulating and guiding how we should think of the natures of creaturely things, including the entities proposed by any hypothesis. By acting as a presupposition to all theory making . . . belief in God can guide every theory and do it in a more pervasive and important way.[12]

One might be uncomfortable with this mentality, precisely because it seems to intimate a dogmatic and fundamentalist application of religious belief to the natural sciences and other disciplines. But while this concern is understandable, it ultimately misunderstands the nature of Clouser's methodology, in which he is trying very carefully to distinguish his approach from fundamentalism. The fundamentalist, argues Clouser, is trying to explain the features of the conditions that produce natural events in a way that necessarily brings God into the explanation. But Scripture doesn't teach that because of God's causal role in the world, scientific investigations will necessarily result in the discovery of inexplicable gaps with no naturalistic explanation. Rather, God is best understood as the *efficient* cause of the universe, with naturalistic explanations playing the role of *material* cause.

In this way, there are at least two answers to the essential question, 'What caused this entity to exist?' One answer points to the fact that God's will and power are ultimately responsible for the existence and structure of physical reality; whereas the other answer provides an account of the means through which God exercised this will and power. Both answers provide insight and knowledge concerning the nature of the cosmos, and yet they clearly use a different methodology in doing so. Indeed, both answers are equally scientific in their orientation, yet only one is capable of being adequately demonstrated through current methodologies.

As Clouser points out, the biblical view is not that natural events and entities, owing their dependence to God, are all fundamentally inexplicable as objects of rational or scientific scrutiny, but that none of

---

12 Roy Clouser, *The Myth of Religious Neutrality* (Notre Dame: University of Notre Dame Press), p. 115.

these events and entities would exist unless God had engineered them and continued to hold them together. This suggests a way of thinking about modern science and the Christian worldview that respects both the naturalistic methodology ingrained in current scientific practice, as well as the intuitive desire to integrate faith with learning. But again, accepting this approach requires a particular conception of the causal role that God plays in creation: "while God is the creator of the causal order which allows us to explain rainfall, he is not himself one of its causes alongside all the other causes—not even its first cause. Strictly speaking, God is not the *cause* of the universe, but the creator of *all the kinds of causality* in the universe."[13]

This mentality, when manifested and applied in scientific practice, would fall perfectly within the boundaries of contemporary inquiry. From the standpoint of methodology, there would be practically no difference between the materialist scientist and the Christian counterpart. To be clear, there might be significant differences regarding the kinds of questions that the Christian asks and how those questions serve to shape the direction that the research ultimately takes. But this is no reason to think that the methodology itself is fundamentally flawed or that the final conclusions are somehow suspect or thereby called into question. The myth of scientific objectivity has been sufficiently established, and it is beyond idealistic to think that projects can be initiated and employed without various background beliefs playing a critical role.

CONCLUSION

On the one hand, the claim that ID represents pseudo-science is unfounded, given the abject failure of philosophers of science to specify the necessary and sufficient conditions of scientific method. And in light of the fact that the ultimate justification for scientific practice comes from philosophy, rather than science itself, this suggests there are sources of knowledge that transcend the empirically observable. The design inference points to an incorporeal entity, incapable of being directly detected by scientific method. In theory, there might be compelling reasons for thinking that such an entity exists, and inference to the best explanation is one avenue through which to substantiate this claim. As such, the process of defending the ID hypothesis, in a very important sense, is thoroughly scientific in nature, even if it involves the use of non-observational based methods of inquiry.

On the other hand, there is some reason to think that ID critics are partially justified in their criticisms of the design inference. Perhaps it

---

13 Ibid.

is correct to be suspicious of arguments that purport to demonstrate the existence of entities that, in principle, are incapable of being empirically detected. It is certainly the case that design arguments, like those employed by ID theorists, are strikingly confused in their attempts to ground the design inference in the specific details of biological organisms. At the very least, it is understandable that critics feel that appeals to design represent "science stoppers" in that they will tend to discourage further analysis of the causal features of the universe. Insofar as science is traditionally centered on the desire to explain the causal connections between various entities and events in the universe, practitioners of this discipline will quite naturally be frustrated with perceived attempts to stifle their progress.

What I have suggested in this essay is a middle ground between these two competing intuitions. Instead of treating the notion of design as the conclusion of an argument or analysis, we should treat it as a guiding principle or hypothesis that provides the conceptual impetus to pursue the relevant projects. Or to speak more broadly, treat the Christian worldview itself as the guiding principle or hypothesis, and thereby position scholars to infuse their religious faith into not only the practice of science but other academic disciplines as well. Such an approach, no doubt, would carry scholarship into some surprising and fruitful directions and, above all, would enable the Christian academician to exemplify the kind of holism and integration that is most becoming of a follower of Christ.

11

MAKING A DIFFERENCE: JOHN GRISHAM AS A CHRISTIAN NOVELIST

John J. Han & Mary C. Bagley

INTRODUCTION

In a recent interview with the Associated Press, the best-selling novelist John Grisham remarked that he writes fiction only for entertainment: "I'm not sure where that line goes between literature and popular fiction. I can assure you I don't take myself serious enough to think I'm writing literary fiction and stuff that's going to be remembered in 50 years. I'm not going to be here in 50 years; I don't care if I'm remembered or not. It's pure entertainment" ("John Grisham"). Despite his diffident public posture, Grisham is not just a popular novelist who tries to please his readers for commercial gain. While the elements of

John J. Han <hanjn@mobap.edu> is professor of English & Creative Writing and chair of the Humanities Division at Missouri Baptist University. He is the author of numerous articles, reference entries, and book reviews, and his poems and creative nonfiction have appeared in the *Mainichi Daily News* (Tokyo), *Mid Rivers Review, Kansas English, the St. Louis Anthology of Verse,* and *In Other Words.* He edits *Intégrité: A Faith and Learning Journal,* for *Cantos: A Literary and Arts Magazine,* and the Rodopi Press collection of critical essays on O'Connor's *Wise Blood.* In addition to a BA and an MEd from South Korea, he holds an MA from Kansas State University and a PhD from the University of Nebraska-Lincoln. **Mary C. Bagley** <bagley@mobap.edu> is professor of English at Missouri Baptist University. She authored nine books, including *The Front Row: Missouri's Grand Theatres* (1984), *Professional Writing Types* (1989), and *The Art of Writing Well* (1995), and edited several more books, including *Nineteenth and Twentieth Century Romantic Literature* (1994). She has published over 200 articles in magazines and journals and used to work as a newspaper editor. She received her PhD from St. Louis University and her BA and MA from the University of Missouri-St. Louis.

entertainment clearly exist in his fiction, he is fundamentally a Christian novelist who embodies—either consciously or unconsciously—a Christian worldview in his writing. When he was asked the question "Do you try to put Christian sentiments into your books?" in a *Newsweek* interview in February 2008, he replied, "I'm a Christian, and those beliefs occasionally come out in the books" ("Ten Questions" 6). As Jimmy Allen states, Grisham is "a Baptist churchman, not only in regular worship but also in active service. The sub-themes of his fiction reveal his understanding of the plight of the poor, his commitment to seek justice in our criminal system, his concerns for environment, and his descriptions of the challenge to reach across the racial lines that divide us" (quoted in Warner).

This paper will investigate three of Grisham's novels in an effort to understand how they embody his Christian faith: *The Street Lawyer* (1998), in which a lawyer leaves his lucrative legal practice to help the homeless; *The Testament* (1999), a story of the positive impact of faith on modern man; and *The King of Torts* (2003), which concerns the evil of greed. In these legal thrillers, Grisham not only entertains readers with a masterful use of suspenseful plot, but also makes them ponder important moral issues from a Christian perspective: inner-city poverty, greed and materialism, environmental concerns, the power of addiction versus the power of faith, and the mistreatment of indigenous people, among many others.

From the Tower to the Street: *The Street Lawyer*

The most prominent theme of *The Street Lawyer* is Christian calling. Thirty-two-year-old Michael Brock, a rich Caucasian lawyer, leaves his lucrative job to fight for the homeless as a poorly paid "street lawyer" in Washington, D.C. The title of the novel is somewhat prescient in that the main character will know what it is like to practice law on both sides of the street—and on both sides of what is right and wrong. The story opens with Brock as a successful anti-trust lawyer with Drake & Sweeney, a major corporate firm composed of 800 lawyers. He thought he was climbing the success ladder and would soon be a partner, but his encounter with a homeless, mentally ill man nicknamed "Mister" transforms his life: he changes from a man who does not have time to empathize with the victim (unless the victim is Brock's wealthy client) to a man who does not care about money, only people.

Mister is a forty-five-year-old Vietnam veteran who has a history of drug use and has been arrested once for burglary. One day Brock and his colleagues are taken hostage by Mister, who shows up at the office with fake dynamite strapped to him. During the next few hours,

Mister asks the millionaire lawyers what they have done for the poor, sick, and hungry; they cannot think of much to prove their generosity. After listening to lame excuses from them, he blurts out, "You are miserable people" (Grisham, *The Street Lawyer* 21). Although Mister is armed and dangerous, he does not kill anyone; rather, he wishes to confront the affluent to awaken them out of their complacency and greed. After a while, the SWAT team surrounds the building, kills Mister, and rescues the hostages.

This incident traumatizes Brock, who begins to re-evaluate his priorities in life. As he ponders what Mister said during the hostage crisis, Brock realizes that he was one of "the rich white guys" (39) pursuing things of this world. In an experience similar to the conversion of Paul the Apostle, Brock becomes transformed after his encounter with Mister. He divorces his wife, from whom he has been estranged for a significant amount of time anyway, leaves his life of "blatant and unshamed greed" (60), and becomes a "street lawyer" crusading for the homeless in the city.

A key phrase in this novel is "a social conscience" (68). Brock realizes that the good acts in his life were perfunctory. He gave offerings to the church because the Bible demanded it, he paid taxes only because the law required it, and he worked hard in the belief that his industriousness would somehow benefit society. He now decides to "work for the good of society"—to "change society"—even if that means making less money (69). He becomes a voice of the disenfranchised, fighting the bureaucrats, government workers, courts, corporate lawyers, and landlords. While working for the poor, Brock loses interest in eating for pleasure and becomes comfortable living in a cheap apartment; in his fight against "injustice and social ills," he has finally found "a higher calling" in life (193).

The Street Lawyer deals with the ideas of what is right/ethical, and what is wrong/unethical. It embodies Christ's teaching in Matthew 25:35–36, in which he explains how he would commend righteous people at his second coming: "I was hungry and you gave me food, I was thirsty and you gave me something to drink, I was a stranger and you welcomed me, I was naked and you gave me clothing, I was sick and you took care of me, I was in prison and you visited me" (NRSV). The novel also reflects Christ's warning against the love of money: "[I]t is easier for a camel to go through the eye of a needle than for someone who is rich to enter the kingdom of God" (NRSV). The novel shows how money can corrupt and how people with less money seem to be better human beings. Michael Brock changes from an unsympathetic lawyer with no social conscience to a champion for the homeless. Rarely do people change so dramatically, especially in their job and personality, yet in *The Street Lawyer*, Brock's change highlights the Christian idea of spiritual transformation and further expresses the worldview of Grisham that has been established through faith.

A JOURNEY INTO THE HEART OF DARKNESS: *THE TESTAMENT*

Like *The Street Lawyer*, *The Testament* is a legal thriller which, on its deeper level, deals with the Christian theme of vocation. The book opens with two highly dramatic chapters involving Mr. Troy Phelan, a self-made billionaire and the tenth wealthiest person in America. Supposedly dying of incurable cancer, Phelan (his name sounds like *felon*) throws a press conference to reveal his last will and testament. His greedy and conniving family, including three ex-wives and seven children, are anxiously awaiting a windfall from him. He hates them passionately, however: "They are vultures circling with clawed feet, sharp teeth, and hungry eyes, giddy with the anticipation of unlimited cash" (Grisham, *Testament* 4). As expected, he reads his will distributing the money generously. After all have left, he tells the cameraman not to turn off the video, but to keep it running. Then he reads a new will, a surprising one, in which he basically disinherits the family, and then commits suicide by jumping out the window of the fourteenth floor.

According to Phelan's last will, the inheritance—eleven billion dollars—will be given to Rachel Lane, Mr. Phelan's illegitimate, estranged daughter who is rumored to serve as a missionary among indigenous people in a Brazilian jungle. After a life-threatening journey into the Amazon, lawyer Nate O'Reily, who has been appointed by Phelan's attorney, finds Rachel and explains the will to her. Surprisingly, however, she shows no interest in the fortune; she neither needs nor wants the money. She "[knows] nothing and certainly [cares] nothing for the events and worries and pressures of the world" (54–55), and feels that she is doing God's work while living with and helping a remote Indian tribe in a region known as the Pantanal.

Grisham's novel is as much about Nate O'Reily as about Rachel, and his transformation is heavily influenced by her Christian testimony. O'Reily has two ex-wives, is an alcoholic who has visited rehabilitation four times, and is being pursued by the IRS for tax evasion. The two trips to the Amazon, however, offer O'Riley an opportunity to reflect on his life and start over again in hope of finding meaning. Touched by Rachel's faith in Christ and her lifestyle, he learns from her that money, sexual pleasure, and worldly fame pale in importance compared with things eternal. At the end of the novel, O'Reily reflects on her influence on his life: "Somehow she'd known he wasn't a drunk anymore, that his addictions were gone, that the demons who'd controlled his life had been forever locked away. She had seen something good in him. Somehow she knew he was searching. She'd found his calling for him. God told her" (532–533). Nate has a chance to redeem himself, and in a sense, his redemption comes at the expense of Phelan's heirs. In its journey motif, *The Testament* is akin to Mark Twain's *Adventures of Huckleberry Finn* and Joseph Conrad's *Heart of Darkness*. Unlike the two works, however, Grisham's novel is a search for a Christian spirituality.

The distinctions between good and evil are evident in *The Testament*. While O'Riley is making a journey by leaving civilization behind, court proceedings are continuing with Phelan's relatives who contest the will. The relatives are pictured as evil and greedy, although one would assume the ex-wives and children are like him since he had greedily amassed the fortune, too, and had treated them unfairly. Their lawyers are also interested only in making money. Hark Gettys is a prime example:

> What Hark desperately wanted was a will contest—a long vicious fight with packs of lawyers filing tons of legal crap. A trial would be wonderful, a high-profile battle over one of the largest estates in America, with Hark in the center. Winning it would be nice, but winning wasn't crucial. He'd make a fortune, and he'd become famous, and that's what modern lawyering was all about. (63)

The greed exemplified by the heirs and their lawyers is contrasted with Rachel's single-minded dedication to the cause of Christ. The novel begins with the testament of Troy Phelan; it ends with the testament of Rachel, who dies of malaria. The opening of her document reads: "I, Rachel Lane Porter, child of God, resident of His world, citizen of the United States, and being of sound mind, do hereby make this as my last testament" (527). Regarding the inheritance from her father, she directs,

> The earnings from the trust are to be used for the following purposes: a) to continue the work of World Tribes missionaries around the world, b) to spread the Gospel of Christ, c) to protect the rights of indigenous peoples in Brazil and South America, d) to feed the hungry, heal the sick, shelter the homeless, and save the children. (527)

Rachel's testament reflects the biblical mandate for the work of international missions, for social action, and for the promotion of human dignity. Through the characters of Rachel and O'Reily, Grisham delivers the story of faith, sin, and redemption in *The Testament*.

THE FORTUNATE FALL: *THE KING OF TORTS*

In *The King of Torts*, Grisham poses a serious ethical question: how should we live in a money-driven society without compromising our integrity? Through the story of a public defender's rise and fall, *The King of Torts* teaches us that greed can ruin a person's life—a lesson taught not only in the New Testament (in 1 Timothy 6:10, for example), but also in numerous fictional stories including Leo Tolstoy's "How Much Land Does a Man Need?" and John Steinbeck's *The Pearl*.

Grisham's main character, Clay Carter, is a smart, handsome lawyer in his early thirties. A Georgetown Law School graduate, he has been working as an underpaid, unappreciated public defense lawyer in Washington, D.C., for five years. He has opportunities, but declines, to move to a lucrative big-time law firm; a vague sense of compassion for underprivileged criminals prevents him from jumping ship. He lives in an old apartment, owns only two suits, and drives a twelve-year-old Honda Accord.

Clay has been going steady with Rebecca for over four years. Rebecca's wealthy father pressures him to accept the staff attorney position offered by the Virginia Speaker of the House. As Clay respectfully declines the offer, Rebecca's father is infuriated and calls him "a loser." Then, he continues, "You're turning down a promising job so you can stay in a rut and work for minimum wage. You have no ambition, no guts, no vision" (Grisham, *King of Torts* 70).

Then, one day, Clay receives a phone call from a mysterious man named Max Pace, who says he is looking for a competent tort lawyer. A former attorney-at-law, Max promises Clay millions of dollars in exchange for successfully pursuing a class action against a pharmaceutical company which tested a potentially fatal product, Tarvan, on ex-drug addicts without their knowledge. After deliberating for a few days, he resigns his public defense position and becomes the lead attorney of a brand-new tort firm. Although Clay is convinced that the company deserves a legal challenge, he is also interested in making quick money: while he is "sick with the thought that a respected company could prey on the weakest people it could find," he is also "thrilled with the prospect of more money that he ever dreamed of" (95–96).

Through the lawsuit, Clay earns ten million dollars in fees. Then, he takes on another lucrative class-action case, making more than a hundred million dollars. Within a short period of time, he becomes a relentless, sensationally successful tort lawyer, earning the nick name "The King of Torts." Once a poor public defender, he now has a $300 million private jet, thousands of customers, and a beautiful trophy girlfriend. Clay's success, achieved through deception and blind ambition, inevitably crumbles, and the rest of the novel deals with his sudden downfall—and his eventual redemption.

In the novel, Clay's role is two fold: he is not only a character with moral deficiencies, but also a moral voice—Grisham's mouthpiece—that exposes the shady world of trial lawyers. While his capitalist greed leads him to temporary moral lapses, he is different from other trial lawyers who are portrayed as "clowns," "vultures," or "thieves" (166, 172, 238). When Max initially offers him millions of dollars, Clay wonders whether he should continue to serve the needy and poor as a public defender, or pursue the money by "selling [his] soul" (120); unlike Max, Clay maintains a sense of decency even while succumbing to the power of money. While he collaborates with other prominent tort lawyers, Clay keeps distance from them, observing them with a critical eye: they are arrogant, shallow, mean, uncaring, and selfish.

Not always a man of integrity, Clay is still portrayed as a likeable character in *The King of Torts*. In his moral struggle and dilemma, Clay is akin to Christian in John Bunyan's allegory *Pilgrim's Progress*. Christian's journey is riddled with temptations and mistakes, yet he eventually reaches the celestial city. Likewise, Clay is fundamentally a good man and eventually regains his integrity—and perceptive readers know that in the end, he will become a better person. The last page of the novel shows that he lost all material possessions but will live a happy life with his love, Rebecca: "Clay longed for two good legs and a clean slate. He was surviving one of the more infamous meltdowns in the history of American law, and it was further and further behind him. He had Rebecca all to himself, and nothing else mattered" (470).

The King of Torts raises important ethical questions for discussion. When Clay mentions the ethicality of a class-action lawsuit, Max Pace responds, "...You are doing nothing unethical. You're getting huge settlements for clients who have no clue that they are due anything. That's not exactly selling your soul. And what if you get rich? You won't be the first lawyer to get a windfall" (120). Of course, Max's idea of ethicality is different from Clay's (and the author's). By "unethical," Max probably means "unlawful," while Clay briefly considers whether so-called ambulance chasing is morally justified. Tempted by multimillion dollars Max offers, however, Clay violates his own conscience, becomes his accomplice, and eventually pays a big price.

CONCLUSION

The Street Lawyer, The Testament, and *The King of Torts* demonstrate that as a fiction writer, Grisham is fundamentally a Christian moralist. The characters in his novels reflect the fallenness of humanity and of this world. In addition to providing excitement, his works embody biblical teachings, mostly in a covert manner: be compassionate toward the poor, needy, and underprivileged; spread the Word of God throughout the world; live a life free from greed and worldly ambition; and practice good stewardship of Creation.

Grisham's villains—sometimes even his heroes—break Christian ideals, and the author does not always punish the bad or reward the good. Although he often does not criticize his characters, Grisham shows through their selfish actions that they are wrong while others who are kind and good are correct. He builds his suspense by showing the ones in the right being threatened by the ones in the wrong, and the reader wants to see justice done. He also uses the law itself to show how it can be twisted and abused by those with money—and to show how truth does not always prevail.

Grisham's fiction typically champions the underdog. His favorite plot pits the righteous little guy, a David figure, against the unrighteous big guy, a Goliath figure; the outcome of their moral struggle ends with the victory for the little guy—perhaps with the exception of his latest novel, *The Appeal* (2008), a political thriller in which evil triumphs. Grisham's faith can be defined as progressive evangelical Christianity. In his emphasis of Christian social conscience, he is in line with former President Jimmy Carter and political activist Jim Wallis, who edits *Sojourner* magazine and convenes Call to Renewal. One may also find parallels between his fiction and Charles Monroe Sheldon's novels *In His Steps* (1896) and *The Reformer* (1902), both of which reflect the teachings of the Social Gospel movement.

Of course, Grisham's Christian ideas for social change as reflected in his fiction are open to debate. His solution to inner-city poverty, for instance, supports a heavy subsidy of government funds while the role of personal responsibility is less emphasized. Homelessness is a complex issue that cannot be simplified as he does in *The Street Lawyer*. Demonizing society in general—Congress, the city, police officers, the courts, the bureaucrats, rich lawyers, etc.—and portraying the homeless as innocent victims may minimize Grisham's well-intended appeal for social change. Another issue in *The Street Lawyer* involves the main character's act of stealing a legal document from his former law firm. He rationalizes his thievery as an action for social justice, yet one wonders if the end can justify the means.

Despite critical acclaim and popularity among readers, Grisham's fiction exhibits weakness in its characterization: his characters are either good or bad; there is little subtlety or ambiguity in them. Corporate lawyers are branded as vultures, while public defense lawyers are stereotyped as moral crusaders. Some characters are also portrayed along racial and ethnic stereotypes. For instance, in *The Street Lawyer*, Michael Brock is described as "a handsome white boy" (300), and in *The King of Torts*, Clay Carter's would-be father-in-law addresses him as "a handsome young man" (51). In contrast, the word *handsome* is never used in reference to the righteous black lawyer and Brock's mentor in *The Street Lawyer*, Mordecai Green. A "warm, caring man who labor[s] on the streets protecting hordes of nameless clients" (50), Mordecai is still portrayed as a large man who looks intimidating, yells and roars, and drives recklessly on the street. Rachel Lane, the Caucasian heroine in *The Testament*, is portrayed as an angelic figure; O'Reily addresses her as "a very lovely missionary who just happens to be the richest woman in the world" (281), while the word *lovely* is never used in reference to indigenous women.

By depending on stereotypes and simplistic moral distinction, Grisham risks the danger of losing credibility as a storyteller; rather than portraying each individual as an independent soul, his novels sometimes fall into simplistic melodrama and hackneyed sensationalism. His works are heavily didactic and do not invite readers to read them repeatedly to investigate multiple layers of meaning. In this regard, Grisham is not a literary but a popular novelist who writes prodigiously to appeal to a broad readership. It is no wonder that despite his tremendous commercial success, Grisham is not considered one of the "best" American novelists by critics. The Modern Library's 100 Best Novels list, for example, does not include any work written by Grisham.

Still, Grisham should be commended for grappling with important social issues that face Christians of the twenty-first century. More than 100 million copies of his books have been sold worldwide, he is considered the most commercially successful novelist of the 1990s, and he still is a towering figure in popular fiction. Despite his success, he still maintains a Christian perspective on life. One of his interviewers asked him whether he wondered how God made him such a famous, successful novelist. In response, he stated:

Yes. I used to ask all the time. I'm getting used to the success, but the questioning still hits occasionally.

I go for long walks in the woods a lot, and I ask myself if I'm handling it the way it ought to be handled. I don't know why it happened to me. God has a purpose for it. We are able to contribute an awful lot of money to his work, and maybe that's why. But I firmly believe it will be over one of these days—five years from now, ten years from now. The books will stop selling for whatever reason. All this is temporary. (Norton)

Grisham does not take his success for granted, and he knows that his success will not last long, and more importantly, he knows that life in this world is temporary.

The *Publishers Weekly* magazine labeled Randy Singer—a Christian novelist—"the Christian John Grisham" (quoted in Walzer). Asked whether he agreed to the label, Singer "gently deflected the praise," saying, "I don't think John Grisham would appreciate that." Singer does not elaborate on what he means by that statement, but what is clear is that *Publishers Weekly*'s label ignores the fact that Grisham *is* a Christian novelist who embeds Christian truths in his fiction while not losing elements of entertainment.

WORKS CITED

The Bible. New Revised Standard Version.

Grisham, John. *The King of Torts*. 2003. Dell domestic mass market ed. New York: Dell, 2003.

_____. *The Street Lawyer*. 1998. Dell reissue ed. New York: Dell, 2003.

_____. *The Testament*. New York: Dell, 1999.

"John Grisham Has No Illusions about Writing." CNN.com. 16 Feb. 2008. 18 Feb. 2008 <http://edition.cnn.com/2008/SHOWBIZ/books/02/15/ books.johngrisham.ap/index.html>

Norton, Will. "Conversations: Why John Grisham Teaches Sunday School." *Christianity Today* 3 Oct. 1004. 8 July 2008 <http://www.christianitytoday.com/ct/1994/october3/4tb014.html>.

"Ten Questions." *Time* 4 Feb. 2008: 6.

Walzer, Philip. "Religion, Faith Play Key Role in Norfolk Lawyer's Novels." PilotOnline.com. 27 May 2008. 15 July 2008 <http://hamptonroads.com/2008/05/region-faith-play-key-roles-norfolk-lawyers-novels>.

Warner, Greg. "Author John Grisham Joins Lineup of New Baptist Covenant Speakers." abpnews.com. 21 Dec. 2007. 14 July 2008 <http://www.abpnews.com/2940.article>.

12

Words, Grammar, and Style: Teaching English from a Christian Worldview

Susan Robbins

All English usages reflect a worldview; no less does professional and academic English, also known as ESP, English for Special Purposes. This worldview carries a message to the readers and hearers of papers given in such usage, quite apart from the subject matter and position on the subject defended by the authors of such papers. Too often, English and linguistics teachers treat academic English usage as a neutral medium completely detached from the ends of the users and as a code, as nothing more than a technological and impersonal instrument, entirely value-free until some speaker or writer infuses his or her own values into the message to be communicated via the language. I hold that this view of language is part of a naturalistic, mechanistic worldview and that consideration of the worldview embedded in various discourses and usages of language must be a priority of those who plan to teach English as academic tentmakers. I defend the view that language, especially scientific and academic language, is not a neutral, merely fact-describing set of terminologies with purely utilitarian grammatical rules. Ethical values and principles, and the worldviews underlying them, are found not just in users of language, but also in language itself as distinct from those of the user.

People can be corrupted, and this corruption can show itself in the language they use. But language itself can also be corrupted, and such

Susan Robbins <profsrobbins@gmail.com> has served as a philosophy and humanities professor at Klaipeda University in Lithuania for five years. Susan grew up in the Central African Republic, and in America she taught philosophy for 13 years in various American colleges and universities. She received her BA from The College of New Jersey, an MA (Systematic Theology) from Denver Seminary, and an MA (Philosophy) and PhD from Temple University.

corrupt language can be used by unobservant people in such a way that the innocent and good messages they wish to communicate to others can be undermined by the worldview of the language they use. I will show that certain conventions of academic usage, such as the elimination of the first person in scientific writing, the heavy prevalence of passive voice, the preference for Latinate words rather than Anglo-Saxon ones, and the long convoluted sentence, collectively produce a language inimical to a Christian worldview and unsuitable for conveying the full reality of the created world. In contrast, a well-ordered language in its vocabulary, grammar, and style not only conveys the truth of reality, but also its beauty and goodness.

I present four points: 1) that professional and scientific English usage is not a neutral subject to teach; 2) that language itself can be corrupted apart from any corruption of the user; 3) that modern standard academic usage reflects a worldview inimical to the gospel; and 4) that academic missionaries, including tentmakers, should defend and teach, not merely correct, but good English that is in accord with a Christian view of the world.

The Non-Neutrality and Worldview of Academic and Professional English

There are several characteristics of academic and scientific English I shall highlight. The first is its *impersonality*. Writers who aim at an impersonal style do it primarily by using passive voice and avoiding the first person. *Merriam-Webster's Dictionary of English Usage* holds that the passive voice is approved for scientific writing "because it helps establish a tone of detachment and impersonality."[1] Tom McArthur, in his article on academic usage, also points out that passive voice serves "to minimize or remove personality."[2] But impersonality is not a neutral quality. Its underlying message is that the world is impersonal, that the human personality is detached and alienated from the rest of creation, and that the science of the scientist ought to be dehumanized and detached from the whole personhood and humanity of the scientist doing it. It is not necessary to value detachment and impersonality as characteristics of good science.

Such a preference for passive voice betrays a serious prejudice against human agency. But we all know that the sciences, and not only

1 E. Ward Gilman, ed. (Springfield, Mass.: Merriam-Webster, 1993), 721. See also the entry "Passive (Voice)," *Oxford Companion to the English Language*, ed. Tom McArthur, (Oxford University Press, 1992).

2 Tom McArthur, "Academic Usage," *Oxford Companion to the English Language*, ed. Tom McArthur, (Oxford University Press, 1992), 8.

the arts, are products of human agency. There is no way to achieve Mr. Gradgrind's goal of "nothing but the facts." What we have in the history of science is not "progress" or a simple accumulation of facts, but one paradigm following another depending on which worldview and philosophical underpinnings of the disciplines prevails in each era. But even in ordinary laboratory reports and articles writing up the findings of various investigations, we have passive phrases such as *a meeting was held, the findings were discussed,* or *conclusions were drawn* without any hint as to who attended the meeting, whose voices and opinions were dominant at it, and how these people drew their conclusions. Such language not only conceals or obscures the human agency involved, but actually shows an unwillingness to accept the responsibility for the results. Its use is an attempt to present them to the reader as indisputable facts rather than disputable human judgments. For the authors of such language to align themselves on one side of the fact-value distinction in this way is to attempt to deny the reader any serious or critical engagement with the material. Rather than an awakening sting of a gadfly, such writing serves to lull the horse even more deeply into sleep.

Fortunately, not all scientists have unthinkingly succumbed to the social pressure to write in the prevailing style. Among others, N. David Mermin, a US physicist, has spoken up against the current. He points out that

> [o]ver the last fifty years or so, scientists have allowed the conventions of expression available to them to become entirely too confining. The insistence on bland impersonality and the widespread indifference to anything like the display of a unique human author in scientific exposition, have not only transformed the reading of most scientific papers into an act of tedious drudgery, but have also deprived scientists of some powerful tools for enhancing their clarity in communicating matters of great complexity. Scientists wrote beautifully through the 19th century and on into the early 20th. But somewhere after that, coincident with the explosive growth of research, the art of writing science suffered a grave setback, and the stultifying convention descended that the best scientific prose should sound like a non-human author addressing a mechanical reader.[3]

The theological objection to impersonal language is that the world was created by God in three persons and thus bears the mark of His

---

3 N. David Mermin, *Boojums All the Way Through: Communicating Science in a Prosaic Age* (Cambridge University Press, 1990), Preface. Quoted in McArthur, *Oxford Companion,* 8.

personhood. Our scientific description or presentation of the reality of God's world ought not to try to remove that mark. Another objection is that we, who are created in the image of God, should do our work in imitation of Him, as sub-creators, representing the truth of the world in our arts and sciences without attempting to erase our humanity or personhood from that representation.[4]

The second feature of academic prose is its *exclusivity*. This feature restricts access to the paper by using a specialized and technical vocabulary that is understood only by specialists in the field. There are two kinds of vocabulary in use in various disciplines and professions. The first is jargon, "the specialized language of a trade, profession, or other group. The term is often associated with law, medicine, and the sciences: *technical jargon, scientific jargon*. To non-members . . . their usage is filled with terms and syntax that are not typical of general English and may therefore impede understanding among lay people."[5] Such jargon is meant for insiders and is meant to exclude the general public from access to it. The audience addressed consists only of colleagues in the field. [According to tradition, such jargon sprang up in the medical field first, so that doctors could discuss the condition of their patients without the patients' being able to understand what was being said of them.] Sometimes such jargon may be used for humane purposes, for surgeons to communicate very quickly with each other exactly what is going on in a patient's heart or brain; or for a lawyer to protect the interests of a client against an injustice that may sneak in through some technical loophole. As Mermin implied, sometimes specialized vocabulary is necessary to discuss some issue of extreme complexity.

But the second kind of vocabulary contributing to the feature of exclusivity is merely a marker to define who is in the profession and who is outside it. It does not serve any humane purpose but merely uses pretentious obscurantist language to say things that could perfectly well be said in ordinary English. This vocabulary is characterized by multisyllabic, Latinate terms, nominalizations, and noun strings. Here is an example from the *Oxford Companion to the English Language*. The second sentence is a translation of the first into ordinary English.

a. Although solitary under normal prevailing circumstances, raccoons may congregate simultaneously in certain areas of artificially enhanced nutrient resource availability.

---

4 Cf. Tolkien "On Fairy Stories" in *The Tolkien Reader* (New York: Del Ray, 1966). In this essay Tolkien defends the right to "sub-create" on the basis of having been created in the image of God. "–'twas our right (used or misused). That right has not decayed: we make still by the law in which we're made."

5 McArthur, *Oxford Companion*, 543.

b. Raccoons live alone, but if you put some food out, they will gather around it in a group.[6]

There may be social or political purposes to such inflated prose, but they clearly don't include communicating with the general reader. Instead, such prose is meant to impress others with the author's authority, prestige or sophistication, or it indicates membership in the profession. There is a long prejudice in favor of words with roots from Latin or French, and against words whose origins lie in Anglo-Saxon or Old Norse, for granting social status to the users. After the Norman Conquest, French was the language of the aristocracy for over 200 years, whereas Old English was the language of the peasants. There is still a feeling that Latinate terms add respectability and are more likely to impress the reader with the author's expertise in the subject. This language style carries the underlying values of the author, that the subject of raccoons isn't interesting or important, so the jargon is put into use to lend an air of sophistication and complexity to a subject actually common and simple. The inflated language serves to prop up the author and the raccoons, because the raccoons by themselves can't carry the day.

One *Calvin and Hobbes* cartoon captures this attitude beautifully. Sitting at a table with a pencil in hand and a paper in front of him, Calvin says to Hobbes, "I used to hate writing assignments, but now I enjoy them." He continues, "I realized that the purpose of writing is to inflate weak ideas, obscure poor reasoning, and inhibit clarity." In the third frame he announces with glee, "With a little practice, writing can be an intimidating and impenetrable fog. Want to see my book report?" Hobbes picks up the paper and reads, "The Dynamics of Interbeing and Monological Imperatives in *Dick and Jane*: A Study in Psychic Transrelational Gender Modes." Leaning on his elbow complacently, Calvin finishes, "Academia, here I come!"[7] Bill Watterson has shown with humor and clarity what we already intuitively knew, that most academic prose is not meant to share some interesting aspect of reality with the reader. Rather it is to impress the reader with the erudition and expertise of the author, while obscuring the fact that the reader is thus being manipulated into accepting the worldview that reality is out of the reach of most readers and accessible only to the expert.

There are strong Christian objections to the use of needlessly exclusive prose. The first comes from the command to allow no

---

6 Tom McArthur, *Oxford Companion*, 544. There are more examples from the fields of politics, business, and management on the website of the Plain English Campaign.

7 Bill Watterson, Universal Press Syndicate. Originally published on 1993-02-11.

unwholesome speech come out of our mouths, but to let our speech always be winsome, seasoned with salt (tasty, refreshing) that it may give grace to the hearers, and that we may be able to answer everyone.[8] The second is that exclusive prose does not welcome the stranger and take him in. Building status or prestige as a scientist on the incomprehension of outsiders to the field is like building a house on the sand. Using puffed-up vocabulary, using Latinate words where Anglo-Saxon ones carry the same meaning indicates a pretentious attitude on the part of the author, and is directly counter to the principles of loving our neighbor in I Corinthians 13:4–6. [*Charity vaunteth not itself; is not puffed-up.*] A third objection is that the heavens (and by extension, all the rest of the natural world including raccoons) declare the glory of God. In God's value system the common and simple things are as important and interesting as the complex and difficult things. In our science, they do not need to be advertized or puffed-up by difficult and complex prose.

The third and final characteristic of academic and scientific prose is its stultifying *dullness*. This is accomplished by the use not only of passive voice and Latinate terms but also of nominalizations and long noun phrases. A "career alternative enhancement program" is letting go several thousand workers; "vertical transportation corps members" are lift operators. Chesterton remarked that "Most of the machinery of modern language is labour-saving machinery: . . . Long words go rattling by us like long railway trains. We know they are carrying thousands who are too tired or too indolent to walk and think for themselves." Nominalizations instead of active verbs carry the weight of the sentences. Using 'implementation' instead of 'implement,' 'discussion' instead of 'we discussed,' and 'arrangement' instead of 'arrange' sound as if nothing is going on and fatigue the readers and listeners. Chesterton also said that he found

> the whole modern world talking scientific fatalism; saying that everything is as it must always have been, being unfolded without fault from the beginning. The leaf on the tree is green because it could never have been anything else.

Such fatalism is also conveyed by passive voice. It presents a static rather than dynamic feeling to the universe. In opposition to this feeling, Chesterton claims that he experiences the world differently:

> Every colour has in it a bold quality as of choice; the red of garden roses is not only decisive but dramatic, like suddenly spilt

---

8 Ephesians 4:29; Colossians 4:6.

blood. He [the fairy-tale philosopher] feels that something has been DONE.[9]

This is a true feeling about the world. The Creator has indeed DONE something in creating everything. But this feeling is obscured, not only by the determinism, but by just the scientific prose used for describing nature. Strong verbs carry a vitality with them that the nominalizations cannot match.

In spite of the discrediting of the fact-value distinction, most professional prose still tries to eliminate any affective import from its content. The language has little elegance, beauty, grace, or liveliness. Strong verbs, taut presentation, clear figures of speech, simple, lucid, and concrete diction, and varied sentence length all add to the readability of a paper. Prose that is interesting, moving, or refreshing is not considered to be sufficiently scientific simply because a bias against affective engagement with the subject matter still prevails in academic circles. In the current conventions, scientific prose must avoid any hint of poetic or literary expression, or its scientific validity and prestige will be undermined. Our society has been so indoctrinated in the belief that value judgments are subjective, private, and disconnected from reality, that any language that evokes a trace of aesthetic or moral response is regarded with suspicion in scientific and professional circles. Both students and professors inhabit an academic culture dominated by a prevailing relativism in which all aesthetic and moral responses are equal, none better or worse than any other, and all equally unwelcome.

But we are commanded to love God with all our heart and soul as well as with all our mind. The whole person should be engaged in loving God through all the means He gives in general and special revelation. We should not fragment ourselves into loving God with our minds in our academics and loving Him with our hearts when privately dealing with poetry and pets. The aesthetic and moral dimensions of our scientific engagement with the world should not be shunted off to the private side of life.

THE CORRUPTION OF LANGUAGE

It is part of my thesis that language can be corrupted apart from any corruption on the part of its user. By this I mean that a professional, without any intention to deceive or manipulate her audience, can deliver her message in a prose style that does indeed manipulate

---

9 G. K. Chesterton, *Orthodoxy*, "The Ethics of Elfland," (Christian Classics Ethereal Library) <http://www.ccel.org/ccel/chesterton/orthodoxy.vii.html>

or deceive her audience. A professional may be so socialized in the conventions of his discipline that he may be completely unaware of how these conventions disrespect the humanity of his audience. And an audience can be so taken in by the propaganda, flattery, and manipulation, that they are unable to distinguish reality from illusion or truth from fiction.

This is not a new phenomenon: it goes all the way back to the opposition of Plato to the sophists. Plato's chief problem with the sophists was that they used language and taught others to use language to impress, to manipulate, and to achieve social success. Language is turned from a representation of reality into an instrument of power. Josef Pieper has divided the corruption of language into two forms: the corruption of the relationship of language to reality, and the corruption of communication.[10]

There are two ways the corruption of the relationship of language to reality takes in modern professional language. The first, called *doublespeak*, stems from the political language of 20th-century totalitarianism. The second is the heavy use of meaningless buzzwords.

According to the *Oxford Companion to the English Language*, doublespeak "diverts attention from, or conceals, a speaker's true meaning, or from what is on the speaker's mind, making the bad seem good, and the unpleasant attractive or at least tolerable. It seeks to avoid, shift, or deny responsibility, and ultimately prevents or limits thought."[11] We use the figures of speech of metaphor, simile, and irony to draw attention to some aspect of reality by referring to something else that is similar or in contrast to it. "I am the door" or "My love is like a red, red rose" enhance our understanding of the speaker's message, while the ironic "Well I like that!" humorously lets us know the speaker doesn't actually like it at all. Even a euphemism such as "the rest room" does not conceal the meaning but merely makes something that would literally be embarrassing more socially acceptable. Doublespeak is a figure of speech that relies on deception and concealment, whereas euphemism simply is a more pleasant metaphor for something whose public literal mention is socially unwelcome. To substitute "unlawful or arbitrary deprivation of life" for "killing" does not conceal the fact of death but does reduce its emotional impact. Using "servicing the target" for killing the enemy, "pacification" for torching villages, "air support" for bombing, "enhanced interrogation techniques" for torture: military jargon is full of doublespeak phrases.

---

10 Josef Pieper, *Abuse of Language Abuse of Power* (San Francisco: Ignatius Press, 1992) 16.
11 Tom McArthur, ed., *Oxford Companion*, 320.

From totalitarian to military jargon, to bureaucratic and management jargon, euphemism and doublespeak have crept into all aspects of professional life. They are especially prevalent in expressing a decision to "let people go." From "career change opportunity" to "skill-mix adjustment" to "work force imbalance correction," dozens of expressions are coined to mitigate an unpleasant reality and render it emotionally more acceptable.[12]

Even in the academic world, this sort of deceptive euphemism turns up occasionally. At a thesis-defense meeting at one university, as an outside reader, I had failed a BA thesis that was severely plagiarized from the Internet. In an attempt to get me to agree to passing the student, one professor argued that "compiling" was regarded as a weak but passing technique for research papers, according to the writing manual produced by their literature department. I didn't realize until later that "compiling" was doublespeak for copy-paste plagiarism in that faculty.

The second corruption of the relationship between language and reality occurs when the technical terms do not actually have any relationship to reality at all. They are not trying to cover up a harsh or unacceptable reality; there is no reality behind them. They are used only to impress the reader with the author's skill and justify the author's status in the profession. Here is an example from sociology:

> Chieftaincy, as a sanctional source, a symbolic referent, an integrational integer, and for ethnic and sub-ethnic definition, represents an orientational base for the charismatic persona.[13]

This may have some meaning to a sociologist, but to most of us it is, in Calvin's words, "an intimidating and impenetrable fog." But the pressure on teachers in social science and humanities departments is to write papers using such language, and the pressure on students is to acquire competence in the terminology of their specialties. The pressure on non-native speakers of English is even greater. I have been teaching overseas for several years, and in several colleges and faculties; so my examples come from a variety of situations. I once showed the *Baffle-Gab Thesaurus*[14] to my management students, but instead of seeing the humor in it, they took it seriously as a means to "improve" their writing. On another occasion I showed my academic writing

---

12 See David Crystal, *The Cambridge Encyclopedia of the English Language*, 2/e, (Cambridge University Press, 2003) 174.

13 Tom McArthur, ed., *Oxford Companion*, 544

14 See <www.angelfire.com/ga2/stepstoinsanity/baffle.html>

students *The Folklore Article Reconstitution Kit*,[15] and they wished they had such a kit for writing their course papers. In one university, several administrators and faculty in the social sciences asked me to teach them the specialized English of their fields so they could read and write respectable scholarly articles. The detachment of the professional language from reality was irrelevant to them. Their goal was not to communicate their ideas and findings; it was to gain status and prestige, to prove themselves respectable scientists in their respective fields. They all understood that in order to gain acceptance to the "in groups" in their field, they had to demonstrate competence in using the jargon in English, even if that jargon was meaningless and the users had nothing to say with it.

Besides the corruption of terminology in relation to reality, there is also the corruption of communication. The two forms go hand in hand to constitute the corruption of language. Any discourse that conceals reality or misleadingly conveys it shows indifference regarding the truth. To be indifferent toward the truth is to be indifferent toward the audience's grasp of the truth. In Pieper's words, it "is the opposite of communication. It means specifically to withhold the other's share and portion of reality, to prevent his participation in reality."[16] Most of the teaching carried on in many departments and faculties is carried on this way. The students are not considered equal partners in the pursuit of truth; instead they are apprentice functionaries, being trained to fill a slot in the secular economy. Even in the pure humanities courses on poetry, drama, history, philosophy, the student is there merely to absorb information and practice technical skills. The teacher speaks, but it is speech without a partner. And Pieper comments that

> Speech without a partner, in contradiction to the nature of language, intends not to communicate but to manipulate. The word is perverted and debased to become a catalyst, a drug, as it were, and is as such administered.[17]

Indeed, in a writing manual in use at another university, the authors indicate (using their own jargon) that the content of student papers at the Bachelor level is of no interest save to demonstrate to the faculty that the student has the ability to use the jargon and understands the norms and conventions of the profession. The Bachelor's thesis is an exercise to prove that the student is qualified to enter the

---

15 David Crystal, *Cambridge Encyclopedia*, 174.

16 Pieper, *Abuse of Language*, 16.

17 Pieper, 22.

profession; it has no other purpose. Such prose has no readers; it has only consultants or evaluators, and very few of those. This manual, without very much hedging, informs the students that their teachers are not interested in what the students actually have to say about their topics. It defeats the inherent purpose of language, which is to communicate from one mind to another.

A WORLDVIEW INIMICAL TO THE GOSPEL

In this section I shall examine an illustration by Orwell in his essay "Politics and the English Language." He took Ecclesiastes 9:11, and translated it into modern English.

> I returned, and saw under the sun, that the race is not to the swift, nor the battle to the strong, neither yet bread to the wise, nor yet riches to men of understanding, nor yet favor to men of skill; but time and chance happeneth to them all.

Here is Orwell's translation:

> Objective consideration of contemporary phenomena compels the conclusion that success or failure in competitive activities exhibits no tendency to be commensurate with innate capacity, but that a considerable element of the unpredictable must invariably be taken into account.

In addition to all the factors discussed above, there is one more factor pertaining to truth to examine here. Orwell himself analyzes the linguistic difference between the two sentences and gives the details:

> The first contains forty-nine words but only sixty syllables, and all its words are of everyday life. The second contains thirty-eight words of ninety syllables: eighteen of its words are from Latin roots, and one from Greek. The first sentence contains six vivid images. . . . The second contains not a single fresh, arresting phrase, and in spite of its ninety syllables it gives only a shortened version of the meaning contained in the first.

But Orwell doesn't address the import of the affective differences between the two. In an oral reading of the sentence from Ecclesiastes, the '*not*' of the phrase *the race is not to the swift* is a stressed syllable. The stress carries the import that the race ought to be to the swift and the battle to the strong, but that what happens and what ought to happen don't coincide. There's a sadness underlying the recognition that justice does not prevail as things are, and it leads the reader to the longing for justice to cover the earth as the waters cover the sea. For the Christian, the sadness can shift to a joyful sense of freedom upon reading this sentence in light of the upside-down value system of the Kingdom where the first shall be last and the last first. Since we are freed from seeking the winning of the race or the battle, for riches or favor, we need not stress out over not being swift or strong or intelligent enough for success in the secular world, or that our strength and intelligence are not properly recognized. "Fret not thyself because of him who prospereth in his way," says the Psalmist, and in that light *the race is not to the swift* can be a positive statement. As Milton said, "They also serve who only stand and wait." Not only does Orwell's translation give a shortened version of the meaning contained in the verse from Ecclesiastes, but it is also a much shallower version of the meaning and a much weaker version of the meaning. Strength, depth, and breadth of meaning are all missing in modern scientific prose.

I showed these two sentences to a colleague of mine to illustrate the power of the first and the tedium of the second, and she exclaimed, "But the first one is poetry!" Everyone expects poetry to convey strength and depth of meaning. But also everyone thinks of poetry as purely private and subjective, not universal or objective enough to carry the truth of the world. Even on academic papers about poetry, she told me that in her department and in the academic culture of her country, students are required to write using the second style of prose, not the first. However curtailed in meaning Orwell's translation may be, that is the style of prose students are expected to master for their academic papers and presentations.

This example shows that academic professional prose with its emphasis on abstraction, passive voice, specialized jargon, and impersonal tone is not adequate to carry the truth of the world and the weight of reality. As such it undermines a worldview at whose heart is God's revelation about reality and about redemption. The secular assumption is that truth must be objective rather than subjective. Genesis 1:31 tells us, "And God saw everything that He had made, and indeed, it was very good." Is God's judgment here objective or (merely) subjective? Can we do justice to the truth of reality in prose that seriously diminishes that truth?

Teaching English from a Christian Worldview

I have three conclusions, or rather recommendations, to draw for academic missions centered on teaching English: both for English as a Second Language (ESL) and English for Special Purposes (ESP). The first has to do with the qualification of those who wish to become academic missionaries by teaching English or by teaching the specialized English of their own fields. It entails having a heartfelt love of language and a sense of the importance of handling it well. It also entails having a sense of the power of language and being able to communicate the ethics of language to one's students. Richard Weaver, in *The Ethics of Rhetoric*, explains:

> [T]he right to utter a sentence is one of the very greatest liberties; . . . The liberty to impose this formal unity is a liberty to handle the world, to remake it, if only a little, and to hand it to others in a shape which may influence their actions. . . . The sentence through its office of assertion is a force adding itself to the forces of the world. . . . The changes wrought by sentences are changes in the world rather than the physical earth, but it is to be remembered that changes in the world bring about changes in the earth. [118–119][18]

This is a profound and awesome liberty, and it requires a clear sense of the responsibility involved. In the *Phaedrus* Plato calls rhetoric "the art of soul-leading by means of words" (261a). The writer is leading the soul of the reader to a new shape to the world that may influence the reader's actions in the world. Ray DiLorenzo in *Peitho: A Classical Rhetoric* says that rhetoric is "the care of words and things."[19] The teacher of English must think of language as not merely a technological and impersonal instrument, entirely detached from the message to be communicated. The care of words and things includes a care for the relationship between words and things, ultimately going back to a love of God, the Creator of all things through the Word.[20]

Tolkien's description of the lack of this care is masterly:

> But Orcs and Trolls spoke as they would, without love of words or things; and their language was actually more degraded and filthy than I have shown it. . . . Much the same sort of talk can still be heard among the orc-minded; dreary and repetitive with hatred and contempt, too long removed from good to retain even verbal vigour, save in the ears of those to whom only the squalid sounds strong.[21]

---

18 Quoted in Scott F. Crider, *The Office of Assertion*, (ISI Books: Wilmington, DE, 2005) 11–12.

19 Quoted in Crider, *The Office of Assertion*, 12.

20 Cf. John 1:1–2.

21 J.R.R. Tolkien, *The Return of the King*, Appendix F, "On Translation."

How something is said can never be completely detached from what is said. The English teacher must be aware and care about what the students say and want to say, as she cares about their skill in saying it correctly in English. As Crider concludes:

> The care of words and things—that is, the care of things through the care of words —in a generous, disciplined forum: this human activity is rhetorical through-out, the true influence of friends who have, as Plato puts it at the close of the Phaedrus, "every-thing in common" (279c), in particular the shared motion toward the real.[22]

The second conclusion or recommendation for the academic missionary is to keep a biblical order of priorities in our care and compassion for the students, especially students of the poorer countries of the world. It is easy to be misled into thinking our task is to "equip students to earn a livelihood or to make a place for themselves in society." We all know the feeling Peter Herbst comments on: "If a teacher is fond of his students, he will not wish them to come to grief in life, and thus he may skimp on their education in order to increase their value in the market."[23] But our purpose is not to merely train students to fill a position in the technical or administrative machinery of a consumer society. It is to make disciples of Christ, first and foremost. Courage is a necessary virtue here. We must always keep in mind the question "What shall it profit a man if he gains the whole world, but loses his own soul?" The pressure and desire to be respected in secular academic circles is very high, for ourselves as well as for our colleagues and students. To resist such pressure we need to gather a list of allies as we seek to take a stand in serving Christ rather than serving the secular conventions of our academic disciplines.[24] Using those allies, we can then be ready to give an answer to everyone who asks why we are bucking the trends in our respective fields.

We also need to guard against a false guilt that cringes from preaching "You cannot serve both God and Mammon" to students much poorer than we are. We must remember the widow and her two mites and the generosity of the Macedonians and not deny to our students

---

22 Crider, *Office*, 14.

23 Peter Herbst, "Work, Labour, and University Education" in *The Philosophy of Education* (Oxford University Press, 1973).

24 See not only those listed in these footnotes, but also Donald E. Hall, The *Academic Self: An Owner's Manual* (Columbus: Ohio State University Press, 2002) , Berel Lang, *Writing and the Moral Self* (New York: Routledge, 1991), and J.R.R. Tolkien, The *Monsters & The Critics and Other Essays* (HarperCollins, 1990).

the opportunity to choose whom they will serve.

The last point follows from the second. The teachers of English need to know something of the history of English if they are to allow their students to make an informed choice concerning the professional usage they will adopt. Mermin points out that "Scientists wrote beautifully through the 19th century and on into the early 20th. But somewhere after that, . . . the art of writing science suffered a grave setback."[25] Students need to understand why it happened, what the language of totalitarianism had to do with it, how that language style has crept into public and professional life,[26] and if they can take their models from earlier scientists rather than later ones. Pieper in 1974 could see how high the stakes are:

> The general public is being reduced to a state where people not only are unable to find out about truth but also become unable even to search for truth because they are satisfied with deception and trickery that have determined their convictions, satisfied with a fictitious reality created by design through the abuse of language.[27]

The situation is even worse now, with many professionals in the humanities denying the existence of truth altogether. The tentmaker in academic English needs to take the office of assertion and the liberty to utter sentences seriously enough that she may become a soul-leader, pointing students to the way out of darkness into light.

---

25 Mermin, *Boojums*, Preface.
26 Berel Lang, *Writing and the Moral Self*, Chapter 18: "Language and Genocide."
27 Pieper, *Abuse of Language*, 34–35.

13

Worldview in the Waste Land: Christian Humanism and the Education of Youth

Rick D. Williams

Toward the conclusion of a recent review of Anthony Esolen's translation of the *Divine Comedy*, the reviewer enthusiastically anticipates the translator's potential to "be for contemporary students . . . what Virgil is for Dante within the narrative: a guide and teacher." His enthusiasm is tempered a bit by an acknowledgment that Dante presents an intellectual challenge far "beyond the unaided capacities of today's . . . students, the victims of television and computer games." An unwritten but nonetheless obvious pause follows, then he continues, "But never has a generation been more lost in a dark wood, more pitifully strayed from the straight path."[1]

What are we, as hopeful guides and teachers, to make of the cultural wasteland that consumes even our most promising pupils? What prospects have we in our quest to convince them of the value of a "liberal education" or the worth of an "examined" life? In truth, our current dilemma is not merely a contemporary crisis; it is the consequence of a much longer story that students need to hear. Blaise Pascal recognized this in the 17th century when he wrote in his *Pensées*, "Truth is so obscured nowadays and lies so well established that unless we love the

---

1 R. V. Young, "Dante's New Guide," *Touchstone*, April 2004, p. 45.

Rick D. Williams <rwilliams@judah.org> is Dean of Students at Judah Christian High School in Champaign, Illinois. He teaches Worldviews, Civics, and Classics, is a curriculum writer, and has published numerous articles on topics related to state and local history. He has won several awards for teaching excellence, and he is currently involved in research examining the impact of the study-abroad experience on Korean students and their families. He received his MS and BS degrees from Illinois State University and has done additional graduate work at Lincoln Christian Seminary.

truth we shall never recognize it." Today's youth wander bewildered in a landscape of lies more deceiving and far more cleverly packaged than Pascal could ever imagine. They have forgotten the most essential realities of who they are, where they've come from, and where they are headed, having lost their true humanity in a quagmire of amusement and consumption.

Students of this generation have been offered more choices than any before it; in fact, "choice" is a defining characteristic of their lives. In every imaginable area—entertainment, education, personal grooming, fashion, belief systems—dozens if not scores of possibilities beckon them. Blessed with unprecedented affluence, leisure, and autonomy, often from pre-adolescence, they have become what one journalist identified in the late 1990s as "A Tribe Apart"—loosely-parented, peer-centered, consumer-driven casualties of reckless overindulgence.[2] The increasing popularity of online social networking over the past few years has added to their technological addiction, resulting in what one author has deemed the "screenager."[3]

When it comes to personal beliefs, most young people, in their intellectual ennui, follow the easiest path wherever it takes them. Many who identify as Christians travel tentatively, if at all, along the faintly marked trail of so-called "moralistic therapeutic deism."[4] They may profess, and even possess, genuine Christian faith, but they lack anything resembling a Christian worldview. All are in desperate need of compass and map to show them the way out of the wilderness. More importantly, they need to learn to love the truth that is most fully embodied in the gospel and best articulated, I believe, through the tradition of Christian Humanism.

The term "Christian Humanist" has been used to describe writers and thinkers ranging from Erasmus and Thomas More to Chesterton and Tolkien. What they have in common, besides their primarily Catholic religious identity, is a dedication to "reclaiming the basic inheritance of our history and the natural connection of culture with the religious vistas of the human being."[5] The same spirit that motivated these well-known Catholic humanists also informed many early

---

2 Patricia Hersch, *A Tribe Apart: A Journey into the Heart of American Adolescence* (Ballantine Reader's Circle, 1997).

3 Jessi Hempel, "The MySpace Generation," *Business Week*, December 12, 2005; Candice Kelsey, *Generation MySpace: Helping Your Teen Survive Online Adolescence* (New York: Marlowe & Co, 2007).

4 Christian Smith, *Soul Searching: The Religious and Spiritual Lives of American Teenagers* (Oxford University Press, 2005).

5 Virgil Nemoianu, "Teaching Christian Humanism," *First Things* (May 1996), accessed online at <http://www.firstthings.com/article.php3?id_article=3867>.

Church figures, prominent Protestants, even modern mystics. I would include Dostoevsky and Solzhenitsyn as well. From medieval mystics like Hildegaard of Bingen to Renaissance humanists like Erasmus and More to the "Hillbilly Thomist" Flannery O'Connor,[6] these creative figures "strongly affirmed Christianity's capacity to be inclusive and to reclaim areas in which its universality could shine forth again."[7]

Speaking more directly to the legacy of Chesterton, Vigen Guroian provides a brief and practical insight that connects the crisis of contemporary culture with the educational deficiencies of Christian students: "Christian Humanism [responds to] a serious breakdown of the fundamental moral suppositions deposited by Biblical faith and Classical tradition."[8] The Classical tradition teaches the value of virtuous living; pursuit of the good, the noble, the beautiful in our humanity. Biblical faith places us in right relationship with our Creator and Lord, revealing our utter dependence on Him. Christian Humanism speaks truth to the lies borne by false understandings of what it means to be a human being, created in the image of God, living in a world ordered by His will yet fallen and in need of His redemption.

This approach to learning is motivated by the scriptural admonition to "love the Lord your God with all your heart, and with all your soul, and with all your mind." Cornelius Plantinga describes loving God "with all one's mind" as "a matter of faithfulness, of intellectual humility, of mere loyalty."[9] Such love involves an acceptance of who He is, a willingness to personally get to know Him, and a genuine effort to understand Him on his terms—to (so-to-speak) listen to his story. Plantinga elaborates:

> To hear in the world both the song of God and the groaning of all creation, to prize what is lovely and to suffer over what is corrupt—to ponder these things and to struggle to understand them and God's redeeming ways with them—these are ways of loving God with all our minds.[10]

---

6 Susan Srigley and Ralph Wood discuss Flannery O'Connor on *Mars Hill Audio Conversation* "Hillbilly Thomist: Flannery O'Connor and the Truth of Things," <http://www.marshillaudio.org/catalog/conversa.asp#con22>. Interviews and/or audio conversations related to many of individuals and "isms" discussed in this paper can be found on the *Mars Hill Audio Journal* (hereafter *MHAJ*) website.

7 Nemoianu, *op. cit.*

8 Vigen Guroian, "Christian Humanism: Truth and the Paradoxical Imagination," accessed online at <http://www.pfm.org/Content/ContentGroups/BreakPoint/Columns/Really_Human_Things/200217/The_Christian_Humanism_Of_G_K_Chesterton.htm>.

9 Cornelius Plantinga, "I Pray the Lord My Mind to Keep," *Christianity Today*, August 10, 1998, p. 51.

10 Ibid., p. 52.

The idea of learning as "an act of flagrant intellectual love" (Plantinga again) is a thrilling possibility to present to young minds. It is also, I think, a much more satisfying and engaging approach for worldviews education than the curricular models marketed to and embraced by much of the evangelical educational world.

In a recent interview, J. Mark Bertrand of *Worldview Academy* likened this common model to a kind of "worldviews as apologetics"—a "dumbed-down, popularized understanding" of a term that Christian students have grown tired of hearing because they've grown up with it. "Youth pastors and speakers have sort of beaten it to death," Bertrand related, leaving students "fatigued" by a fad that has burned its way "through popular Evangelical culture."[11] It is an approach that tends to categorize worldview in "us-and-them" terms, with nice comparative charts and bullet points that line up a "Biblical Christian Worldview" against its enemies, be they Marxism, Liberalism, Secularism, Naturalism, Existentialism or New Age Spirituality. Such "culture wars"-oriented curricula aim, with the best of intentions, at preparing students to be warriors in the "battle for their hearts and minds." *Mars Hill Audio* host Ken Meyers, in the course of the Bertrand interview, expressed his concerns over the inadequacy of this meaning of worldview as merely "a really useful defensive tool to beat the bad guys with"—particularly when it, as properly understood, it "entails so much more."[12]

My personal journey from this apologetics model toward the "so much more" has led me—and through me, my students—toward a great appreciation for Christian Humanism. Rather than merely "mobilizing the troops," I attempt to kindle the love of truth by guiding students through the great story of human history. This process takes the truth-seeker beyond a mere cost-benefit analysis into deeper verities that can best (and sometimes only) be perceived through the literary imagination. Stratford Caldecott writes, "For Christians, it is obvious that the life of Christ . . . is the drama within all drama, the story that all good stories reflect. In the Gospels, literal truth and universal symbolism, history and legend, time and eternity coincide."[13] Most important-

---

11 J. Mark Bertrand, interview with Ken Myers, *MHAJ* 90.1.1, (Mar./Apr. 2008). Bertrand is also the author of *Rethinking Worldview: Learning to Think, Live, and Speak in This World* (Wheaton, Ill.: Crossway Books, 2007).

12 Meyers discusses worldview extensively in two other important interviews: with Nicholas Wolterstorff, on Abraham Kuyper's use of the term and how it relates to "sphere sovereignty" (*MHAJ* 84:1.2, Jan./Feb. 2007); and with David Naugle, on the origins of the term and the religious significance of "worldview thinking" for Christians (*MHAJ* 60.1.1, Jan./Feb. 2003).

13 Stratford Caldecott, "Speaking the Truths Only the Imagination May Grasp," *Touchstone,*

ly, the great story tells us who we really are as human beings, and it reveals Christian truth as not just one choice among many stories, but as the single cohesive metanarrative from which all stories emerge—or diverge.

This approach to worldview education surveys the landscape of seminal cultural movements and introduces students to the most influential creative minds and cultural events of human history. Beginning with archetypal myths and the development of major religious and philosophical systems, the story follows the main themes of Western thought from the classical world through medieval Christendom, Byzantium, and Islam, continuing on to the modern world. Students examine influential ideas and their consequences from Antiquity to Hellenism to the Renaissance; from the Enlightenment to Romanticism and Modernity. They witness the triumphs and tragedies of the human experience as we move from creatures in constant awe of the gods and the cosmos toward the hubris of modern man, subduer of nature through science and reason.

As this tale unfolds, three "essential life questions" are kept constantly in mind:

1. The question of human identity: Who are we? Why are we here? What's the point of our existence?
2. The question of the human condition: Why is life like it is? What gives life meaning? What's gone wrong with the world? What should be done about it?
3. The question of ultimate hope for humanity: What directs us toward and awaits in the future--evolution? progress? utopia? salvation?

Responses to these questions fall on either side of Solzhenitsyn's great dividing line in history that cuts through every human heart. They emerge in the story to be considered by students for what they "really" represent in light of the three essential life questions. Do they align truly with—or are they contrary to—those deep verities of the human experience aptly described by J. Budziszewski as "What We Can't Not Know"?[14]

Of course, the ultimate point Solzhenitsyn makes is that no single worldview, in human terms, holds exclusive possession of either side of that famous dividing line. Worldview is not a landscape of "us vs. them"; it is the reality that all of us, both personally and collectively,

---

September/October 1998, p. 48.

14 J. Budziszewski, *What We Can't Not Know: A Guide*, (Dallas: Spence, 2003).

stand either with or against "the way things are" as ordered and de-fined by our Master and Creator. Honest and truthful answers to the three essential life questions can be seen in the lives of great minds such as Augustine, who responds, "Our hearts are restless until they rest in You." Yet it is this very restlessness that prompts us to find our own answers, on our own terms, and that is a big part of the story as well. We can easily follow that plotline from Hobbes to Hume to Rous-seau to Kant and on to the Big Three of modernity—Marx, Darwin, and Freud.

Another element of the story involves the much-asked question, "Can't you lead a good life without believing in Christianity?"[15] In other words, are all the "right" answers only to be found through a religiously informed worldview? In this light, we might consider Bo-ethius' *Consolation of Philosophy*. Here is a Classically informed dis-course, written by a devout but suffering Christian, in which nary a "Christian" sentiment is expressed on the subject of good vs. evil. In his wonderful analysis of the *Consolation*, Graeme Hunter points out,

> [Dame Philosophy's] view derives from a deeper source, from Plato's morally optimistic alternative to Sophoclean tragedy. No matter how discouraging life may seem to be, Plato thought, cos-mic justice ultimately prevails. Evil never prospers; good is every-where triumphant . . . .[16]

For the next millennium, the Classical ideas of Plato and Aristotle, in their "baptized" Augustinian and Thomistic expressions, remained central to a Western worldview. What the Classicist and the Scholastic held in common was the idea of "a good life." Where they differed was in their understanding of its source.

With the "new views" of the Renaissance, this part of the story diverges into three streams: the "spare" humanism of the early Prot-estant Reformers; Erasmus's and More's Catholic humanism; and a more "exuberant" humanism that proved to be the most diverse of the three.[17] "Exuberant" humanism focused on personal transforma-tion through experience and the idea that liberation leads to truth. Religiously motivated exuberance began with the Anabaptists and continued through waves of pietism and revivalism to the Holiness

---

15 Opening line of C. S. Lewis's essay, "Man or Rabbit," from *God in the Dock: Essays in Theol-ogy and Ethics*, ed. Walter Hooper (Grand Rapids, Eerdman's, 1970), p. 108.

16 Graeme Hunter, "Boethius's Complaint," *Touchstone*, April 2004, p. 27.

17 The terms "spare" and "exuberant" as typologies of humanism come from Ronald A. Wells, *History Through the Eyes of Faith* (San Francisco: Harper, 1989), pp. 73–74, followed by an excellent section headed, "A Christian Humanism?" pp. 75–77.

and Pentecostal traditions of the 20ᵗʰ century. Secularly motivated exuberance gradually co-opted the Scientific Revolution and Continental Rationalism, gaining great influence by the Enlightenment, full intellectual respectability in the 19ᵗʰ century, and cultural dominance in the 20ᵗʰ century.

This final strand of exuberant humanism contributed greatly to the cultural conditions in which contemporary worldviews education emerged. The Fundamentalist/Evangelical response takes aim at the legacy of the "Big, Bad, Three"—Marx, Darwin, and Freud—and rightly so. But the Christian Humanist knows to look farther back and more deeply into the story. Writing about the "ideologies of evil" of the 20ᵗʰ century, John Paul II reaches back into European philosophical history, pointing to Descartes' famous *"cogito, ergo sum."* Before Descartes, he noted, the *cogito,* or "thinking," aspect of human identity was subordinate to the *esse,* or emphasis on "being." The "I Am," was considered the point of departure for all of the created order, including the thinking man. With Descartes' famous declaration, all that changed—

> [P]hilosophy became a science of pure thought: all *esse*—both the created world and the Creator—remained within the ambit of the *cogito* as the content of human consciousness. Philosophy now concerned itself with beings *qua* content of consciousness and not *qua* existing independently of it.[18]

Consequently, over the next few centuries, Christian influence in the ivory towers of culture moved from the center to the margins, and the triumph of secularism seemed at hand.[19]

Still, from Augustine and Boethius to C. S. Lewis, the story also passes through many influential and diverse characters--Dante, Pascal, Berkeley, Kierkegaard, Newman, even William James—for whom religion remained a valid, if not essential, part of the human experience. A more direct and theologically homogenous thread of Christian Humanism runs from More to Chesterton to Eliot and Waugh.[20]

---

18 John Paul II, *Memory and Identity,* (New York: Rizzoli, 2005), pp. 8–9.

19 Discussion of two important recent books on secularism can be found at the excellent "dignitarian" website, *Mercatornet. com.* For an interview with Mariano Fazio, author of *A History of Contemporary Ideas: A Reading of the Process of Secularisation,* 2ⁿᵈ ed. (Madrid, 2007) see "Reclaiming Secularity" (April 9, 2997) at <http://www.mercatornet.com/articles/reclaiming_secularity/>. Randal Marlin reviews (July 2, 2008) Charles Taylor's *A Secular Age* (Cambridge: Harvard U. Press, 2007) at <http://www.mercatornet.com/articles/a_secular_age/>.

20 Chesterton, Eliot, Waugh, even Tolkien, Joseph Pearce asserts, were "wrestling" primarily "against the legacy of two men: Fredrich Nietzsche and Oscar Wilde." "The Christian Humanists," *Christian History* Issue 78 (2002), p. 18.

Of course, the case for a genuinely Christian Humanism most strongly permeates my world, the world of evangelical Christian education, through the life and writings of Francis Schaeffer. His emphasis on cultural engagement at all creative levels stands in the Christian Humanist tradition, but his *style* of engagement, with its challenge to be people of "demonstrated, incarnate love," expresses a bit more of the "evangelistic" impulse of historical Evangelicalism.[21]

The modern "triumphs" (both real and imagined) of secularism, therapeutics, scientism, and ideology—even the so-called "fatigue of culture" known as postmodernism[22]—are well established in the ivory towers of academia and the fertile fields of popular culture. In the midst of their posited certainties (or rejections thereof), a genuinely Christian Humanism points the bewildered to deeper truths lying beneath and behind the clever contrivances—but not beyond the baptized imaginations—of humanity. Within this "grand narrative," students can anchor themselves and find both compass and map, as well as inspiring guides and teachers, to help them find their way in the waste land.

An op-ed piece written after September 11, 2001, asked the question, "How, in our secular times, can we accommodate [an epochal struggle between good and evil] in the story of civilization?" Postmodern culture suddenly seemed lacking in this capacity, the writer noted. "Fundamentalist cultures hold durable notions about the Evil One. But our postmodern condition . . . deprives us of grand narratives." He continued,

> All we have is Harry Potter, whose ultimate victory over Lord Voldemort is the bet that parents place when they buy J. K.

---

21 see Glen T. Stanton, "The Conservative Humanist," *Christianity Today*, April 2006, p. 43–45. Stanton's use of the term "conservative" is perhaps meant to make a clear distinction with Catholic Humanism. This powerful essay, written in conjunction with CT's "Christian Vision Project," provides a strong evangelical framework for real-life application of the ideas expressed in this paper and in my class. Stanton urges, "We must become humanists: people who are unreservedly committed to human life at its fullest and people deeply pained by human life at its worst." I have used his definitions of "true humanism" in the last few weeks class to provide students with a clear vision of social action in postmodern culture. "True humanism," Stanton asserts,

• will demolish our gnostic tendencies to believe in a small God who is only interested in our eternal destiny and our moral behavior.

• will refuse to see people as things to be used.

• will vigorously resist the marketing culture that sees people as consumers to be sold rather than served

• will demolish the iPod society—not the device itself, but the social atomization that it represents.

22 Phrasing from A. J. Conyers, "Can Postmodernism Be Used as a Template for Christian Theology?" *Christian Scholar's Review* 33:3 (Spring 2004).

Rowling's books for their kids. Without even knowing the ending of the seventh volume of the Harry series, we are prepared to bet that it will be happy; its control lies not in the fates, but in its author's hands, and in her readers' confident assumption that Harry's story will not turn out to be tragic.[23]

This is the most valuable lesson we teachers have to share with our bewildered students: that their story is part of a grander narrative that is the human story, and it remains securely in its Author's hands. For those who hear and believe, it will not turn out tragic.

---

23 Martin Kaplan, "Can a postmodern nation write a good-vs.-evil tale?" *USA Today*, November 29, 2001.

14

THE CHRISTIAN WORLDVIEW IN IMAGE-CONDITIONED CULTURE: REFLECTIONS ON HOMILETICAL STRATEGIES

William Renay Wilson II

In the video- and Internet-saturated world, movement from one idea to another seems to require no necessary logical connection. From television to cinema, images change rapidly in video media, sometimes resembling a stream of consciousness. Web sites encourage visitors to explore digital pages in potentially ever new sequences, without ordering that exploration as do books and even, to a lesser extent, print magazines and newspapers. Some homiletical theorists interpret this trend in video and digital communication as expressing a fundamental cultural shift and therefore propose a shift away from rational modes and methods in preaching toward creating primarily emotional experiences through imagery that are only secondarily rational communications. Is this approach an improvement over traditional homiletics for communicating the Christian worldview? This paper explores some of the effects contemporary TV and the Internet have on cognitive formation and the implications these effects have for preaching to communicate the Christian worldview.

TELEVISION

Television is undoubtedly the "most pervasive communication medium our society has ever known."[1] It has also likely conditioned

---

1 Robert G. Finney, "Television," in *Handbook on Mass Media in the United States: The Industry*

William Renay Wilson II <wrenay2@yahoo.com> is visiting professor of Christian Studies at Fudan University, Shanghai, and assistant professor of New Testament for the International Institute for Christian Studies. He teaches and lectures extensively on the Bible and Christian worldview in China and Southeast Asia. He received his PhD and MDiv from Southwestern Baptist Theological Seminary and his BA from Wingate University.

our cultural consciousness to prefer emotional, fragmented, visual stimuli over rational, logical, verbal forms of communication.

Visual and Emotive

The key element in any TV program is drama. Regardless of verbal content, TV is interesting because of the dramatic images, sounds, scene changes, camera angles, attractive announcers, and often bombastic advertisements.[2] The eye is naturally drawn to visual changes; the most striking, the most dramatic changes will generally capture the viewer's attention. Television as a predominantly visual medium uses standard editing procedures to manipulate this natural tendency, drawing viewers in with the "drama" of image juxtaposition.[3] As an involuntary response to stimuli, such a visual-neurological phenomenon is decidedly reactionary and thus perhaps emotional more than rational. According to an analysis published in *Critical Studies in Mass Communication*, juxtaposing images "from diverse contexts weakens their symbolic meaning, leading individuals to respond on a more sensual level. Rational interpretive meaning is displaced by an aesthetic of desire and sensuality rooted in bodily intensities."[4] Such TV images do not invite or demand rational acts of interpretation, explanation, or examination, instead seeking only to conjure emotional experiences. This valuing of emotion over reason drives not only entertainment genres such as feature movies and sitcoms but also broadcast news. "The highest power of television journalism," asserts NBC's Reuven Frank, "is not in the transmission of information but in the transmission of experience . . . joy, sorrow, shock, fear, these are the stuff of news."[5]

Cognitive Fragmentation

In addition to fostering affective response, TV's technique for quickly moving from one subject to another, combining contradictory images in a "flash" of sensory exposure, threatens to strip the habitual viewer of the ability or desire to think critically.[6] Daily exposure to

and Its Audiences, ed. Erwin K. Thomas and Brown H. Carpenter (Westport, CT: Greenwood Press, 1994), 184.

2 Jeremy Murray-Brown, "Video Ergo Sum," in *Video Icons & Images*, ed. Alan M. Olson, Christopher Parr, and Debra Parr (New York: State University of New York Press, 1991), 23.

3 Renee Hobbs, "Television and the Shaping of Cognitive Skills," in *Video Icons & Images*, ed. Alan M. Olson, Christopher Parr, and Debra Parr (New York: State University of New York Press, 1991), 37.

4 John B. Harms and David R. Dickens, "Postmodern Media Studies: Analysis or Symptom?" *Critical Studies in Mass Communication* 13, no. 3 (September 1996): 211.

5 Reuven Frank, quoted in Murray-Brown, "Video Ergo Sum," 27–28.

6 Bernard Reymond, "Preaching and the New Media," *The Modern Churchman* 34, no. 5

unrelated images artificially spliced and connected desensitizes the mind to the linear coherence characteristic of literate culture. Moving seamlessly from famine to deodorant, natural disaster to automobiles, or genocide to cosmetic surgery would seem to demand an explanation. Yet routinely none is given. Often all that remains is a chaotic emotional stream of consciousness without reasonable connection: from sorrow to embarrassment, fear to covetousness, shock to vanity. Program genre itself is increasingly disappearing. Once-distinguishable categories are now collapsing into hybrids: infotainment, edutainment, infomercials, advertorials, simulated news, "reality" TV.[7] Strictly utilitarian programming does not entertain and will not sell. The genres must mix and meld into one massive amalgamation. The boundaries between "serious" TV and entertainment disappear.[8] In this way, TV has revealed its fundamental ruling principle: If programming does not entertain, if it does not "massage" consciousness, no one will watch. The medium has created a surreal and fragmented worldview, a "pseudo-reality" which displaces "unmediated reality" with "show biz."[9]

Unfortunately, critical thinking is often not particularly entertaining. Discerning the fine distinctions that often separate truth and error offers little drama. It is easier and much more entertaining to sit back and allow images, which only need to be recognized, to invoke experience.[10] The demand for constant entertainment nearly free from serious information may soon shape TV culture such that it no longer attempts to distinguish such information from floods of imagery. This direction in TV programming influences culture by moving thinking and communicating into a stream-of-consciousness paradigm in which fluid transition from one bit of information to another unrelated fragment has become normal, and viewers are induced to react emotionally to a bombardment of visual stimuli.[11]

(1993): 23.

7 Harms and Dickens, "Postmodern Media Studies," 211, 214.

8 Gerald Celente with Tom Milton, *Trend Tracking: The System to Profit from Today's Trends* (New York: John Wiley & Sons, 1990), 45–47. Cf. Jon Katz's statement in "Rock, Rap, and Movies Bring the News," *Rolling Stones*, 5 March 1992, 33: The "Old News" is dying out, but the "New News" is a "heady concoction, part Hollywood film and TV movie, part pop music and pop art, mixed with popular culture and celebrity magazines, tabloid telecasts, cable and home video."

9 William F. Fore, "The Contemporary Text: Media and Preaching," *Journal for Preachers* 18, no. 2 (Lent 1995): 35.

10 Neil Postman, *Amusing Ourselves to Death: Public Discourse in the Age of Show Business* (New York: Penguin Books, 1985), 73.

11 William E. Brown, "Theology in a Postmodern Culture: Implications of a Video-Dependent Society," in *The Challenge of Postmodernism: An Evangelical Engagement*, ed. David S.

THE INTERNET

The rise of the Internet further complicates relationships between cognitive formation, communication, and rationale discourse. The Internet has perhaps changed the very nature of knowing and the definition of literacy to include understanding facilitated by video, audio, animated graphics, and hyperlinked text.[12] The nature of "text" is also being redefined in the same terms: "New Media" like the Internet are both integrated and interactive, fusing sound, video, and other forms of data.[13] The "audiovisual variant (texts accompanied by images and sounds)" is gradually overtaking oral and written forms of communication. This in turn further "reveals the central position of the screen and the rise of a culture of images."[14] As a result, within the new "visual culture" dominated by TV, the Internet, photography, cinema, and Youtube video fragments, "a new aesthetic is emerging in which depth, narrative, and meaning are being replaced with the pleasures of sensuous experience and spectacular effect."[15]

Feeling a Text

The integrated qualities of New Media are therefore changing the nature of cognition and learning from linear "book" learning to learning by image-level impression or association (hypertext).[16] This change impinges on culture as a whole. Since at least the Middle Ages, knowledge has been ordered by the book in a linear sequence.[17] Readers' knowledge increases as they follow the linear order determined by the author. The hypertext environment, however, delivers non-sequential reading and writing. Here readers encounters a multi-linear experience that "threatens to overturn the organization and management of knowledge as we have known it to date," from monolinearity to multi-linearity. "Text" as object is deconstructed, and a book is "dissolved into a network of association."[18] Even the process of following

Dockery (Wheaton: Victor Books, 1995), 318.

12 Rachel A. Karchmer, "The Journey Ahead: Thirteen Teachers Report How the Internet Influences Literacy and Literacy Instruction in Their K-12 Classrooms," *Reading Research Quarterly*, 36, no. 4, (Oct.– Dec., 2001): 442.

13 George P. Landow, *Hypertext 2.0: The Convergence of Contemporary Critical Theory and Technology* (Baltimore: The Johns Hopkins University Press, 1997), 3.

14 Jan A.G.M van Dijk, *The Network Society: Social Aspects of New Media*, 2nd ed. (London: Sage Publications, 2006), 213.

15 Martin Lister, Jon Dovey, Seth Giddings, Iain Grant, and Kieran Kelly, eds. *New Media: A Critical Introduction* (London: Routledge, 2003), 97.

16 van Dijk, *The Network Society*, 225.

17 See Walter J. Ong, *Orality and Literacy* (London: Routledge, 2002).

18 Lister, et al. eds. *New Media*, 25.

links and reading hypertext can lead to cognitive overload ("Which link goes where, and how to get back?") and disorientation ("Where am I in this text?").[19] The reader is left to "feel" his way around a text.

Universal "Text"

Traditional writing is a static product, disclosing the author's intended message in its final form. Such writing provides an ideal platform for order and formal structure (or linearity), necessary components of rational argumentation.[20] Published hard copies, for good or ill, are "finished." The argument is finished and ready for examination. The published computer text, however, is perhaps never finished, always open to revision, and therefore much more difficult to evaluate. Theoretically, the hypertext document is an endless "draft." As digital media, Internet "texts" may exist in a permanent state of flux, potentially never existing as "hard copy" and always open to augmentation. Wikipedia, for example, is a collaborative Internet-based encyclopedia to which practically anyone at anytime may contribute new content or editorial revision. "Texts" like these are therefore potentially free from traditional authorial authority and open to free interaction and editorial change, thus becoming "new" texts altogether.[21]

Going far beyond the open authorship of wikis, cyber technologies such as "Automatic Discourse Generation" or "Natural Language Generation" (NLG) access electronic data and attempt to create natural human language automatically by machine, without contemporaneous human agency. NLG literally rewrites and customizes stored and digitized "documents" for the individual reader each time it is accessed by hyperlinks or other mediums. Applied examples include generating weather reports, responses to customer service inquiries, and computer-tailored letters encouraging smokers attempting to quit.[22] Such hypertext links can connect an assertion, not just with a reference point in another text, but with the entire text itself, even with libraries of texts: "In theory, each computer text may incorporate every other electronic text, perhaps leading us to a world with a single, universal text."[23] This way of reading, knowing, and communicating

---

19 Patricia M. Boechler, "How Spatial Is Hyperspace? Interacting with Hypertext Documents: Cognitive Processes and Concepts," *Cyberspace and Behavior* 4, no. 1 (2001): 23–46.

20 Simon Barker, "The End of Argument: Knowledge and the Internet," *Philosophy and Rhetoric* 33, no. 2 (2000): 166–167; 171, 175.

21 Lister, et al. eds. *New Media*, 16–17.

22 John Bateman, "Introduction," Natural Language Generation: An Introduction and Open-ended Review of the State of the Art, http://www.fb10.uni-bremen.de/anglistik/langpro/webspace/jb/info-pages/nlg/ATG01/node2.html. Bateman's introductory article itself was generated automatically from a database.

23 Barker, "The End of Argument," 173–174.

can dissolve the distinction between authors, readers, and texts: What "text" am I reading? Who is reading, and who is writing? How can I follow an argument that is never finally made?

Embodying the Postmodern

The formative impact of these media on consciousness, together with post-Enlightenment philosophies such as that of Friederich Nietzsche,[24] has led contemporary Western culture into a new era characterized by the free acceptance and even preference for contradiction, chaos, and irrationality.[25] The postmodern ethos "swims, even wallows, in the fragmentary and the chaotic currents of change as if that is all there is."[26] Hypertext is the "technological embodiment" of seminal postmodern theorists and disciples of Nietzsche, such as Foucault and Derrida, who proposed literary theories of fragmentation, non-linearity, and "death of the author."[27] In the post-rational image-oriented mind, words no longer carry meaning; they are only "masks of masks and veils of veils" in an "endless drift of meaning" that can never be stopped, much less understood.[28] Television- and Internet-mediated thought patterns "require an order of consciousness that is able to subordinate or relativize systemic knowing;" such patterns eclipse the rational.[29]

Yet language itself must demonstrate systemic coherence. Order in language is crucial to its function. Words must occur in a commonly recognized sequence, or grammar, in order to create meaning. As these media continue to shape consciousness and postmodern sensibilities continue to direct it, emphasis on verbal communication may continue to fade.[30] Communication in this context is best achieved through images: "A picture is worth a thousand words." What a picture actually says, however, may be only a matter of impression or association.

---

24 This paper cannot, unfortunately, also treat the philosophical path that finds fulfillment in the changes in knowledge that video and digital technology encourage. Nietzsche, however, is well known for his radically relativistic view of truth and knowledge: "What then is truth? A mobile army of metaphors, metonyms, and anthropomorphisms" (from his "On truth and lie in an extra-moral sense").

25 Harms and Dickens, "Postmodern Media Studies," 211.

26 David Harvey, *The Condition of Postmodernity: An Enquiry into the Origins of Cultural Change* (Cambridge, MA: Basil Blackwell, 1989), 44.

27 Lister, et al. eds. *New Media*, 28.

28 Mark Taylor, *Erring: A Postmodern A/theology* (Chicago: University of Chicago Press, 1984), 174.

29 Robert Kegan, *In Over Our Heads: The Mental Demands of Modern Life* (Cambridge, MA: Harvard University Press, 1994), 316.

30 Kevin Perrotta, *Taming the TV Habit* (Ann Arbor: Servant Books, 1982), 51–63.

In a culture that often seems to aggressively prescribe pluralism as the only legitimate worldview,[31] these developments have monumental religious implications. An image-conditioned consciousness more naturally ignores or rejects questions of universal truth. Differences between right and wrong are more often decided on existential terms: "What is right or wrong for me!"[32] The notion of absolute truth is merely a human creation designed to exert power over others or alleviate the stress of ambiguous experience.[33] Contradictory viewpoints can be held simultaneously without intellectual disruption. Individuals can freely make the truth claim that there is no truth. One truth is just as good as any other. All that matters is how one feels about any given subject.[34] With this fragmented, pluralist, video-oriented cultural milieu in view, how can the contemporary preacher hope to communicate the Christian worldview?

HOMILETICAL STRATEGIES

These apparent shifts in cultural consciousness have not gone unnoticed by homileticians. Contemporary theorists are proposing, in conjunction with the culture at large, a shift away from rational modes and methods.

Emulating Trends

Adopting electronic media's forms and functions, many homileticians are calling for the creation of an emotional experience. According to Robert Stephen Reid, chair of the communications department at the University of Dubuque (Iowa), "Regardless what people may say, what they appear to want is an experience that moves them. Thus, regardless of theological stripe, this is the rhetorical strategy of preaching that is increasingly commensurate with the emerging postmodern sensibility."[35] The underlying assumption of such preaching theory is that experience rather than understanding exerts greater control over thought and action. Men are moved to faith by their "intuitive and

---

31 Cf. Allan Bloom, *The Closing of the American Mind* (New York: Simon and Schuster, 1987), 25–26; D. A. Carson, *The Gagging of God: Christianity Confronts Pluralism* (Grand Rapids: Zondervan, 1996), 19.

32 Brown, "Theology in a Postmodern Culture," 318.

33 Taylor, 174–175.

34 Jim Leffel, "Our New Challenge: Postmodernism," in *The Death of Truth*, ed. Dennis McCallum (Minneapolis: Bethany House, 1996), 31.

35 Robert Stephen Reid, "Postmodernism and the Function of the New Homiletic in Post-Christendom Congregations," *Homiletic* 20, no. 2 (Winter 1995): 11.

emotive sectors of consciousness."[36] Preaching from this perspective becomes affectively stimulating but intellectually passive. Preaching involving complex logic and detailed argumentation is supposedly "a museum artifact, or should be, if the speaker wants to communicate" in a culture of dwindling attention spans.[37] Such preaching should, in a sense, communicate non-verbally, relying on imagery, symbolism, and emotional appeal.[38]

Pulpit Imagery

New Media seems to have informed, at least indirectly, this new homiletical theory, presenting preachers with a paradigm for achieving non-doctrinal emotional goals. According to such theory, preaching should be "less concerned with conversions and dogma . . . reaching people through their feelings and imagination."[39] According to some theoretical rhetorical structures, sermons should be filled with imagery "flashes" that resemble commercial breaks or camera cuts.[40] Sermons may be designed like hour-long TV programs complete with small blocks of material (scenes) interrupted by musical "commercial breaks" with "God portrayed as our 'sponsor.'"[41] Such structural innovations could resemble a Web page's collage or patchwork quilt pattern, as opposed to a straight line of linear argumentation.[42]

Giving this same basic concept a more sophisticated look, David Buttrick has proposed a rhetorical structure based on his anticipation of a new "visual, or associational logic, something that can best be described as a logic of consciousness."[43] The power of preaching formulated on this basis is its aesthetic or imagistic quality.[44] Preaching is then no longer concerned with discourse on truth but with imaging for response.[45] Buttrick seems to frame his entire homiletic in terms of image, illustration, depiction, story, and metaphor, all in an effort

---

36 Henry H. Mitchell, *Celebration & Experience in Preaching* (Nashville: Abingdon Press, 1990), 23.

37 Raymond Bailey, "Preaching in the Electronic Village," *Review and Expositor* 90, no. 3 (Summer 1993): 351, 357.

38 Reymond, "Preaching and the New Media," 26.

39 Ibid., 28.

40 Reymond, "Preaching and the New Media," 27.

41 Bailey, "Preaching in the Electronic Village," 352.

42 Reymond, "Preaching and the New Media," 27–29.

43 David G. Buttrick, "Preaching Between the Times: Homiletics in a Postmodern World," in *Theology and the Interhuman*, ed. Robert R. Williams (Valley Forge: Trinity Press International, 1995), 153.

44 Harold N. Englund, "Observations on Preaching since 1950," *Reformed Review* 40, no. 1 (Autumn 1986): 54.

45 Buttrick, "Speaking Between the Times," 156.

to "bring into view" what is not readily visible.[46] The sermon is based on an underlying "image grid" that forms the basis of an entire message. Images, illustrations, and concrete examples do not merely function in support of particular ideas; "they interrelate in consciousness to form a whole structure of meaning."[47] This interrelation of images is not for dazzling rhetorical display; the aim is an "all-but-subliminal action in consciousness."[48] Gathering interesting images does not, however, complete the process. They must be strung together in ways patterned after contemporary consciousness. This of course rules out linear reasoning in an image-saturated culture. The connectives are not explanatory material used to specify meaning. Images are juxtaposed through free associations, analogies, contrasts, and plot sequences.[49] The end result begins to resemble "stream of consciousness" techniques, TV's "cut" and "flash" techniques, or hypertext's endless linked associations.

With this exaltation of imagery, contemporary homiletical theory disposes of already-waning modern emphases on reason and instead absorbs the idioms and forms of the technology age.[50] The pulpit becomes less a vehicle for teaching[51] and more a medium for moving listeners by mental "sight" to an emotional crescendo.[52] Because of the growing dominance of image- oriented cognition, "image-rich" narratives are the best place to look for sermonic material.[53] The linear logic of the New Testament epistles is less desirable because they often require explanation. William Willimon, one of the most celebrated champions of the new homiletic, intends to avoid explanation in his preaching all together. For him, narrative is the best preaching material because there is nothing beyond the narrative to be taught. Christian "truth" can only be "experienced."[54]

RESISTING TRENDS

Should preaching be concerned primarily with the shape and direction of culture at large or primarily with shaping the culture in

---

46 David Buttrick, *Homiletic: Moves and Structure* (Philadelphia: Fortress Press, 1987), 113.

47 Ibid., 153, 163.

48 Ibid., 167.

49 David Buttrick, "On Doing Homiletics Today," in *Intersections: Post-Critical Studies in Preaching*, ed. Richard L. Eslinger (Grand Rapids: Eerdmans, 1994), 96.

50 Craig A. Loscalzo, "Apologizing for God: Apologetic Preaching to a Postmodern World," *Review and Expositor* 93, no. 3 (Summer 1996): 412.

51 Englund, "Observations on Preaching since 1950," 54.

52 Mitchell, 82–85.

53 Loscalzo, "Apologizing for God," 413.

54 Stanley Hauerwas, "Explaining Why Will Willimon Never Explains," in *A Peculiar Prophet: William Willimon and the Art of Preaching*, ed. Michael A. Turner and William F. Malambri III (Nashville: Abingdon, 2004): 126.

church? Often overlooked in homiletical theory is attention to ecclesiology. What is the Church's nature and function?

Preaching to the Church

In the broadest sense, the Church universal is comprised of all God's people who have been justified by faith in Jesus Christ. Perhaps more relevant for preaching strategy, however, is a biblical understanding of the Church's functions. At the core of church life stands Christ's evangelistic mandate.[55] Prior to this evangelistic function, however, are the corporate functions of worship and edification. While recognized generally as the "people of God," the local church can also be understood as a specific community of believers. According to the New Testament model, these communities gather together regularly, not for evangelism, but for praise and nurture.[56] The gathered church is designed for the regenerate.

In 1 Corinthians 14, for example, Paul highlighted two aspects of this communal gathering. The church at worship turns toward God through praise and thanksgiving. In this context, the unintelligible gift of tongues should be restricted. Otherwise, individual "giving of thanks" will not lead others to focus their attention on God (vv. 15–17). In terms of a horizontal concern for other believers, Paul declares, "When you assemble . . . [l]et all things be done for edification" (v. 26). Paul assumes that gathering together as a church is for the edification of Christians. An unbeliever is free to enter (v. 26), but the assembly is not intended primarily for their benefit.[57] Preaching in the church should be fundamentally for the church, equipping the "saints for the work of service" (Eph 4:12).

Reasonable Doctrine

Image-conditioned culture demonstrates a built-in disdain for questions of truth. Effective communication in this pluralistic context seems to rule out the pursuit of doctrinal clarity or the distinction between truth and error. In fact, Willimon essentially derides any effort to tell the definitive truth about anything: "If you think that truth has to be consistent, or universally valid, or objectively true or some other nonbiblical definition of true, then you ought to go worship that definition of truth and not bother with trying truthfully to serve the Trinity."[58]

---

55 Stanley J. Grenz, *Theology for the Community of God* (Nashville: Broadman & Holman, 1994), 638.

56 Millard J. Erickson, *Christian Theology* (Grand Rapids: Baker Book House, 1993), 1052–1057.

57 Ibid., 1054–1055.

58 William H. Willimon, "Postmodern Preaching: Learning to Love the Thickness of the Text," *Journal for Preachers* 19, no. 3 (Easter 1996): 35.

Despite skepticism regarding the existence or availability of truth, contemporary preaching must pursue and proclaim it, for Jesus said "I am the truth." Preachers must frame the world theologically, regardless of current cognitive fragmentation, offering ultimate meaning to a culture desperate for solidity.[59] Disjointed video culture in its clamor for structure has adopted the rhythms of TV time slots and aimless web surfing as "reality maintenance" techniques providing a shallow form of psychological order.[60] Contemporary preaching must offer instead the coherence of a reasonable Christian worldview.[61]

It is not enough simply to believe in Jesus. Who is Jesus? An effort to answer that question is an effort to make a doctrinal statement, and doctrinal statements inevitably involve old-world linearity and argumentation. Knowledge of the true God can be specified only through doctrine. As Alister McGrath has argued, "The teaching of Jesus has authority on account of who Jesus is—and the identity and significance of Jesus can be spelled out only in doctrinal terms."[62]

To the chagrin of image-conditioned culture, however, doctrinal preaching will inevitably involve reason. As the pendulum swings in homiletical theory toward holistic and therefore more emotional preaching,[63] preachers must not forget the role of reason. If we are to preach to the whole man, there must be a place for rational, logical, and systematic theological formulation. In the church universal, the image of God within men is being restored.[64] Though this image should not be described wholly in terms of intellect or reason, this aspect of regenerate man's makeup must be taken into account.[65] Emotion and reason might seem incompatible in any initial assessment, yet emotion without reason, an irrational response to stimuli, is not an acceptable

---

59 Loscalzo, "Apologizing for God," 416.

60 Robert Kubey and Mihaly Csikszentmihalyi, *Television and the Quality of Life: How Viewing Shapes Everyday Experience* (Hillsdale, NJ: Lawrence Erlbaum Associates, 1990), 182–186.

61 Alister McGrath, *A Passion for Truth: The Intellectual Coherence of Evangelicalism* (Downers Grove: InterVarsity Press, 1996), 241–244.

62 Alister E. McGrath, *Understanding Doctrine: What It Is and Why It Matters* (Grand Rapids: Zondervan, 1990), 103.

63 See Mitchell, 15–36.

64 Note Calvin's statement in *Institutes* 1.15.4: "Now God's image is the perfect excellence of human nature which shone in Adam before his defection, but was subsequently so vitiated and almost blotted out that nothing remains after the ruin except what is confused, mutilated, and disease-ridden. Therefore in some part it now is manifest in the elect, in so far as they have been reborn in the spirit; but it will attain its full splendor in heaven."

65 Martin Luther could list reason explicitly as one aspect of the *imago Dei* (*Luther's Works*, vol. 1, Lectures on Genesis: Chapters 1–15, ed. Jaroslav Pelikan [Saint Louis: Concordia Publishing, 1958], 337). For a helpful survey of the "image of God" in historical theology see James Leo Garrett, *Systematic Theology: Biblical, Historical, and Evangelical*, vol. 1 (Grand Rapids: Eerdmans, 1990), 391–405.

Christian paradigm for faith at all.[66]

Sound, rational, biblical argumentation, coupled with imagery, can stir experience in a video-dependent culture.[67] The doctrines of revelation, incarnation, justification, sanctification, and glorification, clearly narrated, explained, applied, and Spirit illumined can flood the heart with exhilarating wonder that surpasses the New Media's merely emotional conditioning both in its intensity and, more importantly, in its life-transformative power. The story of Jesus Christ crucified, resurrected, and exalted contains enough imagery to glut even the most insatiable appetite for spectacle. Yet, it is the explanation, rational and propositional, that drives the meaning of these narrative images home to the heart: "For Christ also suffered for sins once for all, the righteous for the unrighteous, in order to bring you to God. He was put to death in the flesh, but made alive in the spirit," (1 Peter 3:18 NRSV). Emotive imagery and reasoned argument are interdependent in a holistic Christian worldview. Perhaps the key to gaining a hearing is not so much accommodation to an emergent cultural consciousness, but emotional and rational balance energized by Spirit-led gravity in the pulpit.[68]

---

66 Diogenes Allen, *Christian Belief in a Postmodern World* (Louisville, KY: Westminster/John Knox Press, 1989), 128.

67 H. Armin Moellering, "Creating an Experience," *Concordia Journal* 22, no. 3 (July 1996): 258.

68 John Piper, *The Supremacy of God in Preaching* (Grand Rapids: Baker Book House, 1990), 49–51.

15

SQUASHING SCREWTAPE: DEBUNKING DUALISM AND RESTORING INTEGRITY IN CHRISTIAN EDUCATIONAL THOUGHT AND PRACTICE

David K. Naugle

"But the Christian . . . cannot split up his life into water-tight compartments. The common denominator is to be sought in thought and practical living in an integrated attitude to life."
– Dietrich Bonhoeffer, *Letters and Papers from Prison*

INTRODUCTION

Of all the various temptations to which Christian men and women are regularly subjected, one in particular seems to go unnoticed all too often. Yet it is one of the most serious of all and just may be at the root of all the others. The temptation of which I speak is that of religious or spiritual compartmentalization. With multiple causes and effects, Christian believers of every stripe in every age are often inclined to restrict faith and its influence to the overtly spiritual areas of their lives such as church involvement and private devotions. But then they proceed to go about the real business of daily life on their own independently of God. For many, private life is, indeed, spiritually engag-

David K. Naugle <dnaugle@dbu.edu> is chair and professor of philosophy at Dallas Baptist University, where he has worked for seventeen years in both administrative and academic capacities. He is also the director of the Paideia College Society, serves as a Fellow of the Wilberforce Forum, and is on the advisory board of the International Institute for Christian Studies. He has authored *Worldview: The History of a Concept* and *Reordered Love, Reordered Lives.* He earned a BA from the University of Texas at Arlington; a ThM and ThD (Systematic Theology) from Dallas Theological Seminary; and a PhD (Humanities) from the University of Texas at Arlington.

ing. But faith quickly becomes irrelevant in that same person's public world. Such an individual draws a sure and certain line of distinction between what he or she considers to be sacred and secular. Religious pursuits are eternally significant to be sure, but all other activities are temporal in character. There is the church and there is the world—the Bible study and the corporate Board meeting—but these two domains are kept in isolation from each other at a comfortable distance. Christianity is well ensconced in its particular silo as a special, spiritual realmof life, rather than as a wise and godly way of life for every realm.[1]

Compartmentalization is quite common, even among the deeply devout. And I am convinced that it is a temptation to which Christians who labor in the academy are particularly vulnerable. For a variety of reasons—and the pressures are very real—professors and administrators who are Christians are easily persuaded to check their faith at the campus gate or office door, to hide their light under their tweed coats or in their leather brief cases, and to go about their scholarly, pedagogical or administrative work on the same basis and in the same manner as their non-Christian counterparts. Though such people may be active Christians on weekends and in private life, when it comes to the push and shove of their academic vocations, for the most part they function day to day as practical agnostics or atheists. Though they realize that Jesus is Lord over all, that Christian commitment is to be total, and that living out the faith is supposed to be a 24/7 affair, nonetheless, because the pressures within and without are so great, they succumb to the temptation of compartmentalization and simply jettison the faith in their culturally influential roles as scholars and professors. The cost of Christian consistency is just too high professionally. On the other hand, the cost of inconsistency may be even higher, for at the end of the day it amounts to serious hypocrisy and to a glaring lack of integrity.

This is the problem—the huge and challenging problem—I want to address in this essay. I would like for us to understand the nature, kinds, causes, and consequences of a compartmentalized faith. I also want to respond to this issue from the vantage point of a biblical worldview, especially by focusing on the essential doctrinal elements that abrogate compartmentalization and establish a basis for Christian holism, with an emphasis on Colossians 1:15–20.

A LETTER FROM BELOW

But first I thought it would be interesting to take a look at this matter from the demonic point of view. It seems to me that

---

1 I owe this idea to Kenneth Hermann.

compartmentalization has been one of the most effective strategies ever employed by the underworld to hamstring the Church's redemptive mission and to maintain control of the public square, including our colleges and universities and their students. If the demonic powers can establish compartmentalization (which I will also refer to as dualism) as a fundamental category of religious thought and life, and accordingly, if they can tempt and persuade Christians to limit the expression of their faith to their personal lives, then they have essentially achieved their goal. Eschewing compartmentalization and maturely grasping and applying a biblical worldview across the whole spectrum of life, including the life of the academy, is the last thing—the very last thing—evil spirits would want to ever happen. With this in mind, I thought: *Wouldn't it be interesting to write a new Screwtape letter (with apologies to C. S. Lewis) in which Screwtape, as the veteran tempter and Undersecretary of the Infernal Lowerarchy, writes to the inexperienced enticer Wormwood about his "patient" who is in jeopardy of abandoning his compartmentalized Christianity and beginning to flesh out a biblical worldview across the whole of his life, including his life and work as a professor. What would Screwtape have to say to Wormwood about this situation and how to handle it?* Here is what I think he might have to offer (*indicates words or phrases originally used by Lewis):

My Dear Wormwood:

I have just returned from our weekly meeting of the Infernal Lowerarchy* where before my peers I was utterly humiliated to report that that 'patient' of yours has registered for the IICS worldview conference in Kansas City, Missouri. For hell's sake, how could you let that happen? He was supposed to go on holiday that week. You are on the verge of letting that subject of yours slip through your scaly fingers. At that conference, they intend to discuss how they as professors can be salt and light for—uh, ugh—I can barely make myself say it—"Jesus Christ" in our academic fields and at our universities. They have lined up some keynote speakers and conference presenters who oppose our work to assist them in these matters. Even worse, they plan on discussing how a Christian worldview can impact the academy and not only the academy, but the real world. The theme is something like: "From the Ivory Tower to World Wide Impact" or maybe it's "Global Impact" or something stupid like that. They may, hell forbid, discover how the Enemy's word establishes a lucid vision for scholarship and teaching, not to mention student change and cultural transformation. This cannot happen!

As you might imagine, our Father below* is not pleased with these developments. He fears that the fragmented version of faith and life that we have successfully imparted to them through multiple avenues may be undermined, not only in your patient, but also in others who attend this gathering. Consequently, he has told me to take immediate action, else the consequences will be unusually severe for both you and me.

You know very well that from the time of our cosmic takeover, our fiendish Father has inspired us with a shrewd vision of disintegration. The Enemy (GOD), who has a slight advantage over us as the Creator of the universe, has stamped His triune nature on the world He has made. All things reflect the unity and diversity of His own miserable character, and He wants those loathsome little replicas of Himself* to apprehend His creation as a "uni-verse" with its proper distinctions and overarching integrity. Our goal, however, has been to undermine this coherent vision of reality, pitchfork and tail. We have aspired in all things everywhere to put asunder that which the Enemy has joined together, to halve the whole, to fragment and divide, to exacerbate the diversity and destroy the unity. Or if this doesn't work, we will go the route of monism and make everything the same! Most importantly, we must work to keep faith isolated from real life. That has always been our primary goal, and our success rate over the centuries has been extremely high.

Various unconscious human recruits have served us admirably in promoting our lies. Slubgob* is famous throughout our kingdom for prompting both Plato's forms/world distinction and the dualism of the Gnostics and Manicheans, not to mention his success in adequately infecting the thought of that sexually repressed, neurotic bishop of Hippo with a residual Neoplatonism. Triptweeze* caused these wonderful divisions to endure throughout the Middle Ages, with only a slight scare when Aristotle's philosophy revived and was embraced by that Dumb Ox Dominican who tried to tie nature and grace too closely together for comfort. Fortunately, William of Ockam's nominalism kept them apart and isolated reason from faith. Descartes and Kant contributed unwittingly to our covert cause to ontologically divide and conquer through their respective mind/matter and noumena/phenomena distinctions. The rise of idolized science (how we love to twist the Adversary's gifts!), especially in its evolutionary form (Zozezas' work on Darwin should be noted here), has undermined the notion of creation itself (next to redemption there is no more important doctrine for us to destroy) and made it certain that facts and values are forever severed. Marx, Freud, and Nietzsche, who by then required very little coaxing from us, took things the rest of the way home. How excited we were when the latter of this triumvirate—our favorite infidel—announced to the world that God was actually dead!

But our crowning achievement has been in the churches. Under the well-intended influence of their hoodwinked leaders, they actually believe our lies are the truth! They think they come out of the

Bible. The stupid little Christians have confused creation with sin (or ontology with ethics, to use some fancy talk), and now they can hardly wait to evacuate the planet and head off to heaven where they think they really belong! How joyfully they sing, "This world is not my home, I'm just a passin' through." They gleefully promote heaven over earth, the spiritual over the physical, grace over nature, the soul over the body, the eternal over the temporal, faith over reason and so on. They see everything as essentially sacred or essentially secular. They think that Christianity is its own distinct realm of life rather than a way of life for every realm. They separate their faith from the bulk of their lives and oppose Christ to their cultures. How proud they are of their resulting superspirituality, nicely ensconced in their cozy, well-fortified Christian ghettos! They have bought into our grand vision of disintegration and are compartmentalists, par excellence!

As a result—and how delicious this is!—they slam dunk all vocations except church-related vocations, ministers and missionaries and the like. They think Christians who become professors, and certainly politicians, are virtually apostate, destined to deny the faith. They have substantially abandoned cultural life and essentially turned it over to our control. They have denied the value of the Enemy's creation and their own bodies, and seriously diminished the scope and richness of human experience. Their mental framework enables them to find all the support they need for these perspectives in the way they misread the Bible. How we have caused them to twist many passages to serve our deceptive ends! In short, we have enthroned a good, solid resounding lie at the center of their lives!* We are the kings and queens of twists!

To be sure, my dear Wormwood, we must maintain this dualism, not only in the Christians' churches, but most certainly in their universities. After all, next to the church and the family—our prime targets of subversion—their educational institutions are most influential in shaping the young and affecting culture. Here we got off to a slow start and took some early losses when many of their schools first began—cursed be Luther, Calvin, and those damn Puritans! But thanks to our Department of Miseducation—Chairman Glubose* in particular—we have successfully recaptured the universities and are effectively using them for our own purposes. We have also convinced them, like most of the world, that education is an objective, scientific, worldview-neutral enterprise. We must prevent them from ever discovering that all aspects of scholarship, teaching, and learning are grounded in a diversity of metaphysical assumptions, especially nowadays in the prejudices of naturalism. This kind of blindness makes education one of our most powerful weapons in destroying the tender faith of unsuspecting students. We already have the professors in bondage to this deception.

Above all, we must keep the Christian convictions of these professors quarantined—compartmentalized as it were—from the real business of the academy. We will allow our Christian patients to be professors, but we must not and cannot allow them to be truly Christian professors. They must pursue their respective tasks of scholarship and teaching just like their non-Christian counterparts, remaining oblivious to the fact that their academic work is proceeding on the basis of non-Christian presuppositions and performed in service to the idols of the age. We must never let them recognize their essential spiritual infidelity in their scholarly endeavors. We must never let develop an integrated Christian perspective on their work. Their Christianity and their academic pursuits must be kept in separate spheres. Dualism must rule their lives. Otherwise, our victories in this domain may soon end.

This is why I am so shocked that you, Wormwood, of all tempters, would allow your patient to attend this ridiculous worldview conference. You know good and well that what they are espousing is diametrically opposed to what you and I believe in. We must seek to suppress its effectiveness as much as possible.

So, regarding your patient, I suggest you employ weapons of mass distraction, say with anxieties about matters back home, or with sexual preoccupations, or with silly things, like people with shoes that squeak, or double chins, or odd clothes, or funny hair, or voices out of tune.* That should keep that patient of yours from profiting from this conference, the one thing we can't allow. In any case, report back to me when the conference ends, and I expect to hear of significant success. Or else.

Your affectionate uncle,
Screwtape

DEBILITATING DUALISMS

On the basis of several key passages in Scripture (Col. 2:16–23; 1 Tim. 4:1–5; 1 John 4:1–3) reinforced by reason and experience, I am convinced that compartmentalization (or dualism[2]) which divides reality into the two intrinsically distinct categories of the sacred and secular, is a satanic temptation and, indeed, a doctrine of demons. It is certainly a superlative theological error and should be designated as a "material heresy."[3]

---

2 Though it is possible to distinguish dualism as a metaphysical concept that divides reality into two different and opposing categories from compartmentalization as a practical religious consequence of this division, I will forsake these technical matters and use the two words interchangeably, more or less as synonyms, for a general perspective that sharply segregates sacred and secular life.

3 According to *The Oxford Dictionary of the Christian Church* (3rd ed.), pp. 758–59, Catholic teaching asserts that a "material heresy" "means holding to heretical doctrines through no

Dietrich Bonhoeffer, who would certainly know, calls compartmentalization the most "colossal obstacle" to a unified conception of the Christian faith, noting that in all dualist schemes "Christ becomes a partial and provincial matter within the limits of reality." Here is how Bonhoeffer in his book *Ethics* describes, and, in fact, condemns, this debilitating assumption that has plagued the Church throughout her entire history.

> However great the importance which is attached to the reality of Christ, [in a compartmentalized context] it still always remains a partial reality amid other realities. The division of the total reality into a sacred and profane sphere, a Christian and a secular sphere, creates the possibility of existence in a single one of these spheres, a spiritual existence which has no part in secular existence, and a secular existence which can claim autonomy for itself and can exercise this right of autonomy in its dealings with the spiritual sphere. The monk and the nineteenth-century Protestant secularist typify these two possibilities. The whole of medieval history is centered upon the theme of the predominance of the spiritual sphere over the secular sphere, the predominance of the regnum gratiae over the regnum naturae [grace eats up nature]; and the modern age is characterized by an ever increasing independence of the secular in its relations with the spiritual [nature eats up grace]. So long as Christ and the world are conceived as two opposing and mutually repellent spheres, man will be left in the following dilemma: he abandons reality as a whole, and places himself in one or other of the two spheres. He seeks Christ without the world, or he seeks the world without Christ. In either case he is deceiving himself. Or else he tries to stand in both spaces at once and thereby becomes the man of eternal conflict, the kind of man who emerged in the period after the reformation and who has repeatedly set himself up as representing the only form of Christian existence which is in accord with reality.[4]

This ontological schizophrenia is undoubtedly the mental illness of the West and of the Western Church. It is a mental illness that continues to afflict us today. In passing, it is important to note that to the

---

fault of one's own, 'in good faith,' as is the case, e.g., with most persons brought up in heretical surroundings. It constitutes neither crime nor sin, nor is such a person strictly speaking a heretic, since, having never accepted certain doctrines, he cannot reject or doubt them." Most well-meaning, evangelical dualists or compartmentalists are "material heretics" who should be distinguished from "formal heretics" who intentionally and obstinately deny or doubt, after baptism, any historically defined doctrine of the orthodox faith.

4 Dietrich Bonhoeffer, *Ethics* (New York: Macmillan, 1975), pp. 196–97.

extent that dualism is a product of secular thought, it is a worldly and ungodly point of view, even though most dualists in the church or in Christian academies embrace it as a mark of super-spirituality. The irony is palpable.

To be sure, in academic settings, dualism results in the loss of integrity and wholeness, that is, in the forfeiture of being complete and undivided in educational thought and practice, among both teachers and students. It means a failure to make our Christian convictions central to our academic work.

Dualism's impact on individuals who aspire to an academic career is powerful. For example, Deborah Moreland, who is chair and professor of philosophy at Mountain View College, in Dallas, Texas, explains in these autobiographical words how dualism nearly prevented her from pursuing an academic career.

> Like many other lovers of God, my most devastating misunderstandings caused me to become so heavenly minded that I was no earthly good, because that's what I thought the Bible required of me. I read Colossians 2:8, "Beware of philosophy," and believed human thought to be evil. I read Colossians 3:2, "Set your minds on things above . . ." and concluded I should avoid the activities and institutions of physical life. I read Matthew 6:33, "But seek first his kingdom and his righteousness . . ." and thought I should obsess about heaven and resign myself to poverty. I read the Great Commission and thought Christianity was only about saving souls for the Great Beyond. I believed that serving God meant avoiding all earthly endeavors and investing myself in missions or full time ministry, so that's what I did. But a funny thing happened on the way to the ministry . . . .[5]

Or consider this recent testimony from Jeremy Shepherd, a former student of mine at Dallas Baptist University, who nearly left the University *because* it sought to integrate faith and learning.

> When I came to Dallas Baptist University, I had a rather violent reaction to what I thought was a profound category mistake. Coming from the public school system, I had a deeply embedded idea of how . . . "religion ought to be privately engaging but publicly irrelevant." . . . My reaction to the university's holistic vision of life was so serious that I almost left the university to go get myself a "real" education. . . . My worldview lenses saw "education" as

5 Debbie Moreland, "In His Intelligent Image," *Worldview Church E-Report*, a publication of the Wilberforce Forum and BreakPoint, August 2003.

something totally separate from my "faith." . . . [This] was only a small part of something much deeper and much more profound, the separation of my "faith" from the rest of my life. Over the last years, I have come to know that this split vision of reality and life is not Biblical and is actually sin. Nonetheless, I would character-ize my former self as a methodological religious dualist."[6]

Finally, for DBU alumna Jennifer Latham, dualism was particu-larly pernicious in its effect on her university studies. She arrived on campus as a freshman with one primary goal in mind: to land a well-paying job upon graduation. Aside from this, education held modest value, and she was convinced that her faith had little if any bearing upon it. God was concerned exclusively about spiritual matters, she reasoned, and He couldn't care less about biology, psychology, the fine arts and so on. In her own words,

> Dualism, I discovered, is essentially separating life into two op-posing spheres—things pertaining to God, and things that are not. It's precisely this type of split-level thinking that led me to erect a distinct barrier between my faith and my academic endeavors. What hit smack dab in between the eyes my junior year is that this mindset is most definitely rooted in an incorrect understanding of the Scriptures and of God Himself.[7]

Now I could easily multiply similar testimonies from colleagues and students I have known over the years. I would also have to num-ber myself among the dualists for the first dozen or so years of my own Christian journey, as I rather proudly elevated the explicitly spiritual domain over all other aspects of life. Yet I must admit that when I came to understand and believe differently on the basis of a comprehensive biblical vision of reality rooted in the themes of creation, fall, incarna-tion, redemption, and consummation, it was like a second conversion experience, a paradigm shift of the greatest magnitude, and a transi-tion to a whole new outlook and way of life! I have not been the same kind of Christian . . . or educator since.

Yet I find that this illegitimate division that rips the fabric of reality into unrelated and unequal parts persists in the thinking and living of countless numbers of well-intentioned believers, not the least among educators and those whom they seek to educate. Indeed, the basic,

---

6 Jeremy Shepherd, "Christian Dualism," an unpublished paper presented at the Paid-eia College Society Student Conference, April 2004, Dallas Baptist University. Available at <http://dbu.edu/naugle/pcs_conference_sp04.htm#studentpapers>.

7 Personal correspondence with the author, January 15, 2000.

generic dichotomy between sacred and secular expresses itself in a variety of dualistic species or specific forms of compartmentalization, of which the most insidious for Christian educators are the following four.

1. *Metaphysical dualisms:*

    The *sacred/secular dualism* identifies specific realms of reality as intrinsically religious and related to God, or as intrinsically non-religious and unrelated to Him;

    a. the eternal/temporal dualism divides time and history, along with all human actions and events, as spiritually meaningful and enduring or as physically transitory and insignificant;
    b. the spirit/matter dualism classifies all human experiences as sacred and eternal or as secular and temporal, depending upon whether or not they are spiritual or material in character and involve the activities of the soul or the body; and
    c. the heaven/earth dualism radically bifurcates the connection between this and the other world, spatially depicting God and His kingdom at a virtually infinite distance, far removed from this world.

Many Christians, educators included, tend to view academic pursuits in secular, temporal, natural, and earthly terms, unrelated to the sacred, eternal, spiritual, and otherworldly affairs of human life.

2. *Anthropological dualisms:*

    a. The *soul/body dualism* distinguishes between the mental and physical components of the human person as radically different kinds of things with diverse properties. In a Christian context, the soul is often associated with the true self, the seat of spirituality, and that which is saved and survives the death of the body, whereas the body is regarded as the soul's container, the source of sin, and that which succumbs to death and returns to the earth; and
    b. the *spirit/flesh dualism* is essentially the same, with its affirmation of the spirit as good and the source of life, and its denigration of the flesh or body and physicality as the source of sin and death.

Many Christians, educators included, are thus inclined to elevate the spirit, denigrate the body, to pursue a life of asceticism (or quasi-asceticism), and think that the highest task in life is to save souls, and that, eternally speaking, study, teaching, and learning is a secondary, if not inferior enterprise.[8]

3. *Epistemological dualisms:*
    a. The *faith/reason dualism* sharply contrasts belief and knowledge, viewing faith as subjective opinion and the basis of religious and ethical life, and reason as objective truth and the source of a scientific understanding of the world;
    b. the *fact/value dichotomy* similarly ascribes trustworthy facts or genuine knowledge to reason and science, and relegates personal values and metaphysical preferences to faith and religion;
    c. the *head/heart dualism* separates thought and feeling and roots faith and values in the subjective faculty of the human heart and grounds rationality and facticity in the objective operations of the human mind; and
    d. the *freedom/authority dualism* asserts that intellectual autonomy is necessary for the pursuit and discovery of truth, whereas any form of heteronomy squelches and distorts the scientific quest for human understanding.

Many educators, Christians included, believe that faith, values, the

---

8 Contrary to this belittling of the physical aspect of human nature is this great affirmation of the goodness of the body from the pen of Lin Yutang, *The Importance of Living* (New York: John Day, 1937), pp. 25ff. "The most obvious fact which philosophers refuse to see is that we have got a body. Tired of seeing our moral imperfections and our savage instincts and impulses, sometimes our preachers wish that we were made like angels, and yet we are at a total loss to imagine what the angel's life would be like. We either give the angels a body and a shape like our own—except for a pair of wings—or we don't. . . . I sometimes think that it is an advantage even for angels to have a body with the five senses. If I were to be an angel, I should like to have a school girl complexion, but how am I going to have a school girl complexion without skin? I still should like to drink a glass of tomato juice or iced orange juice, but how am I going to appreciate iced orange juice without having thirst? How would an angel paint without pigment, sing without the hearing of sounds, smell the fine morning air without a nose? How would he enjoy the immense satisfaction of scratching an itch, if his skin doesn't itch? And what a terrible loss in the capacity for happiness that would be! Either we have to have bodies and have all our bodily wants satisfied, or else we are pure spirits and have no satisfactions at all. All satisfactions imply want.

"I sometimes think what a terrible punishment it would be for a ghost or an angel to have no body, to look at a stream of cool water and have no feet to plunge into it and get a delightful cooling sensation from it, to see a dish of Peking or Long Island Duck and have no tongue to taste it, to see crumpets and have not teeth to chew them, to see the beloved faces of our dear ones and have not emotions to feel towards them. Terribly sad it would be if we should one day return to this earth as ghosts and move silently into our children's bedroom, to see a child lying there in bed and have no hands to fondle him and nor arms to clasp him, no chest for his warmth to penetrate to, no round hollow between cheek and shoulder for him to nestle against, and no ears to hear his voice."

concerns of the heart and the dictates of authority belong in the church and private life, but that the school or college is the place where human reason, unencumbered by any form of personal faith or system of values, is deployed freely in search of genuine knowledge about the empirical world.

4. *Ethical-political dualisms*:
    a. The *private/public dualism* dissociates personal character and public conduct and argues that the kind of person one is morally and spiritually is unrelated to professional performance and the content of one's public ideas and actions;
    b. the *belief/behavior dualism* separates what we know from how we actually live, theory from practice, and argues that knowledge as facts, information, and data is value-neutral and has no ethical implications;
    c. the *individual/community* dualism, especially in the West, promotes the well-being of the private person and demotes concern for the common good;
    d. the *church/state dualism* builds a wall of separation between religious influence and the public square and seeks to keep ecclesiastical and political affairs in their respective silos; and
    e. the *Christ/culture dualism* either pits the church against the world, relates them hierarchically (one over the other), or places Christians in a relationship of paradox and tension with society.

Many educators, Christians included, believe that the private lives of public educators is a matter of indifference, that knowledge incurs no ethical obligation, that the individual reigns supreme, that the church is the church and the state is the state, and that Jesus Christ and the Christian faith play little if any role in the transformation of human culture and social institutions.

CAUSES

Obviously, we humans must have a deeply ingrained dualistic streak and are quite adept at sawing things in two. If we add all these dualisms up, we would find here enumerated four metaphysical dualisms (sacred/secular, eternal/temporal, spirit/matter, heaven/earth), two anthropological dualisms (soul/body, spirit/flesh), four epistemic dualisms (faith/reason, fact/value, head/heart, freedom/authority), and five ethico-political dualisms (private/public, belief/behavior, individual/community, church/state, Christ/culture)—fifteen in all. I suspect that this is just the tip of the proverbial iceberg.

While it is certainly legitimate to distinguish ontologically *between* the Infinite, Creator God and His finite creation, and to recognize various appropriate, biblically-based distinctions and dualities in faith and life (e.g., present and future, wisdom and folly, obedience and disobedience, etc.), it is a mistake to draw a line of demarcation *within* the creation to undermine the inherent goodness of the things God has made. Indeed, we tend to forget that everything God made is very good, and in our forgetfulness we promote some aspects of God's handiwork (like the soul) and demote others (like the body). We have come to view spiritual things as good and physical things as inferior, and to regard certain aspects of God's creation with suspicion or even as sinful. We have confused creation with sin, essential structure with moral direction, ontology with ethics.

Why is this the case? Where do these multiple compartmentalizations come from? Why have we become committed dualists? I can think of seven causes that have generated our disconnected approach to faith and life.

1. *The metaphysical effects of sin.* Ultimately, sin is the root cause of the breakdown of creation, the shattered human condition, and the source of our malicious dualisms. God's purpose of shalom—soundness, wholeness, integrity, well-being—for humanity, the earth, and all its creatures has been vandalized, resulting in corruption, disintegration and death. Alienation and incoherence have replaced the divinely intended unity and peace between God and humanity, within the self, among people, and in the earth. A great disturbance has occurred and rendered the entire world, all people, and the whole of life abnormal. The creation itself has undergone a vast process of decay and dissolution. The cosmos has become chaos. Things are no longer the way they are supposed to be.[9] The words of a well-known English nursery rhyme capture well our original state and the now fragmented human condition and world situation: Humpty Dumpty sat on a wall, / Humpty Dumpty had a great fall. / All the kings' horses / And all the kings' men / Couldn't put Humpty together again.

---

9 This idea and the notion about the vandalism of shalom are from Cornelius Plantinga, Jr., *Not the Way It's Supposed to Be: A Breviary of Sin* (Grand Rapids: Eerdmans, 1996), chp. 1.

2. *The noetic effects of sin.* Sin is not only the root cause of a disrupted cosmos, but has also blinded the human mind, and generated faulty, dualistic views of reality. The existence and nature of God, the identity of human beings as His image, the character of the world as His creation, and the residual goodness and integrity of all things remain unknown because of the profound ignorance of the fallen mind. As John Calvin writes in his *Institutes of the Christian Religion* (1.5.11), "But although the Lord represents both himself and his everlasting kingdom in the mirror of his works with very great clarity, such is our stupidity that we grow increasingly dull toward so manifest testimonies, and they flow away without profiting us." So people instead suppress the truth in unrighteousness, are actively engaged in futile speculations, are darkened in their foolish hearts, and are deceived in thinking themselves to be wise when in fact they are fools. For its proclivity to falsehood, the whole human races stands under the judgment of God (see Rom. 1:18–32). Nonetheless, humanity's native religious impulses prompt it to manufacture alternative faiths and philosophies in place of God and the truth. Humanity reinvents reality industriously and is responsible for the existence of a multitude of fallacious worldviews, including those characterized by serious forms of compartmentalization. Sin, by its impact on the mind, is the source of dualistic interpretations of God, human life, and the world.

3. *The volitional effects of sin.* Sin affected things metaphysically and mentally to be sure, but it has also has had its impact morally as well. We will give God a portion of life typically labeled "religion" but the rest we want to keep for ourselves. We are in love with our autonomy and reserve the right, a la Frank Sinatra, to do things our way.

4. *The powerful influence of dualistic philosophies and religions.* Various religious and philosophical systems of dualistic persuasion, generated by the fallen human mind throughout history, have corrupted proper Christian perspectives and generated compartmentalized views of life. Platonism, with its strong contrasts between soul and body and the visible and invisible worlds, is a chief culprit in this regard, so much so that Friedrich Nietzsche once described popular Christianity

in his day as nothing but "Platonism for the people."[10] The Gnostic heresy, past and present, has unfortunately infected orthodox Christianity especially with its severe denigration of materiality, as well as its faulty Christology and doctrine of secret knowledge. Plotinus's Neoplatonism, with its teachings of a hidden God, asceticism, mysticism, and multiple levels of reality, has influenced the Church dramatically, especially through traces of this philosophy in St. Augustine, who was influenced by this movement. Other diverse philosophical and religious schools of thought, including Zoroastrianism, Aristotelianism, Philonism, Manicheism, Docetism, Marcionism, Bogomilism, Paulicianism, Aristotelian Thomism, Catharism, Cartesianism, Kantianism, Pietism (Quietism and Fundamentalism), Existentialism, Liberalism, and Secularism each in their own way have contributed to a split vision of reality by which so many people in the West and in the Western church order their daily lives. The Church has failed, under these overwhelming intellectual forces, to prevent believers from adopting compartmentalized views of faith and life that have sadly undermined Christian experience and short-circuited the Church's larger redemptive purposes in the world.

5. *The pressures of secular culture.* Compartmentalization often results from a hegemonic secularity that seeks to keep public culture religion free. While "grace ate up nature" in the medieval period, resulting in a profound other-worldliness, in these modern and postmodern times, "nature has eaten up grace," resulting in a profound this-worldliness. In the former, over-spiritualized, medieval world, earthly concerns were downplayed and shuffled to the side; in the present, over-secularized, contemporary world, spiritual concerns are undermined and relegated to the periphery. Religion is an unwelcome guest in the public square, and must be kept sequestered in the individual, home and church. As is often said, it is acceptable for faith to be privately engaging, but it must remain publicly irrelevant. Many believers have capitulated to the pressures of the reigning social order, and in compliance, have limited the scope and exercise of their faith to altar, heart, and hearth.

---

10 See the preface to Nietzsche's *Beyond Good and Evil*, trans. Helen Zimmern, intro. W. H. Wright (New York: The Modern Library, 1927, 1954), p. 378. Thanks to Russ Hemati and Chad Kidd for helping me locate this quotation.

6. *The restrictive consequences of sloth.* Limiting faith to the conveniences of altar, heart, and hearth can result, not only from the external pressures of a secular society, but also from internal spiritual listlessness. As the hatred of spiritual things that require work and hardship, sloth or *acedia* can also account for a compartmentalized Christian lifestyle. It just takes too much effort—too much blood, sweat, and tears—to think through and live out the implications of the Lordship of Christ over the whole of life. This inordinate lack of love for kingship of God, this failure to hunger and thirst for righteousness in all things, this sin of omission rooted in spiritual apathy balks at the far-reaching implications of the biblical metanarrative, reduces the faith to tiny proportions, and leaves it securely nestled in the individual believer's comfort zone. This "noon-day demon," which haunts us all about lunch time, is typically not a temptation of the young, but is apt to overcome the middle-aged who have grown weary of doing good and are on the verge of coasting in their callings and ignoring their spiritual aspirations and goals.[11]

7. *The quest for personal holiness.* If believers are not to love the world or the things within it (1 John 2:15), if they are to keep themselves unstained by the immoral influences of the world (James 1:27), and if Christians are to come out from the midst of unbelievers and be separate (2 Cor. 6:17), then surely personal piety demands a compartmentalized life. Holiness consists primarily of the regular practice of the spiritual disciplines and also entails a negation of the world, public affairs, and the social order. After all, the City of Man—whether Nineveh or Babylon, Athens or Rome, London or New York, Sydney or Singapore—is occupied by pagans, heathens, and apostates and poses a million threats to the people of God. The chief concern is this: How can the Church maintain her moral and doctrinal purity in the midst of such temptation and corruption? Yes, the Bible says believers are to be in but not of the world. But those who live in it are soon of it. Thus, according to this view, it is better to live prophylactically, practice the principle of Christian separatism, and protect the gifts of faith, hope, and love that Christ has given to His

---

11 Several ideas in this section are from *Moral Compasses for Modern Leaders: The Cardinal Virtues and Deadly Vices in Everyday Life,* The Trinity Forum Series of Seminar Curricula, vol. 3 (The Trinity Forum, 1994).

church. Sanctity and worldly isolation belong together in an inseparable union like husband and wife.

Perhaps there are other explanations for this debilitating problem of compartmentalization, but these seven—(1 & 2 & 3) the metaphysical, noetic, and moral effects of sin; (4) the powerful influences of dualistic religions and philosophies; (5) the pressures of secular culture; (6) the restricting consequences of sloth; and (7) the personal quest for holiness—are certainly critical ones.

As educators, we must ask ourselves which, if any, of these causes keeps us from pursuing our tasks with Christian integrity and thoroughgoing wholeness. Faithfulness to Christ and our callings—which involves both our disciplines and our students—demands that we identify and remove any obstacles that would prevent us from consistently basing our academic endeavors on the bedrock assumptions and philosophic implications of a biblical *weltanschauung*.

CONSEQUENCES

Whatever the precise explanations of compartmentalization and whichever ones may thwart the Christian consistency of our educative enterprises, one thing is for sure: compartmentalization has certainly wreaked havoc in the Church, the world, and in individual human lives. I will mention three consequences in particular.

First, the life-denying, body-bashing, creation-condemning, otherworldly orientation that often accrues from *dualistic, compartmentalized Christianity has turned many gifted, influential human beings (as well as lesser figures) away from biblical religion, sometimes generating remarkable animosity toward God and the Church.*

Friedrich Nietzsche is a classic example. This one, who philosophized with a hammer and announced to the modern world that God was dead, held unspeakably hostile attitudes toward the Christian faith, in part because he understood it as an anti-art and anti-life religion. In a revealing passage in a short work titled *Attempt at a Self-Criticism*, Nietzche explains that he deliberately ignored Christianity in his very first book which happened to be on the arts—*The Birth of Tragedy*—because he believed Christian moralism relegated every art to the realm of lies and that Christianity in general does nothing but negate, judge, and damn art. Behind this aesthetic condemnation, however, Nietzsche perceived something deeper *in the Christianity he knew* which he characterized as "a *hostility to life*—a furious, vengeful antipathy to life itself." In the following passage, he elaborates on his overall understanding of the Christian faith that had seemingly been infected with a dualistic poison that estranged it from everything Nietzsche himself held dear, more of a "Platonism for the people" as he called it, than a truly biblical conception of the world.

> Christianity was from the beginning, essentially and fundamentally, life's nausea and disgust with life, merely concealed behind, masked by, dressed up as, faith in "another" or "better" life. Hatred of "the world," condemnation of the passions, fear of beauty and sensuality, a beyond invented the better to slander this life, at bottom a craving for the nothing, for the end, for respite, for "the sabbath of sabbaths" . . . at the very least a sign of abysmal sickness, weariness, discouragement, exhaustion, and the impoverishment of life.[12]

As a case study, I cannot help but wonder if Nietzsche—the son of a Lutheran minister, turned nihilist, in whose mouth are found the fiercest accusations ever leveled against Christianity—would have turned out differently if the Christianity to which he had been exposed had been holistic rather than dualistic? What would have been his outcome if the Christianity he knew had biblically and rightly embraced life, affirmed the arts, gloried in creation, reveled in beauty, celebrated the passions, and in short, truly loved the good world and human life that God had made. Perhaps nothing could have altered Nietzsche's spiritual trajectory, but his story potentially reveals what is at stake for many people when reductionistic versions of Christian faith are substituted for a genuine biblical vision.

Second, the error of Christian dualism may also provide a clue to understanding the religious motivation of radical Islamic terrorism. According to Paul Berman in his book, *Terror and Liberalism*,[13] *the spiritually arid, dehumanizing conditions of modern secular life have been generated by its divorce from sacred, transcendent realities that radical terrorists are trying to rectify by the violent imposition of the Islamic worldview and way of life that will create a new social order based on ancient Qur'anic principles.* Berman bases this thesis on the writings of an Egyptian Muslim thinker named Sayyid Qutb,[14] who in the mid-twentieth century became Islamism's chief theoretician and philosopher of Islamic terrorism (Ayman al Zawahiri, who is the man behind Osama bin Laden and

---

12 Friedrich Nietzsche, *Attempt at a Self-Criticism*, trans. and commentary Walter Kaufmann (New York: Random House, Vintage Books, 1967), p. 23 §5.

13 Paul Berman, *Terror and Liberalism* (New York: W. W. Norton and Co., 2003).

14 pronounced KUH-tabh

the brains of Al-Qaeda, was one of Qutb's students). His *magnum opus* is a fifteen-volume work, *In the Shade of the Qur'an*, whose title suggests that the divine revelation in the Qur'an provides a refreshing spiritual oasis amidst the spiritually destitute conditions of modern life.

Qutb argues that because Judaism as a comprehensive system of laws degenerated into a rigid and lifeless ritual, God sent another prophet in the person of Jesus of Nazareth. Under Greek influence, however, the religion of Jesus was thoroughly spiritualized and had little to say about bodily existence, social organization, human action, and temporal life. Because Christianity erroneously separated the sacred and secular, the spiritual and physical, the religious and profane, and the church and state, God raised up the prophet Mohammed to proclaim a reunifying religious message that brought the totality of human life under the authority of Allah and the Qur'an. If necessary, it must be proclaimed and obeyed at the point of a bloody sword, that is, by jihad.

However, Greco-Christian dualism eventually triumphed in Europe where God and spirituality were privatized and sharply separated from the growing autonomy of science, commerce, politics, and military power. Imperialistically, Europe spread its "hideous schizophrenia" throughout the world. This kind of religious compartmentalization eventually became the source of liberal, secular societies that were devoid of substantive spirituality and insubordinate to divine authority, a derelict condition ultimately rooted in Christian error.

Qutb's analysis eventually inspired Mohammed Atta and the suicide warriors of September 11, 2001, who, along with others like them, are seeking through violent means to spread Islamic civilization throughout the world. From this perspective, therefore, radical Islamic terrorism is a religiously motivated crusade, and its goals and methods, however misdirected, are aimed at overcoming the effects of Western religious compartmentalization and restoring the whole of life under Qur'anic principles and the rule of Allah.[15]

Finally, in addition to the menacing effects of compartmentalization at personal and global levels, *perhaps its greatest nefarious impact has been on the life of the Church herself, in the lives of believers and their callings, and on the ecclesiastical potential to transform cultural life and social institutions.* A whittled down, fragmented version of Christianity prevents the Church from establishing her essential theological identity as the people (New Israel) of God and from recognizing her larger

---

15 I have based this discussion on a letter written by Ken Myers on behalf of Mars Hill Audio *Journal*, May 2003.

cosmological and soteriological purposes on the basis of the total biblical metanarrative. How impoverishing a truncated vision of the faith can be on the Church theologically, liturgically, ministerially, and missionally. A faith restricted to sacred precincts also denies the full range of human experience to Christian believers and prevents them from knowing, serving, and enjoying God in every aspect and calling in life. How frustrating such a narrow focus can be for believers who long to embrace the richness of their God-given and God-redeemed humanity in all that they are and do. A siloed Christianity tends to limit the redemptive purpose of the Church to the salvation of souls. It also thwarts her larger mission as the instrument of the kingdom of God in overcoming social injustices, renewing cultural life, and restoring various public institutions to their God-ordained purposes. How depressing and unfortunate it is that the Church has allowed its redemptive vision to be limited to private, pietistic concerns.

How great, then, are the consequences of compartmentalization—individually as Friedrich Nietzsche reveals, globally as Islamic terrorism shows, and ecclesiastically as seen in the loss of the church's identity and purpose. In education, the effect has been profound as well, for many Christian educators, whether intentionally or not, have found ways of disintegrating rather than integrating faith, study, teaching, and learning. This has generated what is often called the "two spheres view" in education, by which faith is kept neatly in one sphere and academics is well ensconced in another.

Toward Christian Holism

There is a great irony, however, associated with this viewpoint, for it assumes, wrongly so, that bracketing faith allows academics to proceed objectively without interference from any encumbering subjective considerations (religion, politics, gender, race, class, culture, language, etc.). This methodology, however, is not only ironic, but also naïve because it assumes an essentially non-religious view of human nature and it supposes that academic enterprises are worldview neutral.

But as Christian Smith has argued in his recent book, *Moral, Believing Animals: Human Personhood and Culture,*[16] human beings are animals with an inescapable moral and spiritual dimension. They cannot avoid a fundamental moral orientation in life or escape living by one or another sacred narrative. Along the way, Smith severely critiques naturalistic theories of humanity as reductionistic, asserting that they

---

16 Christian Smith, *Moral Believing Animals: Human Personhood and Culture* (New York: Oxford University Press, 2003).

badly misunderstand the character of the human. By contrast, Smith argues that all people are at bottom believers whose lives, actions, and institutions are constituted, motivated, and governed by narrative traditions and moral orders on which they inescapably depend.[17] As literary critic Henry Zlystra has put it, "No man is religiously neutral in his knowledge of and his appropriation of reality."[18] We can step out of one orienting experience only by stepping into another. If we exit one particular worldview perspective, then by necessity we will enter another. Neither life nor scholarship is possible without a foundational point of view. Even Richard Rorty, though a lifelong "militant secularist" and no friend of traditional religion, has nonetheless converted recently to a particular spiritual outlook and designated himself to be a romantic polytheist.[19] Undoubtedly this outlook influences his scholarship (not to mention his personal life).

In academic affairs, therefore, the question isn't *whether or not* a worldview of some kind will be integrated with learning. The only real question is *which worldview* will be integrated with learning. Here, then, is the punch line to this essay:

> If Christian educators are to avoid compartmentalization and recover personal and profession integrity, then that worldview perspective that undergirds their academic work must be solidly biblical and deeply Christian.

Both Alvin Plantinga and Nicholas Wolterstorff as prominent Christian philosophers have argued persuasively that, for integrity's sake, believers who are scholars and teachers ought to make their biblical commitments foundational to their scholarship and teaching. If it is incongruous for a naturalist to adopt a Christian (or some other) perspective in his or her academic work, then why would a Christian choose to adopt naturalism (or some other perspective) as the basis for his or her scholarly endeavors? Thus in his famous address "Advice to Christian Philosophers," Plantinga has advised Christian academics (philosophers in particular) to take certain biblical doctrines as the foundational assumptions in their scholarly work. Similarly, Wolterstorff in his equally influential *Reason within the Bounds of Religion* has

---

17 This description of the contents of this book were taken from the publishers notes online at <http://search.barnesandnoble.com/Moral-Believing-Animals/Christian-Smith/e/9780195162028/?itm=1> (Accessed September 25, 2003).

18 Henry Zylstra, *Testament of Vision* (Grand Rapids: Eerdmans,1958), pp. 145–46.

19 See Jason Boffetti, "How Richard Rorty Found Religion," *First Things* no. 143 (May 2004), pp. 24–30.

argued that the religious commitments of the Christian scholar ought to function as "control beliefs" in the devising and weighing of academic theories.[20] If acted upon, this vision will require not only theological sophistication, but also moral and spiritual courage in the face of considerable opposition.

The critical burden, then, is to identify and explain those biblically based doctrines and control beliefs that ought to guide and govern Christian scholarly endeavor. The crucial adjunct concern will be to fortify and encourage those who know the right thing to do to actually do it. If successful, this process has the potential to eliminate compartmentalization and restore the faithfulness and integrity of teachers and professors claiming to be seriously Christian.

Here then are the essential elements of the biblical vision or meta-narrative that abrogate compartmentalization and establish the basis for Christian holism.

1. *The sovereignty of the triune God over every aspect of reality and the whole of human life.* God's rule or kingdom is not a partial reality but encompasses all things. Psalm 103:19 states, "The Lord has established His throne in the heavens and His sovereignty rules over all." Abraham Kuyper in his inaugural address at the Free University of Amsterdam affirmed this truth in these practical words: "There is not a square inch in the whole domain of our human existence over which Christ, who is sovereign over *all*, does not cry out, Mine!"

2. *The doctrine of the original, comprehensive goodness of creation.* According to Genesis 1, everything God made is good in all its parts (v. 4, 10, 12, 18, 21, 25), and is in fact *very good* as an ensemble of parts according to Genesis 1:31. In 1 Timothy 4:4, St. Paul affirms the same thing in a post-lapsarian world when he affirms that "everything created by God is good." These texts declare unequivocally the positive character and unqualified benevolence of the whole of reality, a teaching that distinguishes biblical faith from other religious and philosophical systems that trace evil and the human condition to some defect in creation.

3. *A sacramental perspective on reality in which the glory and goodness of God is present and detected in everything.* This means that the world as a whole and in its development culturally and historically is a revelation of God and His wise and benevolent character. Psalm 19:1 states that "The heavens are telling of the glory of God." Isaiah 6:3 affirms that "The fullness of the earth is God's glory" (marginal reading).

---

20 Alvin Plantinga, "Advice to Christian Philosophers," *Faith and Philosophy* 1 (1984): 253–271; Nicholas Wolterstorff, *Reason within the Bounds of Religion*, 2d ed. (Grand Rapids: Eerdmans, 1984).

Romans 1:20 teaches that "since the creation of the world, God's invisible attributes, His eternal power and divine nature, have been clearly seen through what has been made." In this vein, John Calvin refers to creation as the *"theatrum Dei"* or God's theatre, and Russian Orthodox theologian Alexander Schmemann asserts that the whole world is "shot through with the presence of God."[21] All things make Him known.

4. *The incarnation of the Son of God.* That the Word became flesh and dwelt among us (John 1:14) affirms the abiding goodness of God's creation, the essential dignity of the human person, and the value of concern for and immersion in human activities and concerns.

5. *The cosmic character and comprehensive scope of Christ's redeeming work.* What Jesus achieved on the cross was co-extensive with creation and the effects of sin, and has brought about reconciliation and the renewal of all things (Col. 1:15–20). He has come to make His blessings flow, "far as the curse is found" ("Joy to the World"). The redemptive focus of the kingdom of God through Christ by the Holy Spirit applies to every nook and cranny of human existence and renews it all from within. Sanctification is a personal and cultural enterprise.

6. *The doctrine of resurrection and the new heavens and the new earth.* Christ's bodily resurrection and the bodily resurrection of believers (Phil. 3:20–21) along with the restoration and renewal of the whole cosmos as the new heavens and earth at Christ's return testifies to the unlimited scope of God's creative and redemptive purposes and the boundless nature of biblical faith and its impact. Colossians 1:15–20 is crucial to this vision. It reads as follows:

> [15] And He is the image of the invisible God, the first-born of all creation. [16] For by Him all things were created, both in the heavens and on earth, visible and invisible, whether thrones or dominions or rulers or authorities —all things have been created by Him and for Him. [17] And He is before all things, and in Him all things hold together. [18] He is also head of the body, the church; and He is the beginning, the first-born from the dead; so that He Himself might come to have first place in everything. [19] For it was the Father's good pleasure for all the fullness to dwell in Him, [20] and through Him to reconcile all things to Himself, having made peace through the blood of His cross; through Him, I say, whether things on earth or things in heaven.

---

21 Alexander Schmemann, *For the Life of the World* (Crestwood, NY: St. Vladamir's Seminary Press, 1963), p. 16.

In this remarkable passage, which New Testament scholars say is an early Christian hymn, St. Paul presents the Christ of Colossians on a cosmic scale as the Creator, Upholder, and Reconciler/Redeemer of all things. For present purposes, we ought to place the accent on the latter of these Christological works. That which God has created and sin has divided Christ is reuniting or reconciling, and this includes the divisions generated by our multiple dualisms and compartmentalizations. Our gracious, redeeming God is putting Humpty Dumpty back together again! For Christian scholars and teachers, this magnificent truth is fraught with implications for us both personally and professionally.

First and foremost, it means that we ourselves can be reconciled to God. The greatest compartmentalization of all has been between each one of us and God. We have been estranged from Him, and at enmity with Him, because of our sin. We have had no peace with or knowledge of God. But as Colossians 1:21–22 says,

And although you were formerly alienated and hostile in mind and engaged in evil deeds, yet He has now reconciled you in His fleshly body through death, in order to present you before Him holy and blameless and beyond reproach.

If you are already reconciled to God through Christ, then thank Him for His mercy, and grow in understanding what it means to know and serve Him as instruments of reconciliation in all things. But if you are not reconciled to God, then as an ambassador of Christ, as if God was speaking through me to you, I urge you on behalf of Christ to be reconciled to God on the basis of His grace through faith in Him.

Second, Christ's cosmic work of reconciliation means the substantial healing of the brokenness of our lives. Psychologically, reconciliation means healing our broken souls and experiencing considerable healing of the mental diseases and the emotional disorders of our hearts and minds, and enjoying peace within. *Relationally,* reconciliation means healing broken relationships, expressing forgiveness and becoming reconnected to friends, children, and family members from whom we have been estranged, and enjoying peace with others. *Maritally,* reconciliation means the healing of broken marriages, reconnecting us with our spouses and enjoying peace in the home. *Culturally,* reconciliation means the healing of the world and the restoration of our roles as stewards of earth, and enjoying peace in creation. In short, reconciliation means the restoration of shalom, and so we exult in God through Christ by whom we have now received the reconciliation (Rom. 5:11).

Third, Christ's cosmic work of reconciliation means a new vision and new forms of educational wholeness. Foundationally, reconciliation means reconnecting the cosmic Christ and education in a vital, integral, and redemptive manner. *Substantively,* reconciliation means healing the bogus comparmentalizations that have wreaked havoc in the areas of God's creation which we study including the sacred and secular, eternal and temporal, spirit and matter, heaven and earth, soul and body, spirit and flesh, faith and reason, facts and values, head and heart, freedom and authority, private and public, belief and behavior, individual and community, church and state, Christ and culture. *Interdisciplinarily,* reconciliation means grasping how all subjects fit together as a unified whole and form a complete vision of the world. As John Henry Newman writes in *The Idea of a University,* "That only is true enlargement of mind which is the power of viewing many things at once as one whole, of referring them severally to their true place in the universal system, of understanding their respective values, and determining their mutual dependence."[22] *Relationally,* reconciliation means building bridges of faith, hope and love between ourselves as educators and our administrators, co-workers, colleagues, and students. It means being an active agent of shalom in the community to which God has called you providentially.

Now to be sure, we must not only *know* these things, but we must also *do* them. We must cultivate the courage of our convictions. We must indwell them, and they in us. There will likely be considerable opposition, stemming from both human and superhuman sources. Neither the City of Man nor the kingdom of darkness will cheer us on in this battle, and that is exactly what it is. So, we must avail ourselves of every resource, including the Holy Spirit, Scripture, prayer, the spiritual disciplines, and the encouragement of the body of Christ, in order to fight this good fight of faith.

Let us, therefore, resolve with God's help to live out our Christian confession consistently and effectively, not only in private but also in public, not only in the home and the church, but also in our communities and in our schools. By the grace of God, we will triumph over compartmentalization through the restoration of a biblical vision of integrity, serving God faithfully and fruitfully in our callings as Christian teachers and professors, and thereby dealing a blow to Screwtape and Wormwood, and their Father below, from which they will not recover!

---

22 John Henry Newman, *The Idea of a University,* Rethinking the Western Tradition, ed. Frank Turner (New Haven: Yale University Press, 1996), p. 99.

16

An American Dream from God's Perspective

Kumiko Takeuchi

Introduction

I was born and raised in an industrial city on Shikoku Island of Japan. Strangely enough, my family members began to die one by one until I became a sole survivor of the Takeuchi family by the time I reached the age of fifteen. It started with my sister's death just prior to my birth, followed by my father's, mother's, and then brother's, each due to unrelated illnesses. Both sets of my grandparents were gone by then as well. It looked as though my life was cursed by God or some unseen powers. Religion was not a familiar subject or interest in my surroundings, though, as my relatives who raised me struggled to make ends meet. Their simple belief was that material wealth and comfort would bring happiness to life and there would be no more to life than that. In spite of growing up in an environment of scarce love and material comfort for a young child, I never believed that money or material wealth could make me happy. Though puzzled by, or maybe because of, so many deaths around me, somehow I believed that there had to be more to life than that; that life had to lead to a truth; and

(Jean) Kumiko Takeuchi <ktakeuchi@att.net> is a research scientist, retired (2008) from Eli Lilly and Company in Indianapolis, Indiana. She has spent twenty years in drug discovery research at Lilly Research Laboratories and published over thirty publications in peer-reviewed journals and filed over thirty US patents during her tenure there. She was involved in the identification and development of five clinical candidates at Lilly, of which two have advanced in human clinical trials as potential therapeutic drugs. She earned her PhD in chemistry from the University of South Carolina, her MA in chemistry from the College of William and Mary, another MA in Bible and Missions from Columbia International University, and her Diploma in chemical engineering from Niihama Technical College in Japan.

that man's life was to pursue the truth, though I had no idea what the truth was. Unbeknownst to me, God indeed had a plan for this orphan child, not only by taking her out of the traumatic childhood environment to the land of dream and opportunity, but also by bringing her to a personal encounter with her God and Savior and to a global vision and purpose that He has for her life. In this testimony, I would describe how God led me to come to a saving knowledge of Jesus Christ as my personal Savior and Lord, how He has graced my life with His abundant provision to make an American dream a reality in my life, and where He is leading me to fulfill His commission for global evangelization by utilizing the benefits of an American dream from God's perspective.

In the spring of 1999, a preview of the made-for-television miniseries by CBS caught my eye. The story behind the scene told us that the French-Canadian director Christian Duguay even made a trip to Notre Dame Cathedral in Paris, France, to read some of the original documents of Jeanne d'Arc's trial as a heretic in order to make his movie as authentic and true to the facts as possible. I eagerly waited for the evenings when the miniseries "Joan of Arc"[1] actually broadcasted in May of that year. It was over 45 years ago when I read about Joan of Arc's story. I do not recall any inkling that I had ever been affected by the story for all those years gone by. In fact, I even didn't know much about other movies that were made on her short life. The CBS miniseries unfolded exactly the same content of "The Maid of Orleans" that I read when I was about seven years old shortly after I learned to read. My memory was awakened so vividly that it triggered my interest to explore and read all about Joan of Arc once again. I read several books including Pernoud & Clin's "Joan of Arc: Her Story"[2] and Mark Twain's "Personal Recollections of Joan of Arc,"[3] which Twain claimed was the result of his twelve years of research.

Later that summer, taking advantage of my trip to a scientific meeting in Vienna, Austria, I decided to go to France and trace the life of Joan of Arc. I traveled to the southwest of France to visit her birthplace, Domremy, continued from the battleground Orleans through Paris, and then on to the final destination of Rouen in northern France, where Joan of Arc was burned at the stake at the age of nineteen. Reflection from the re-reading on Joan of Arc and the trip to France made me realize how intensely I had been captured by her faith and life. And I began to wonder if reading of "The Maid of Orleans" at the age of seven could have been my first awareness about spiritual matters and most likely my first spiritual awakening.

Childhood: A Life Cursed by God?

August sixth was one of the saddest days in Japan when I was growing up. Wherever we might be, we were to pause for a moment of silence at 8:15 a.m. on this particular day every year. It was the day when the first atomic bomb dropped on Hiroshima in 1945. I once visited the memorial park and museum in Hiroshima. Pictures displayed and remains survived from the bomb depicted an unspeakable atrocity. They made it easy to imagine what a hell could be like. I was born exactly a year later on the nation's saddest day in Japan, and the day foreshadowed my unusually tragic childhood to come. Deaths in the family started with my older sister who died of diphtheria shortly before I was born. I was told that my father died when I was three from an injury he suffered while working. My mother's death followed short five years later, which was the biggest blow and shock, as I understood what her death meant. I still remember it was as if yesterday that I told myself on the morning after my mother's death, "I have Father or Mother no more. I must stand firm on my feet and walk through life on my own from now on." I was about eight years old then, but it appeared as though I grew up overnight. I even didn't cry any more when my brother, who was five years older than me and the last immediate family member, died of tuberculosis with flu complications at the age of sixteen. Both sets of my grandparents were also gone before I reached my fifteenth birthday, and I became the sole survivor of Takeuchi family by the age of fifteen. It was not a circumstance that a child should normally experience in a peaceful time.

Not only was my life plagued with a series of immediate family member's deaths, but also it was as if my life was not much valued by those around me. When my mother died, none of my relatives wanted to take two children left behind into their home. One of my uncles and his family reluctantly took us in because my grandfather, who lived with them, angrily declared that he would take care of his grandchildren who needed a caretaker. I once overheard my aunt-in-law telling a neighbor that she wished that I had taken my brother's place shortly after he had died. It was understandable in a way. My brother was a clown. He was a friendly likable child, and everyone liked him. I was introverted by nature and kept much to myself. I was not likable in my demeanor or appearance. I was not at all beautiful according to a Japanese standard, a fact of which my relatives made it very clear to me. My uncle, in particular, often said to my face that I was ugly looking when he got drunk. I told myself that an inner beauty was much more important than the outer appearance and that's what I should strive for. Death became a familiar scene in my life and it looked easier than life. My life appeared as though it was cursed by God or plagued with some unknown forces.

During those formative years, I still could find a bright spot in my life. I loved to learn, and the school was almost like a heaven. Very easily I could immerse myself in books and art works, and I even dreaded the summer vacation because I couldn't go to school. Thanks to my mother's discipline, I never procrastinated with my homework during the school in session and even during summer vacation. One of the happiest memories I have is the day when our neighbor who ran a convenience store handed me a brand new hardcover out of a stack of books on a shelf. The books were given to children who bought and reached a certain number of boxes of candies, as a prize sponsored by the candy manufacturer. We were poor. Besides, I knew my mother would have never allowed me to buy candies.

Nevertheless, I frequented the convenience store as the old couple, who didn't have children of their own, treated me like their own grandchild. From time to time they treated me with leftover candy or cookies. But I never expected that "Grandpa" would give me one of those books, since I had not bought even one box of candies. It was a fairly thick volume for the first grader who just began to learn to read. I was so happy and eager that I read the book to my mother every evening in bed. I still vividly remember one of the pictures inserted in the book—a girl in a red dress kneeling before two angels (two patron saints of hers). "The Maid of Orleans" was the title of the book. I do not recall, however, if it had any bearing in my life while I was growing up. Maybe I was too young to recognize what effect it had on my thought process. I didn't know how profoundly Joan of Arc's faith and life had impressed upon my heart until 45 years later when I watched the made-for-television miniseries about her life.

JESUS CHRIST IS THE ABSOLUTE TRUTH

My uncle who took my brother and me in after my mother's death was a heavy drinker. He was a somewhat quiet man when he was sober, but he rambled over his life's aspiration and disappointment that followed every time he got drunk. One thing he always emphasized to his children and to us was education. He declared he would send us to any college if we did well in school and if we wanted to get further education, even though he didn't have much money. It was because he could not go to high school when he was young, even though he was dying to do so. My grandfather was a farmer, and he didn't see

270

the need of education for farmers. My uncle wanted to see his dream realized in the lives of his children, including us. His children were average or somewhat below-average students while growing up. My uncle had a lot of hopes and dreams for my older brother, but he did not live to realize my uncle's aspiration.

Ironically, among the kids I was the one who excelled most in school and survived. When I was a 9th grader, I won a competitive national scholarship and passed an entrance examination to Niihama Technical College, while skipping three years in senior high school. After earning a diploma in chemical engineering at the age of 20, I started working as an analytical chemist because there was no job for a woman engineer in Japan. Several years later, I decided to come to the United States when my conversational English instructor encouraged and urged me to do something with my English-speaking ability rather than making it just a hobby. In my ignorance, I applied to only one school, the College of William and Mary in Virginia (W&M). I didn't know how difficult it was to get accepted in this prestigious institution, the second oldest institution among US colleges and universities. Nonetheless, I was accepted as a transfer student. Shortly after my arrival, however, the chemistry department promoted me to its master's program, having recognized that I was far advanced from my five years of undergraduate education in Japan, although I never officially completed a bachelor's degree.

Fate has it that I got acquainted with a lot of undergraduate students on campus that fall because I lived in a student dormitory during the first semester, thanks to my initial acceptance as a transfer student (there was no graduate housing on campus in those days). Students who lived on campus were expected to eat meals at the school cafeteria. One Friday evening I was eating alone when an undergraduate student with whom I was recently acquainted approached my table and joined me for dinner. During a course of our conversation, he asked me if I would be interested in going to a meeting that he was going to, unless I had other plans for the evening. As a foreign student, my evenings were occupied with homework, while I was still trying to overcome the language barrier. I agreed to join him that evening since it was Friday, although still somewhat hesitantly.

I had never before attended the kind of meeting that I went to that evening. Students sang a lot of songs that I had never heard, and then there was a speaker who spoke from the Five Books of Moses. In those days, I was so dead tired from being immersed in English all day that I could hardly absorb anything at an evening meeting or gathering.

I can still remember to this day that the man in a turtleneck sweater underneath his jacket spoke in such plain English that I could comprehend what he was saying at that meeting. My friend asked me how I liked the man's talk at the meeting, while escorting me back to my dormitory. I said to him, "It was very interesting. . . .You know, I think I would like to know more about the Bible." The rest is history. Three weeks later I accepted Christ as my personal Lord and Savior. During those three weeks, I dug out a lot of questions about life that I had contemplated in the past, particularly about the absolute truth for which I was searching. Having seen too many deaths around my life at such an early age, I had been wondering about life's meaning, if there was any at all. Death looked much simpler and less painful than life. During my college years in Japan, a chemistry professor told his students that we must pursue the truth; of course, in this case it was the truth through science. He even told us that our life's purpose was to search for the truth. But what is the truth?

My friend, who took me to that first Intervarsity Christian Fellowship meeting that I ever attended, witnessed and testified to me about Jesus Christ. He explained to me step by step what it meant to live a life intended by God, using a small booklet called "Have you heard of the four spiritual laws?" He pointed out to me that Jesus was the way, and the truth, and the life. After watching his life that was based on his belief and was very real, I concluded that Jesus might indeed be the truth. I was searching for the truth and there I was confronted with the truth. I knew I had to make a choice. As a scientist, I have to think of things logically. It was very clear to me that refusing the truth, which I was looking for, was totally illogical. So I made a logical decision to accept the truth presented. There was nothing emotional about it at the time, but I felt the matter was settled when I prayed to acknowledge and accept Christ into my heart. It was on a cool Thursday evening of December 3, 1973, when I accepted Jesus Christ by praying aloud for the first time in my life in front of my friend.

I hardly knew who Moses or King David was when I came to know Christ. I was pretty much ignorant about the Christian life. Shortly after I accepted Christ, I noticed my friend was always looking for opportunities to share Christ. He was witnessing all the time on campus. Being ignorant, I thought all the Christians were doing the same and I began to witness. He told me that he read the Bible every day, had a quiet time, and kept a spiritual journal. Well, I began to do these things because I thought I had to do the same if all the Christians were doing that! What a role model I had! What an example I saw! A young student who knew no science cared enough to share Christ with me. The Holy Spirit did His work through him, and I came to know Christ as my personal Lord and Savior.

As my graduate study for an MA degree at W&M was nearing its completion, I felt a need to get a biblical education. I applied to Columbia Graduate School of Bible and Missions (CGS, now a part of Columbia International University) in Columbia, South Carolina, and was accepted, even though I had told them openly and honestly that I didn't have any money to go to another school. Early in my Christian life, I was tested to trust in God in the matter of finances. I even didn't have enough money to complete my graduate study at W&M, much less start at another school. Yet God proved Himself to be faithful by providing for all my needs time and again. I stated simply in my application to CGS that as a young believer I believed that God would somehow bring necessary funds for my biblical education. In time, I have come to trust and believe that God is responsible to provide food, clothing, and a shelter as long as He wants me to stay down here on earth and live for His purpose. If He didn't provide or stopped providing for these basic needs, then it's time that He wanted me to come home to heaven. It was simple logic by a simple faith. Subsequently, I earned my MA in chemistry from W&M, another MA in Bible and missions from CGS, and later my Ph.D. in chemistry debt-free, although I could not legally work in this country, nor did I receive a penny from Japan.

"WHAT ARE YOU DOING AROUND HERE?"

From early on in my Christian life I became acutely aware of the importance of witnessing. My friend who led me to the Lord was a better example of someone sharing Christ at every opportunity than anybody else that I know of to this day. He was natural and gifted in evangelism. I have often observed firsthand how casually he starts talking to a stranger and then shares the gospel message before one knows it. He told me that there was always clear prompting by the Holy Spirit whenever he had an opportunity to share Christ. His lifestyle was a clear message to me that witnessing was also my responsibility as a Christian, regardless of what stage of Christian walk I was treading. It soon became my conviction that witnessing was a part of a Christian life. So I began to witness shortly after I became a Christian and always sought opportunities to witness. I also prayed for non-Christians, especially unsaved families of my Christian friends. I knew full well that none of my family members went to heaven, without knowing Christ.

And, therefore, I knew how important it was for one's family to hear the gospel before it's too late. I didn't pay much attention to the fact that I was not bearing fruit in my witness in those days, however. To me the most important thing was that I was burdened and willing to witness if at all possible when I had such opportunities. Then, a revelation came during my second year at CGS.

I was less than a two-year-old Christian when I started at CGS to earn my MA in Bible and missions. Studying at CGS was extremely challenging. I felt I could never grasp everything in the classroom because of my handicap in English as well as my total lack of Christian background. I was also constantly frightened that I could never catch up with all the readings and writings that I had to do as part of the course study. I studied extremely hard for every hour available and did surprisingly well in almost all the courses. When I finished my MA degree, I felt like I could go to any school after CGS. "Bring me Harvard; bring me Yale. Now I could tackle any school after CGS," I mused to myself.

During my second year at CGS I took a course on spiritual gifts taught by the president Robertson McQuilkin. He gave a definition of spiritual gifts as follows: "If you have a spiritual gift, you will consistently bear fruit as you exercise your gift. You may have a ministry and you may bear fruit even without a gift sometimes. But the difference is that you will bear fruit *consistently* if you have a gift and exercise it." In one of the class sessions, he asked us to do three things: (1) list spiritual gift(s) that you believe you have; (2) list spiritual gift(s) that you know you don't have; and (3) list a gift among those you don't have but wish to have, if God would grant you one. We turned in our paper with our answers to his instructions at the end of the class.

At the beginning of the next class, Mr. McQuilkin expressed his grave concern about our answers. "It disturbs me a great deal that none of you claimed that you had a gift of evangelism and yet none of you wished to have a gift in evangelism! God promises us, 'Ask, and it shall be given to you.' We can certainly ask God for a gift of evangelism so that we could win souls consistently. Here you are at this graduate school to be trained as future missionaries, pastors, and Christian workers, and yet none of you thinks about the gift of evangelism as important? " He spoke these words at a higher pitch, and I felt as if a bucket of cold water had been dumped on my head, and I thought, *How foolish I am! How can I be so stupid in all these years. I am not bearing fruit in my witnessing because I don't have the gift and have not asked God if He would grant me the gift of evangelism!* That day I prayed to

God, asking for His forgiveness and for the gift of evangelism because I wanted to bear fruit for His kingdom. Has He granted me the gift of evangelism? I can only testify for the things that have changed in my life since then.

I began to always wonder where a person was spiritually whenever I met someone and began to seek opportunities to find that out. Whenever I have an opportunity to interact with someone, be it over dinner, going to a concert together, or being invited to a small gathering especially by a non-Christian friend, I began to consider it an opportunity to witness. I stopped assuming that anybody is a Christian even in the church unless I hear that person expresses his or her personal relationship with Christ in some way. My outlook in witnessing changed. I became aware of the importance of bringing someone to a point of decision for Christ. At the same time, I realized that I never had to coerce anyone into a decision. The decision is theirs, between God and them. I also began to realize that it is good to share the gospel as long as a person is responding to it either positively or even negatively. Either way, that person is reacting to, thinking about, or evaluating the message. I began to realize "No" is as good an answer as "Yes," and I need to respect either response by a person when I present the gospel. The important thing is to help that person realize that one has a choice to make and one needs to make a decision. I also have realized that I do not have to save anyone; in fact, I cannot save anyone because it is God's job to save. All I need to do is share the gospel message with clarity, to enable a person to come to a point of decision. Once a person makes a moral decision not to believe, then it is futile to witness to him or her any longer. Such a person would not believe no matter what the evidence because he or she has already made a moral decision not to believe.

These understandings have freed me from fretting about witnessing or being rejected. It has become absolutely clear to me that I am not the one who is rejected when someone rejects what I share about Christ. It is Christ and His message that they are rejecting. And there is a consequence for their decision or rejection, for which I am not responsible. Being a witness for Christ whenever or in whatever way possible has become my lifestyle. Everything that I do now is intentional with a purpose for Christ.

After completing my graduate study at CGS, I went back to Japan and worked with TEAM missionaries for a church planting ministry for two years. I returned to the United States briefly after that but had to go back to Japan, having no job prospect and without a green card to work in the United States. Upon arriving in Japan I stayed at the TEAM Center in Tokyo for several days. It so happened that Carl F. H. Henry[4] was visiting Japan and staying at the TEAM center at the same time. He was on his lecture trip in Japan. I decided to go and hear his lecture.

We were on the train together to go to the place of his lecture, when he began to ask me about my background. No sooner had I told him that I had a Master's degree in chemistry than he exclaimed, "What are you doing around here? You should go back to school and get your Ph.D. in chemistry. We need Christians in every profession!" Carl Henry went on to tell me about his conversion experience in his early 20s while he was working as a newspaper journalist and how it changed his life. It took me yet another two years before I took his advice seriously and arrived on the University of South Carolina (USC) campus for my Ph.D. work. Those who do science know how much one can get behind after one has been out of the field even for a short period. I was out of the chemistry field for several years when I got back to school for my Ph.D. work. Moreover, I decided to change the field of research from my Master's work within the chemistry discipline. I felt I had to start chemistry all over again. Besides taking make-up courses for the qualifying exams that I missed, I had to take required courses and cumulative qualifying exams during my first two years before my Ph.D. candidacy.

Professors at a secular university typically give exams on Mondays, assuming that students would spend more time for study and prepare for their exams over the weekend. At CGS, students were not allowed to study on Sundays, and professors were kind enough not to give any exam on Mondays. My lifestyle was pretty much established to keep the Sabbath by the time I arrived on the USC campus. I decided not to study on Sundays at the outset of my Ph.D. work at USC, knowing full well that exams would be given on Mondays. My lifestyle became different from my fellow graduate students at USC. I worked for my research in the chemistry laboratory from 9 a.m. to midnight Monday through Saturday. I studied for exams on Saturdays until midnight, but never on Sundays. On Sundays, I went to church in the morning, and relaxed at my apartment or visited with friends for a ministry opportunity for the rest of the day.

What was the consequence? I maintained grades of all As except one B for the coursework and earned my Ph.D. degree in synthetic organic chemistry within four years, while others were averaging six to six-and-a-half years before they could successfully complete their Ph.D. work.

During my graduate studies, I got acquainted with a couple of Japanese students on campus with whom I shared the gospel. One of them later became a Christian, with whom I still keep contact. Interestingly, I also got acquainted with Carl Henry's daughter Carol and her husband Bill Bates during my USC years. Akiko, one who later became a Christian, and I even audited Carol's music appreciation course in the evening. These things happened because Carl Henry informed me that the Bates were music faculty members at USC when I wrote to him that I finally followed his advice and enrolled in the Department of Chemistry at USC. The Bates are committed Christians and have asked me about Akiko for many years after we left USC, for whose salvation they prayed.

Were these things mere coincidence or God's plan? I moved to the University of Michigan for my postdoctoral research for two years after earning my Ph.D., during which time I obtained my permanent residency (so-called green card) in the United States.

Working in Corporate America

I started working at a major pharmaceutical company in Indiana in August of 1989. I have been engaged in drug discovery research for the last twenty years. Over the years, I have learned how difficult and challenging it is to discover a new drug. It usually takes 10–15 years and billions of dollars worth of research funding. It also requires a huge amount of manpower, and yet much of our research efforts does not bear fruit. Only one out of ten thousand compounds could become a drug in the end, which would amount to only 0.01 percent success. In other words, in the line of my research where a chemist designs and creates a new molecule, most chemists could not come up with one molecule that would become a drug in their entire career simply because we would not be able to make 10,000 compounds in our lifetime. A successful medicine sold in the drug store or used in the hospital is a result of a multi-million dollar, multi-team, and multi-year research effort. I often explain to friends that my work is built on failures rather than on successes.

Why do we then even bother to devote our lives and work on an endeavor with such a slim chance of success? It is because the fruit of that one success out of ten thousands is enormous. It outweighs all the challenges, difficulties, disappointment or discouragement from the many failures because one medicine could literally change or even save millions of lives. Good medicine not only prolongs but also improves many people's lives with quality.

How privileged and gratifying it is, then, if one can contribute to such an endeavor! I am grateful to the Lord that He has given me intelligence, tenacity, and strength to be engaged in one of the most challenging research efforts. Even more amazing and also humbling is that God has enabled me to create and discover a couple of molecules that have advanced to human clinical trials for two therapeutic applications. I have often prayed that God would bless those molecules so that they would one day become a drug that could help millions of people. I am now experiencing firsthand the over ten-year wait before I will know whether the molecules that I discovered through my research will become a drug. Years after my research career has ended, if all goes well, the FDA may announce that it has approved one or both molecules as a new drug. The judgment is still to be made whether one or both will officially become medicine to treat people.

For the last several years, I have been contemplating what I should do after my career in the pharmaceutical industry. I have always been interested in teaching, and I began to wonder about opportunities especially in the European or former Eastern bloc countries. In my thinking, I would rather go to a place where I could have the greatest impact in advancing both science and the gospel than stay in the United States where the resources for both science and the gospel message are abundant. I would like to help and train young people for good science, but more importantly, reach out to the future leaders of a country that is struggling to catch up with the leading countries of the world.

As a scientist, I go to a couple of scientific meetings every year. For the last several years, I specifically began to look for international scientific meetings in my discipline that would be held in a country in those regions. I have been looking for an opportunity to test the water, so to speak, and to find out where I could strategically place myself to train and reach out to future leaders in scientific disciplines after my current career. I have visited Russia (Moscow), Czech Republic, Hungary, and Turkey, besides Austria, England, France, Germany, Holland, and Spain, by taking advantage of what my chemistry discipline could lead me to as a business trip or even as a pleasure trip. And the time and place to pursue such an opportunity appears to be jelling and fast approaching in my mind.

"Help Me Become Filthy Rich!?"

Financial independence has been an important aspect in my life ever since I lost my mother at the age of eight. I was a financial burden to my relatives who took me in and raised me and made me very much aware of this fact. My uncle's family struggled to make ends meet because he did not manage his finances wisely. From a very early age, I promised myself never to live in debt when I grew up. I learned basic bookkeeping when I was in the fourth grade, and I have kept my accounting book ever since. I also learned the difference between "need" and "want" as I managed to live under my income through the years. I lived most of my life poor until I got my current job as a research scientist. I bought a brand new house after five years of my employment at a pharmaceutical company. This was indeed a place of my own that I could call "home" for the first time in my life. I reasoned that I, a single woman, should own this 3500-square-foot house for the following two purposes: (1) for the resale value and (2) for opening it to ministries. I mused that I even could have a group of 50 people for a Bible study when I saw the spacious finished basement.

I wondered what Christmas tradition I could establish, while living alone in my house. Over the years, I noticed that each family had a Christmas tradition when I was invited to homes of my friends during the Christmas season. I decided that I would hold an annual Christmas Open House to celebrate Christ's birth with co-workers, neighbors, and friends. I had a very low-key evangelistic outreach in mind and invited both Christians and non-Christians to mingle and visit with one another at my Christmas Open House. I wondered if I could handle the crowd when I received sixty positive responses to my invitation for my first open house! The great success in the first year has kept me going every year since 1995, usually hosting 60–90 guests. It has indeed become a Christmas tradition not only to me but also to some of my friends. My home also has become a place for a small-group ministry and an evangelistic Japanese Bible study. I never dreamed that one day I could have a beautiful home where I could entertain and minister to others.

As I began to contemplate what I should do after my career as a research scientist, I felt financial independence and freedom would enable me to focus on what's most important without distraction. More and more I feel I would like to get engaged in global evangelization through teaching ministry but without asking for financial support from churches. As I shared my vision with my financial advisor and he appeared to be supportive of my idea, I began asking him half-jokingly, "Help me become filthy rich so that I can go all over the world and teach or do whatever as an outreach without asking a church to support me financially. I only want to ask churches for prayer support."

Though my request was nothing serious, I began to think about the

Bible characters that were indeed "filthy rich": Abraham, Jacob, and Joseph were all abundantly blessed with material wealth.[5] Moses was raised as Pharaoh's son, lacking nothing.[6] Kings David and Solomon established powerful and wealthy kingdoms.[7] And there was Job. He was definitely filthy rich. And though for a time he lost everything and suffered a great deal, Job became even more filthy rich at the end of his life.[8] The amazing thing is that God never seemed to dictate to them as to how they should use or spend their wealth. There seemed to be absolutely nothing wrong with being filthy rich because for some it meant being blessed by God.

I was also reminded of more than a few verses in the Bible, which described God's concern for orphans and widows and His commands to take care of the destitute.[9] I have realized that I am living proof of His care. There I was once in a very poor circumstance grown up without a single family member of my own who was supposed to take care of me. There were times when I yearned for an earthly family and was angry with God that He kept me alone. But now I realize that God has taken care of me all through my life as my Father. Now I feel extremely rich in every way, like a princess, because I am a daughter of the King. I have freedom to do whatever and to go wherever. God's presence has become extremely real, maybe because I have remained single. I sense His presence constantly in my life, and I can freely talk to Him just as I do with friends.

The Lord has blessed me abundantly beyond my basic needs or even beyond my imagination. For the last twenty years, I have focused on science. I have strived to make life better for people physically and emotionally. God has blessed me with the means and opportunities to engage in global evangelization without being distracted with earthly concerns. I would like to focus on God in whatever I do for the next twenty years, should He allow me. I would like to strive and impact spiritual lives of the lost. If this is not an American dream from God's perspective, then what is?

NOTES

1. *Joan of Arc* (VHS) Artisan Studio, 1999.

2. Pernoud, R; Clin, M.-V. *Joan of Arc: Her Story*. New York: St. Martin's Press, 1998.

3. Twain, M. *Personal Recollections of Joan of Arc*. New York: Oxford University Press, 1996.

4. Henry was an American theologian, journalist, and evangelical leader of the twentieth century, who lived from 1913 to 2003. He was the founding editor

of *Christianity Today*, in 1955. See <http://www.christianitytoday.com/ct/2003/decemberweb-only/12-8-14.0.html>.

5. Gen 25:5–7; 30:43; 45:8–11.

6. Exo 2:10; Heb 11:24.

7. II Sam 7:8–16; I King 10:23–29.

8. Job 42:12–17.

9. Exo 22:22; Deut 14:29, 24:19–21; Psa 68:5, 146:9; etc.

www.ingramcontent.com/pod-product-compliance
Lightning Source LLC
Chambersburg PA
CBHW031242090426
42742CB00007B/287